HARVARD
BEATS
YALE 29-29

HARVARD
BEATS
YALE 29-29

...and Other Great Comebacks
from the Annals of Sports

BARRY WILNER & KEN RAPPOPORT

TAYLOR TRADE PUBLISHING
Lanham • New York • Boulder • Toronto • Plymouth, UK

Published by Taylor Trade Publishing
An imprint of The Rowman & Littlefield Publishing Group, Inc.
4501 Forbes Boulevard, Suite 200, Lanham, Maryland 20706

Estover Road, Plymouth PL6 7PY, United Kingdom

Distributed by NATIONAL BOOK NETWORK

Library of Congress Cataloging-in-Publication Data

Wilner, Barry.
    Harvard beats Yale 29-29 :—and other great comebacks from the annals of sports / Barry Wilner and Ken Rappoport.—1st Taylor Trade Pub. ed.
       p.   cm.
    ISBN-13: 978-1-58979-331-6 (pbk. : alk. paper)
    ISBN-10: 1-58979-331-5 (pbk. : alk. paper)
    1. Sports upsets—United States.   2. College sports—United States.
    3. Professional sports—United States.   I. Rappoport, Ken.   II. Title.

GV583.W548   2008
796—dc22   2007020803

∞ ™ The paper used in this publication meets the minimum requirements of American National Standard for Information Sciences—Permanence of Paper for Printed Library Materials, ANSI/NISO Z39.48-1992.

Manufactured in the United States of America.

*For all those who have made comebacks, whether in
sports or otherwise, and breathed
the air of high achievement*

CONTENTS

ACKNOWLEDGMENTS

The authors would like to express their thanks to the many contributors to this book: Nancy Armour, Scott Berchtold, Mike Clark, Brian Dowling, Doug Ferguson, Mike Fitzpatrick, Jon Jackson, Brent Kallestad, Paul Montella, Jim O'Connell, Alan Robinson, Bill Shannon, and Ben Walker.

May all of their comebacks be successful.

Ken Rappoport and Barry Wilner

INTRODUCTION

Man, did this look familiar. The Patriots were toying with the Colts again, something New England had made a habit of in this decade.

Seemingly headed for their fourth Super Bowl appearance in six years—they won the other three—the Patriots owned a 21-3 lead at the RCA Dome. They were befuddling Indianapolis quarterback Peyton Manning once more, and when the Pats took control against the Colts, they never would let go.

Well, almost never. There was something different about the 2006 Colts.

They had more spunk, more versatility, and more resolve than previous editions. They had all the makings for the kind of comeback that never fades from a sports fan's memory.

"Some of that stuff is a little deep for me," Manning said. "I just wanted to do my job and do my job well. I didn't think I needed to be super. I just needed to be good."

Not quite. He and the Colts needed to be very good to stage a rally. And they were.

Down by 18, the Colts went on an 80-yard march of 15 plays, and Adam Vinatieri, the hero of two of New England's Super Bowl wins who was now kicking for Indy, made a 26-yard field goal.

"We had to get some points there," Manning admitted. "It was big for our confidence going into halftime."

Even bigger was the way the Colts came out after the break. They immediately covered 76 yards in 14 plays, Manning scored on a 1-yard run, and it suddenly was 21-13.

"You could feel it after that," star receiver Reggie Wayne said. "You could feel that something special was coming."

Something that marks any champion: a display of will that won't be denied.

Another 76-yard drive capped by an even more unusual 1-yard score than Manning carrying it in—defensive tackle Joe Klecko, lined up as a blocking tight end, catching a pass—and a 2-point conversion pass to Marvin Harrison tied it.

"Even when we were up 21-3," said Manning's New England counterpart, Tom Brady, "you knew at some point they were going to come back."

But so would the Patriots, a club steeped in postseason achievements. Brady, a two-time Super Bowl MVP, threw a 6-yard TD pass to Jabar Gaffney to take back the lead.

More resilient than ever, Indy returned the favor with a fluky TD as center Jeff Saturday recovered Dominic Rhodes's fumble in the end zone for his first score since peewee league. With 12 minutes left, it was 28-28.

"It just shows that this ship didn't sink or sail with one guy," Saturday said. "Every guy has to show up and do their job.

"Things are sometimes unexplainable. I was blocking my guy to the left, and he (Rhodes) spins back and the ball is loose. It hit me in the foot and I just laid down and got it."

Back came New England for Stephen Gostkowski's 28-yard field goal. And back came Indy for Vinatieri's 36-yarder.

As expected, the Patriots didn't flinch, and when Gostkowski hit again from 43 yards, they led 34-31 and were 3 minutes, 49 seconds from the Super Bowl.

Manning is a student of football history and a true sports fan. He certainly knew about the great comebacks of the NFL: Buffalo over Houston in the playoffs after the 1992 season; Pittsburgh's rally to a Super Bowl title a year earlier.

He probably knew all about the 1973 Mets and 2004 Red Sox; maybe even Notre Dame over UCLA in basketball, or the Maple Leafs storming back from a 3-0 deficit to beat the Red Wings for the 1942 Stanley Cup.

So now was the time for Manning and the Colts to dig out their own little corner on the comeback trail.

They had to be brilliant against such an imposing opponent, and they were.

Indy surged 80 yards in 11 plays. After Manning threw a laser for a 32-yard completion to Bryan Fletcher, a roughing-the-passer call moved the ball to the 11, then Manning handed off to Joseph Addai three times, with the rookie scoring from the 3 with a minute left.

"I watched the drive with Elway, you never get tired of seeing that," Manning said of Denver's rally to win the 1986 AFC championship game at Cleveland. "I'm not comparing what we just did to that, but it sounds pretty good."

It would sound and feel a whole lot better if the Colts could stop Brady and their tormentors for another 60 seconds. Even Manning recognized how difficult that could be.

"I said a little prayer on that last drive," Manning admitted. "I don't know if you're supposed to pray for stuff like that, but I said a little prayer."

And it worked. The Patriots sputtered, Marlin Jackson jumped in front of Brady's pass and fell to the ground with it, and the Colts had scaled their biggest hurdle with a memorable rally.

"I'm so proud of the way our guys fought," Dungy said. "I'm very happy for Peyton. He was very, very calm. He had to bring us from behind three or four times. It's just fitting. Our team went the hard way the whole year."

They would need a mini-comeback in the Super Bowl before beating the Bears for the championship. But by climbing back against New England, the Colts had eliminated any doubts—from the outside and within the team—that they were fully capable of rallying.

It's what great comebacks are all about. It's what this book is all about.

1

HARVARD BEATS YALE 29-29

The Game, 1968

It looked like a typographical error: "Harvard Beats Yale, 29-29."

But the headline in the *Harvard Crimson* made its point. If any game in the long and storied series felt like a victory for the Crimson, it was the one played in 1968. The most incredible comeback of them all.

As for Yale, the reverse was true. Brian Dowling, the Bulldogs' quarterback that day, would later refer to that contest as "the first time I lost at Yale."

And Carmen Cozza, the Yale coach, said, "That was the worst loss of my life, even though it was a tie."

In a rivalry known snobbishly only as "The Game," surely this was the Game of Games.

Trailing 29-13 in the final minutes and hopelessly out of contention, Harvard incredibly scored 16 points in 42 seconds to stave off defeat. The result of the battle of unbeaten teams left the longtime rivals sharing the Ivy League title.

"It was a frustrating game and a blemish on my career at Yale because I thought we had a better team," Dowling says. "But if we would have won the way we could have, no one would have remembered us, or that game. They would have said it was just another undefeated Yale team.

"But because of what happened, it was a mixed blessing for us. The notoriety lasted, and it added to the lore of the rivalry."

In 1965 Dowling sat on the bench as a freshman watching his first Yale-Harvard game. He wasn't impressed.

"It was the most boring thing I had ever witnessed," he said of Harvard's 13-0 victory. "I thought the object of the game was to score points. After the first two games, I was beginning to wonder."

Dowling missed the 1966 game, won 17-0 by Harvard, because of injury. As a sophomore he had his share of health problems: a bruised kidney, chipped backbone, a torn knee, broken collarbone, broken nose, and broken hand. Those injuries cost him seven and a half games in his second year and three more in his junior year.

That didn't stop him from becoming a campus hero as a junior. When he did get back in the lineup, he led Yale to victories over Columbia, Cornell, Dartmouth, Penn, Princeton, and Harvard to give the Bulldogs their first Ivy League championship since 1960.

For drama, the win over Harvard in 1967 topped them all—at least until '68's epic. With time running out, Dowling hurled a 66-yard touchdown pass to Del Marting for the winning points in a thrilling 24-20 Yale victory.

Reflecting on that final drive, Dowling said, "I wanted to end the game with more completions to Yale than to Harvard. I think I had four interceptions at the time. I only had three completions. The only bad thing was that we scored so quickly that Harvard had a chance to drive down the field, which they did, and they ended up fumbling on the 10-yard line as time ran out."

With his scrambling ability to make plays on the fly, the 6-foot-2, 190-pound quarterback reminded many of Navy great Roger Staubach, the 1963 Heisman Trophy winner.

"Without a great amount of exaggeration, he can be called the most exciting back in the Ivies since Princeton's Dick Kazmaier (the All-American of the 1950s)," *Sports Illustrated* said.

The star quarterback from Cleveland's St. Ignatius High School had scholarship offers from more than 100 schools, including Southern Cal, Michigan, Ohio State, and Notre Dame. But his father, Emmett, president of a steel-door company in Youngstown,

Ohio, paid for his son to go to Yale. "Why not go first class?" he said to Brian.

Dowling did, but wasn't so sure he had made the right decision at first. "I really wanted to play big-time football," he said.

That feeling soon changed when Dowling saw all the great talent that surrounded him at Yale.

"We had a lot of depth," he remembered. "We had a lot of good players. The major conferences had two or three good teams. The rest of them weren't that great. We could have beaten a lot of those schools."

Dowling was in the middle of a football revival at Yale—one reason why the Yale Bowl bulged with 68,000 fans for the 1967 game with Harvard.

All right, Game with Harvard.

"That was pretty special," Dowling remembered. "We had already clinched [the Ivy League championship], but we had a full Yale Bowl, which was pretty exciting."

All of a sudden, normally sober students usually more concerned with the stock market and the devaluation of the British currency were holding pep rallies, wearing buttons, and marching in parades. "Brian Dowling is our hippie," noted Yale publicity director Charley Loftus.

To be sure, Brian was the big man on campus. The *Yale Daily News* featured him in a comic strip—he was the inspiration for "B.D." in Gary Trudeau's *Doonesbury*. The usually insouciant student body treated him with almost godlike reverence. When it rained at the Yale Bowl, the students called on Dowling for help. "Make it stop, Brian," they would chant during games.

Dowling couldn't do that, but he could make the offense go. After Yale was shut out by Harvard in 1965 and 1966 without Dowling, he had the Bulldogs' offense in high gear in 1967 and 1968.

Dowling shared star billing with Calvin Hill, one of the country's great running backs and a future NFL first-round draft pick. In 1968, the dynamic pair had led a high-powered offense that was ranked No. 3 nationally and would be Harvard's toughest challenge of the season.

Harvard was built on defense. Nicknamed the "Boston Stranglers," the Crimson led the nation with fewest points allowed, 61 in eight games.

"I remember that I had a particular challenge," Dowling remembered. "Harvard had a great defense and they were talking about how they were going to stop us. That was me, of course, because I ran the offense."

There was the usual trash-talking rhetoric before the game. Yes, even in the Ivy League.

"The biggest reason Harvard is No. 1 in defense," snarled Yale tackle Tom Bass, "is because they haven't played us yet."

The Crimson countered.

"We hope to hit them real hard early, just so they will know," said John Emery, a 200-pound Harvard linebacker with a Fu Manchu mustache.

But this Yale team wasn't used to being intimidated. It wasn't used to losing, either. Going into the '68 game, the Bulldogs sported a nation-leading 16-game winning streak, and were ranked No. 19 in the nation.

Both teams had 8-0 records in 1968. Yale's perfect record was expected, Harvard's wasn't.

"The experts said this was going to be our first losing season," said Harvard coach John Yovicsin of his tenure at Cambridge, "but there's something about putting a challenge to Harvard."

The Crimson did have some hard-nosed running backs, including fullback Vic Gatto.

But Harvard had no one in its backfield with the reputation of Dowling and Hill. Yovicsin's teams were known for their sound, but unspectacular, play.

The Crimson would have to be extremely sound to beat this Yale team.

"From the start, we were forced to look at it as a special game," Gatto said. "We were both undefeated."

Dowling said he and his teammates were well aware of Harvard's success as the Ivy League season progressed.

"I tried to take each opponent at a time," Dowling said. "But after four weeks, you sort of knew what everybody's record was. We kept an eye on Harvard. They didn't win big every week, they had two or three close games. They were still undefeated. We knew it was going to come down to the last game."

While Dowling was thinking about Harvard, Foge Fazio, who coached the Crimson's special teams and defensive line in 1968, was thinking about Yale.

"All year long you could feel the buildup of the two teams," he said.

The lure of the game attracted a sellout crowd of 40,280 fans to ancient Harvard Stadium, along with a blizzard of print and electronic media—250 journalists in all.

There were a number of scalpers, as well. The normal scalping prices that day: $50 to $175 for a pair of tickets. One fan reportedly paid $1,000 for a block of eight seats, an incredible amount of money for the time.

The game, uh, The Game began . . .

Dowling was in top form, leading a 79-yard drive and racing around right end for a touchdown in the first quarter.

Early in the second period, Yale had the ball on the Harvard 4-yard line. Dowling, trying to pass, was trapped for an apparent loss. But he squirmed free and fired a touchdown pass to Hill. Later in the period, he hit Marting with a 5-yard pass in the end zone after another scrambling adventure to give Yale a 22-0 lead.

It wasn't what the fans were expecting. The classic they were hoping to see had turned into a one-sided romp as Dowling and Hill scored almost at will against one of the country's great defensive teams.

Dowling, the scrambler, had made all the difference with his fast footwork, running up the score against a team that allowed an average of less than 8 points a game.

"The plan had been to keep Dowling in the pocket," *Sports Illustrated* wrote, "but Harvard was having trouble keeping him in Cambridge."

The Crimson weren't able to contain Hill, either. When he scored that touchdown for Yale, he passed the legendary Albie Booth as the leading scorer in Yale history with 144 points.

Harvard's starting quarterback, George Lalich, meanwhile, was being kept under wraps by the Yale defense. Desperately, Yovicsin turned to second-string quarterback Frank Champi. "OK," the Harvard coach said, "you try it for a while."

That was a surprise to just about everyone in the stadium—including the Harvard football team itself.

"We knew Frank had the arm, but we felt he was a little inexperienced for the job," said Harvard guard Tom Jones, later known as the actor Tommy Lee Jones. "He was a junior and he was sort of nervous all year."

Champi had completed only five passes in his three seasons at Harvard and spent most of his time on the bench. Football hadn't been as much fun for him as it was when he starred at Everett (Massachusetts) High School.

Now, ice-cold, the disgruntled Champi was thrown into a game in a desperation move by Yovicsin.

"We needed to be shaken up," Gatto said.

So Champi, a balding history major, made some history of his own.

With 39 seconds left in the first half, Champi threw a 15-yard touchdown pass to Bruce Freeman to cut the Yale lead to 22-6. A poor snap from center cost the Crimson the extra point, but Harvard's players went into the locker room a fully confident team.

"At halftime, we knew we could win," Yovicsin said. "I told our boys that all we had to do was shut out Yale while getting two touchdowns and a field goal."

The Harvard players believed in themselves, if not their coach. Before the season, Yovicsin had a near mutiny on his hands when most of the 22 seniors almost walked out in a furor over playing time.

"We'd been the forgotten guys on this club," one of the seniors said. "Ever since our freshman year, we've been ignored. We changed our minds about walking out after Vic Gatto was elected captain. We held a meeting in January and decided to rally around Vic. We wanted to show the school, the coaches, and the experts that we were a lot better than any of them gave us credit for."

When the second half began, Yovicsin put Lalich back in the game. Not for long. When the Harvard offense stalled, the ball was back in Champi's hands on Harvard's next series.

A Yale fumble gave Harvard great field position on the Eli 25. Three plays later, Champi had Harvard back in the end zone.

Yale's once-significant lead was now down to 9 points, 22-13.

The score remained that way going into the fourth quarter, which was notable for one big reason. Before the Crimson shut out Yale in the third period, the Bulldogs had scored in 22 straight quarters.

It was a great effort by Harvard, but seemingly not enough, when Dowling carried the ball over the goal line on a 5-yard roll-out in the fourth quarter. Cozza looked at the scoreboard and waved in Bob Bayless to kick the extra point.

Yale 29, Harvard 13.

"After the third touchdown, I figured 2 points would put it out of reach," Cozza said. "After the fourth one, I figured what difference does it make? There was no way they could come back. No way they could win."

Especially with Yale driving toward the Harvard goal line for yet another score.

From Harvard's 32, Dowling completed a screen pass, but Harvard's Steve Ranere recovered a fumble at the Crimson 14 with 3:31 remaining.

Enough time to score a touchdown, sure, but Harvard needed more than one, plus a couple of 2-point conversions just to tie. By Ivy League logic, or logic of any kind, it was an absurd calculation.

But Champi was back in the game, ready to prove his own theory of conversions.

Suddenly, things got interesting. In later years Hill remembered it as a "free fall. It was like watching a big, old tidal wave."

The Harvard quarterback moved the Crimson steadily downfield. The drive seemed doomed when Champi fumbled. However, a Harvard tackle picked up the ball and rumbled 17 yards to the Yale 15.

Still, it didn't seem to matter. There was now less than a minute left. And the Yale students were taunting their Harvard counterparts, waving white "victory" handkerchiefs across the field and chanting, "You're Number 2."

Not even the most loyal Harvard fan could possibly think the Crimson had a chance.

Think again.

Champi, who could throw a football 85 yards with his right arm and 50 with his left, eluded a bunch of white-jerseyed Yale players and rifled a 15-yard TD pass to Freeman with 42 seconds left.

Sure, time was tight, but things were going Harvard's way—even officials' calls. When the Crimson missed their try at the 2-point conversion, a Yale penalty gave Harvard an extra opportunity. Gus Crim took it in to reduce Yale's lead to 8 points, 29-21.

"They started waving those white handkerchiefs and yelling," Gatto said. "That got to us."

Harvard had only one chance left: an onside kick.

The ball went toward a Yale lineman, who couldn't control it.

During the scramble, Harvard's Bill Kelly fell on the ball at the Yale 49.

Despite the sudden turn of events, Dowling wasn't worried.

"Looking back, after they recovered the onside kick, I looked up at the scoreboard and saw us with an 8-point lead," he said. "I felt there was no way we could lose."

But he didn't figure on Champi, exhausted as he was, directing an irresistible force. The Harvard quarterback ran 14 yards for a first down. A Yale face-mask penalty gave Harvard 15 more yards, moving the ball to the Yale 20.

Time left: 32 seconds.

Champi threw two passes into the end zone, both incomplete. Then he sent Crim up the middle on a surprising draw play covering 14 yards.

Three seconds remained, enough for one last play.

As the play unfolded, Champi appeared to be trapped.

"He played ring-around-the-rosey with Yale's defenders," reported the *New York Times*. "He ran around in circles for what seemed like 10 seconds."

Then he spotted Gatto alone in the end zone and fired. The pass settled in the Harvard captain's arms as time ran out. It was a special moment for a special player who became the first back in Harvard history to rush for 2,000 yards.

Yale 29, Harvard 27.

"I thought the pass to Gatto was high," said Champi, also a javelin thrower on the Harvard track team. "I just threw it in his general direction."

Gatto had been injured earlier and his left knee bothered him.

"But when I saw the pass, I knew I just had to love it. Just take it in my arms and love it," he said.

Harvard fans swarmed onto the field to mob Gatto. The game was held up while officials cleared the area. They couldn't keep the noise down, though.

"It was the loudest I'd ever heard in a stadium," Cozza said.

As Harvard prepared to go for the 2-point conversion, the public address announcer implored the crowd, "Quiet, please!"

Harvard still had to make that conversion to tie. No distracting noise needed.

Champi, meanwhile, was confident he could finish the job.

Harvard's Pete Varney celebrates a touchdown to bring the Crimson to
within two points of tying Yale in their classic 1968 comeback.
Photo by Jerry Cooke.

"At this time," Champi said, "I was so tired, I wasn't even nervous."

But not too tired to complete a pass to Pete Varney for the tie that left Yale's Hill with a "sick, sick feeling."

Harvard beats Yale 29-29.

"It was a simple curl pattern," Varney said of the final play. "We had run it all year long. I was usually matched up against a small defensive back and I could screen him out. We had run it the previous game. It made the final one even easier."

The play may have been routine, but Champi saw the game in mystical terms.

"Astrologically, it was a big day," said Champi, who believed in "karma, reincarnation, and God."

Years later, Dowling had the opportunity to watch films of the game for a TV show that chronicled great competition, and thought the quality of play was "pretty good. I was proud of that fact."

It only happened to be one of Dowling's greatest games as a

collegian. The Yale quarterback scored twice and passed for two TDs, and would have probably had another if that receiver hadn't dropped the ball on the way to the goal line in the fourth quarter. Dowling also racked up 116 yards through the air in a magnificent performance against a tough defense.

As for the game's historical impact, Dowling noted, "People are still talking about it almost 40 years later. The circumstances became larger than life the farther away from it you go. If everybody went to the game who said they did, there were probably 250,000 people there."

That game personified the rivalry, as far as Gatto was concerned.

"It is a rivalry among equals and friends," Gatto said. "The rivalry has no bitterness that you associate with others. There's a sense of mutuality that you don't find in other rivalries.

"You never play as well until you're threatened, and we always felt that way against Yale, and I know Yale felt that way about us."

Upon graduation, Dowling and Hill went into professional football. Gatto later went into coaching at Tufts and also did some TV work with Dowling broadcasting the Yale-Harvard game to alumni.

Champi dropped out of school after the second game of his senior year, disenchanted with football, and became a high school teacher.

Scattered as they were, they were still a part of each other's lives, and a part of football history.

2

REVERSING THE CURSE

2004 Boston Red Sox

Now this must be fiction. Maybe even science fiction.

The film *Fever Pitch* was sitting in the can, ready for final editing and release. But the story of a maniacal Red Sox fan—fan is short for fanatic, after all—and his relationship with a woman who doesn't quite grasp his mind-set required a brand new ending. Like all movies about baseball, the Red Sox were lovable losers in this one. Even if everyone else lived happily ever after, the Sox couldn't provide that tableau, right?

Then they did something, well, miraculous. Not only did the Red Sox reverse the Curse of the Bambino, they did it in historic fashion. They vanquished the "hated Yankees"—you spit out those two words if you are from New England—by coming back from three games down in the American League championship series.

And then they swept the St. Louis Cardinals to win it all.

The Sox? The Boston Red Sox? The perennial underachievers (read "chokers")?

So there were actors Jimmy Fallon and Drew Barrymore kissing on the Busch Stadium field while the Sox celebrated their first World Series title since 1918.

"Until then, we didn't allow ourselves to dream that it could happen," said Bobby Farrelly, who along with brother Peter made the comedy that, had they written it the way things turned out, probably would have been lambasted from the Back Bay to the Bronx. "You know how superstitious everyone is in Boston. We felt like if we started writing before that, we'd jinx them.

"It works brilliantly at the end. We didn't want to try to fictionalize it, but now it's reality."

How in the world did it become reality? That is the story of one of pro sports' greatest and most unexpected comebacks.

The Yankees' domination of the Red Sox through the decades was very real, most dramatically and emphatically punctuated by the names Bucky Dent (1978 playoff game) and Aaron Boone (2003). But other teams had destroyed Boston's hopes for a baseball championship, too, including the Cardinals (1946 and '67), Indians (1948), Mets (Bill Buckner, 1986), and the 1975 Reds, despite Carlton Fisk's Game-6 home run that remains the most memorable shot in Fenway annals.

But the way the Bronx Bombers regularly battered the Bosox was the stuff of legend, dating back to when Red Sox owner Harry Frazee sold an outfielder/pitcher named Babe Ruth, on the day after Christmas in 1919, to the Yankees, who would win 26 World Series in the next 81 years while the Sox would chase futilely for one.

"Ruth had simply become impossible, and the Boston club could no longer put up with his eccentricities," Frazee said. "While Ruth, without question, is the greatest hitter the game has ever seen, he is likewise one of the most selfish and inconsiderate men that ever wore a baseball uniform."

Bostonians so devotedly believed in the Curse that they were certain Ruth, who brought Frazee an unheard-of in those days $100,000, was watching their team from on high, toying with the players, the managers, the team executives and, most cruelly, the die-hard fans.

And those fans died hard every time the Yankees drove another stake deep into their hearts and psyches.

In mid-June 2004, divers attempted to find the sunken remains of a piano the Babe supposedly dumped into Willis Pond in Sudbury, Massachusetts, after the 1918 World Series. They came up as empty as the Red Sox had for more than eight decades.

Also in mid-June, it became apparent the Yankees and Red Sox were among the elite of baseball once again. The Yanks already had scored a major victory in the off-season when they outbid the Sox for Alex Rodriguez, who was playing alongside superstar shortstop Derek Jeter on New York's dynamic left side of the infield instead of manning the hole at Fenway. New York sneaked in to make the deal when it appeared the Sox would acquire A-Rod from Texas.

That prompted a war of words between The Boss, Yankees owner George Steinbrenner, and two Boston executives: team owner John Henry and Sox president Larry Lucchino. Henry said the trade was proof baseball needed a salary cap, and Steinbrenner called it "sour grapes" while comparing Henry to the Scarecrow in *The Wizard of Oz*. You know, no brain.

Steinbrenner also said of Lucchino: "I have nothing against him except I wouldn't want him in my foxhole. . . . He's not my kind of guy. Not a good man."

In midseason, New York swept a series with Boston, only to then go to Shea Stadium and lose three in a row to the Mets, after which Steinbrenner wondered how his team could be so flat for a matchup with its rivals from Queens. To which one player said: "We have only one rival, and we swept them."

Including an incredible 5-4 win in 13 innings that required three straight hits with two outs in the bottom of the inning to overcome a 4-3 Boston lead established by Manny Ramirez's homer.

"That was the greatest ballgame I've ever seen or been involved in," Rodriguez admitted.

The Yankees also fought with the Red Sox. In a July game at Fenway Park, catcher Jason Varitek shoved A-Rod in the face after Bronson Arroyo hit Rodriguez with a pitch and the Yankee shouted threateningly at the pitcher. When Varitek stuck his mitt in Rodriguez's mug, the benches emptied and a wild melee ensued.

"It just shows you how much both teams were hyped up," Rodriguez said. "You can't really control your emotions."

Added Varitek: "He challenged my pitcher and he has no right and no business doing that. I just told him to take his base, but he wouldn't stop mouthing off."

Later in the season, with the Yankees cruising to their seventh straight AL East crown and the Red Sox headed for a wild-card berth, the Bronxites bombed Sox ace Pedro Martinez, who afterward eloquently said:

"What can I say? Just tip my hat and call the Yankees my daddy. They're that good. They're that hot right now, at least against me. I wish they would disappear and not come back.

"I can't find a way to beat them at this point."

Nor did the Sox figure to find a way as the postseason began.

"They have the (best) record, so you can call them the favorites," Varitek said of the Yankees, who would play the AL Central-winning Twins in the best-of-five opening round, while Boston played the Anaheim Angels. "We're just concentrating on what we have to do against the Angels."

The Yankees took care of Minnesota in four games of the opening round, while the Sox swept the Angels.

Hello, friends.

"Clash of the titans for the pennant," said Boone, who had been released after the Yankees claimed he violated his contract by playing off-season basketball and injuring his knee. "I think a lot of people wanted to see this. I'm looking forward to following it."

Nearly all of the Yankees were eager to be playing in it. After the previous year's dramatics, culminated by Boone's 11th-inning home run to win Game 7, which capped a rally from 4-0 and 5-2 holes, the Yanks felt somewhat invincible against Boston. And, of course, there was the good old Curse, with Boone's belt—actually, a rather lazy fly ball that found the seats in left field—the latest incarnation.

But there were rumblings of negativity, too. And some tragedy.

Mariano Rivera, the best relief pitcher in baseball, had flown home on the weekend after two of his wife's relatives were electrocuted in his pool in Panama. A weeping Rivera attended the funeral, then said: "At this moment, my family is my priority. I stopped thinking about baseball the moment I got on the plane."

But Rivera vowed to return to his team for the start of the ALCS, which pitted Mike Mussina on the mound for New York against 21-game-winner Curt Schilling. And he did, although his

grief somewhat compromised the Yankees' glee at facing a traditional foe that had become a traditional flop against them.

For their part, the Sox seemed relaxed and ready, buoyed by
how well they played against the Angels.

"We're playing good ball now. I think we're the best team,"
outfielder Johnny Damon said. "Hopefully, the best team wins. But
we know they're no slouches."

Of course, it wouldn't be Yankees-Red Sox without a little
venom, which Schilling provided.

"I'm not sure I can think of any scenario more enjoyable than
making 55,000 people from New York shut up," said Schilling,
who was bothered by tendinitis in his right ankle, if not by the
pressure of Game 1 of the playoffs at Yankee Stadium. Schilling
had won Game 7 of the 2001 World Series against New York when
he was with Arizona, and he signed as a free agent with Boston in
part because of "the thrill" of pitching as a visitor in the Bronx.

Boston brought out the big guns off the field, too: Patriots
owner Robert Kraft was Henry's guest, with the belief that maybe
the Pats' good fortunes—two Super Bowl titles in the past three
seasons—would rub off on the accursed Red Sox.

"Any team in sports would like to emulate them," Henry said
of the Patriots.

The Bronx fans didn't want any part of the Pats transferring to
the Sox. One fan wearing a Yankees shirt yelled: "Hey, Kraft, keep
your winning streak with the Patriots, not with the Red Sox."

Boston led the majors in slugging percentage (.472), on-base
percentage (.360), and runs (949), and tied for the lead in batting
average (.282) in 2004. The Yankees brought a loaded lineup featuring Rodriguez, Jeter, Gary Sheffield, Hideki Matsui, Bernie Williams, Jorge Posada, and a deep bench into the series. But their
pitching wasn't as strong as in previous years.

That showed late in Game 1, although Schilling and the Sox
couldn't take advantage, in great part because Schilling got shelled
and the Sox fell behind 8-0 through six innings.

Matsui tied an ALCS record with five RBIs. Four came off
Schilling, who yielded six runs in three innings and clearly struggled on his damaged ankle which, it turned out, had torn tendons.

But things did get tight at the end.

"It was like it was too good to be true," Yanks manager Joe
Torre said of the huge lead.

Mussina was untouchable for six innings before he tired. Boston reached Mussina and reliever Tanyon Sturtze—a bloodied victim in the fight between Varitek and Rodriguez during the season—for five runs.

In the top of the eighth, Boston kept coming back. David "Big Papi" Ortiz, developing a reputation as a Yankees killer, hit a two-run triple off Tom Gordon, making it 8-7. As much as Torre hated to do so, he made the call for his closer, Rivera.

"Turns out, we really needed him," Mussina said. "I'm sure glad he came back. I know it was tough for him."

Very tough. Rivera had found himself near tears in the bullpen before the game, and admitted his mind wandered during the action.

But when the Sox began scoring and the need arose, he was ready.

"My teammates needed me there," Rivera said. "I wanted to stay home and stay with my family, but I have a job to do, and I have 24 players that were waiting for me."

As was Kevin Millar, with Ortiz 90 feet away with the tying run. Had Millar come through, it could have been an early crushing blow to the hosts.

Rivera got him to pop out, then retired the Sox in the ninth after Williams's two-run double made it 10-7.

"What he did tonight was phenomenal with all the tragedy he's been through," Millar said.

So much for comebacks.

Yeah, right!

Game 2 was the next night, and the fans displayed their readiness in the third inning—of Game 1. That's when the "Who's Your Daddy?" chants and songs began, even though Martinez wasn't pitching.

The three-time Cy Young Award winner would be in the second game of the series, carrying to the mound a 1-2 mark and 5.47 ERA in four 2004 starts against the Yankees. Overall, one of the most dominant pitchers of his era, he was 10-10 with a 3.24 ERA vs. New York.

"I expect him to be on. We need him to be on. There's no way we can come back to Boston down 2-0," Damon insisted.

Manager Terry Francona wasn't concerned about Martinez's mind-set, either.

"I thought he was a little frustrated that night," Francona said of the "daddy" comments. "You see so many times players say something after a game or they think something else, or they are half-dressed going somewhere in a hurry, they say something that they probably wish 10 minutes later they would not have said. I guess I put more credence in his pitching the last 10 years than I do one sentence when he was a little frustrated."

The Sox had every reason to be frustrated heading into the second contest, because they didn't give themselves a fair shot in the first. Schilling had nothing, they couldn't solve Mussina early enough, and their late spurt came up short.

Ah, but this matchup looked like a mismatch. Sure, the Yankees often owned Martinez, but New York was using Jon Lieber, a totally unproven postseason item. Lieber went 5-0 in the final month of the season and was 11-3 in home games. None of those, of course, were playoff games.

"I knew coming into this game what Pedro has done in the past in situations like this, so there was no room for error," Lieber said.

So he made none. And Martinez was pretty good, as well. Even playful, despite a 3-1 loss that, fulfilling Damon's worst fears, dropped Boston behind 2-0 heading to Fenway for three games.

"It actually made me feel really, really good," Martinez said of the chants. "I actually realized that I was somebody important because I caught the attention of 60,000 people . . . plus the whole world. . . . If you reverse time back 15 years ago, I was sitting under a mango tree without 50 cents to actually pay for a bus. And today, I was the center of attention of the whole city of New York."

Well, sort of. Lieber got plenty of accolades from the sellout crowd by limiting Boston to a single in the third, another in the seventh, and one to Trot Nixon leading off the eighth that brought on Gordon. And brought the fans out of their seats in tribute to Lieber.

Gordon was ineffective again and after the Sox scored a run, Rivera once more was summoned in the eighth. He fanned Damon, who still hadn't gotten a hit in the series, then closed it out in the ninth.

Sheffield's RBI single in the first and John Olerud's two-run homer in the sixth provided the New York offense.

"I'll take responsibility for this . . . 0 for 8 with five strikeouts,"

Damon said, practically spitting out the numbers. "I'm the catalyst of this team. I'm the guy on this team that gets us going, gets on base and creates some havoc, but I haven't been able to do that."

Of course not, Johnny. Not against the Yankees. Not with the Curse hanging there like one of the meaty curveballs Schilling had delivered the previous night.

While the Yankees weren't getting cocky, they sensed this play-off series would be much easier than the previous year, when they were five outs from elimination. They'd already beaten Boston's aces, and they had no fear of Fenway.

And the Sox?

"There's no panic with this team—we're still calm and re-laxed," Damon said. "We're down 2-0. Big deal. We've won four in a row before."

But down 3-0, now that would be a big deal. Only in hockey had any team come from such a deficit to win a seven-game play-off series, and that happened only twice in more than 80 years.

As for baseball, as they'd say in the Bronx: "Fuhgedaboutit."

The gloom in New England over the plight of the Sox matched the weather for Game 3. A steady rain forced postponement, add-ing more mental anguish to the region.

"If we're not able to overcome some adversity," Francona said, "we're not a good enough team."

They also would be weakened by Schilling being unavailable for Game 5. If, of course, the ALCS got to a Game 5.

So it was up to Arroyo to keep the Yankees from building the "insurmountable" 3-0 lead.

Boston could have done worse than having the guitar-strumming part-time singer on the mound. Arroyo had won eight of his last ten decisions in '04, and never lacked for confidence.

"I don't feel the weight of the entire season," Arroyo said. "I obviously feel a lot of pressure from this series. But, you know, we're not down 3-0, but obviously we're backed into a corner and there's going to be a huge, huge game."

A game in which Arroyo came up tiny, very tiny. So did New York starter Kevin Brown, but it hardly mattered because, on this night, the Yankees paid tribute to Bronx Bombers of all genera-tions with an unfathomable 19-8 win.

They scored three times in the first, but Boston got four in the second. So the Yankees added three more in the third—both starters were gone by then—and the Sox got two.

OK, 6-6 after three. At least the Sox's bats had awakened.

But awake and ablaze are entirely different things, and the visitors got five runs in the fourth, two in the fifth, four more in the seventh, and two in the ninth. They had 22 hits, including an astounding 8 doubles.

Sheffield broke the 6-6 tie with a three-run homer off Curtis Leskanic. Matsui had a triple-quint if there is such a thing: five hits, five RBIs, and five runs scored. Rodriguez homered and scored five times.

"I'm not surprised the way our ballclub is playing, but no question, you can't expect to go in against the Red Sox and do—especially what we did tonight," Torre said.

Time of game was 4 hours, 20 minutes, the longest nine-inning game in postseason history. Not that many of the Fenway faithful stuck around until the bitter end.

And while the venerable ballpark would be filled for Game 4, just about everyone sensed the true bitter end would come that night in the form of a sweep. Supply your own adjective (ignominious, embarrassing, brutal).

"It starts to look daunting if you look at too big a picture," Francona said, shaking his head. "You just have to believe this was one game, nothing more than one game we lost."

Yes, but routs like this tend to take a toll on the victim.

"To get destroyed like that and have a football score up there, it's definitely embarrassing," Arroyo admitted.

"I think we're definitely upset, definitely stunned. . . . It's not fun," said Damon, who had nicknamed the wild bunch of Sox "The Idiots," and whose team was looking pretty dumb (and dumbfounded).

Team owner Henry was so shocked at being behind 0-3 that he went on the Internet to find the last team to dig its way out of such a chasm and win a series. The search didn't take long; he quickly discovered it had never occurred in baseball and only the 1942 Maple Leafs and 1975 Islanders had done it in hockey.

Ever the optimist, Henry insisted it would happen in baseball someday, so why not in 2004?

A cynic might have told him even the Babe was probably chuckling at that one.

As for the Yankees, life couldn't have been better, the prospects for title No. 27 very bright.

Jeter even believed the Boston fans were gaining a measure of high regard for his team.

"To be honest with you, you get them one-on-one, I think they respect us," he said. "Obviously, they don't pull for us, but I think they have respect for how we go about playing the game. If you get a group of them—that's trouble."

The only ones in trouble, it appeared, were the Yankees-haters.

Because of the rainout before Game 3, Torre could have sent Mussina out for the clincher on four days rest, but chose to give him another day off and turned to "El Duque," Orlando Hernandez.

It was an easy decision; even if Hernandez had not pitched in 16 days because of a tired shoulder. El Duque was 8-2 after joining the team in midsummer, and was 9-3 in postseason games, including a win over Boston. And with Rivera not used in the third game, he would be well-rested for the clincher.

Without Schilling, the Red Sox turned to Derek Lowe, who wasn't even a planned starter in the series, but got the ball after Tim Wakefield was used in the 19-8 debacle. Lowe was a 14-game winner who struggled mightily down the stretch of the season, but he won the clincher against the Angels.

For many Sox fans, avoiding a sweep was paramount. That's about all they could hope for.

Not so the players, who insisted there was still hope.

"Anybody who says you are done isn't a professional athlete," Damon said, emphasizing professional. "There's always a chance."

Slim, after all, is a whole lot better than none.

Except for A-Rod, the Yankees didn't have their power swings in gear in Game 4, but they weren't exactly invisible at the plate. New York took a 2-0 lead in the third inning on Rodriguez's second home run in two nights. The silence in Fenway was deafening.

But the Yanks would waste a variety of opportunities to add to the lead, stranding 14 runners. They let Boston hang around, and the Sox snatched up the chance to stay alive, using small ball: three walks, Orlando Cabrera's RBI single, and Big Papi's two-run single.

Still, the celebrations were relatively muted. The folks in the stands were like thousands of Wily Coyotes, well aware the anvil would drop on them before they could catch Roadrunner.

The Yankees took the lead in the sixth on Matsui's triple and a few infield hits. The countdown had begun.

Soon, either the Yankees would pad their lead—perhaps with an explosion like the previous night. Or they would bring on Rivera to mow down what little hope and faith remained for the Bosox and their legions.

New York's bats stayed silent, and Rivera was summoned in the eighth inning. Usually, he would save games with one inning of work after being set up by Gordon. But Gordon was struggling, and Torre believed Rivera could handle two innings—and hand the Yankees another pennant.

"I think it was a matter of Torre trusting Rivera so much," said Mike Fitzpatrick, baseball writer for the Associated Press. "They'd been together so many years and Rivera came through in so many big spots for him. Torre was just thinking, 'Let me just get the game to Rivera, get the ball to him as soon as I can.' Rivera had plenty of postseason saves with more than one inning of work."

Rivera got through the eighth and into the ninth—his neighborhood, his province, his realm—with the 4-3 lead.

"Any team in baseball would want Mo on the mound in the ninth inning," Jeter said. "I'm sure all those guys would tell you they don't like to face him."

First to face him was Millar, who walked. Rarely used Dave Roberts pinch-ran, and Rivera paid extra attention to him. Three times he threw to first base, and each time Roberts got back safely.

When Rivera finally threw a pitch to Bill Mueller, Roberts took off.

Had Posada thrown him out, it almost surely would have been the last deflating blow, and Rivera likely would have cruised to the save—and into the World Series. But Roberts slid in safely, Fenway shook with cheers (yes, you could feel the ancient ballpark moving), and the tying run was on second base.

Mueller promptly singled home Roberts to tie it.

Boston had life, and nearly won it right there, loading the bases before Rivera got Ortiz on a fly ball.

"We scored a run off the best relief pitcher in the history of baseball with our backs against the wall," Doug Mientkiewicz said.

Actually, their backs were nearly through the wall and into the off-season.

Having reached everyone's nemesis, Rivera, for the critical run, the Sox now faced their own crisis. Their ace reliever, Keith Foulke, had gone two and two-thirds innings and Francona was left with lesser arms in his bullpen. He brought in Alan Embree, then Leskanic nearly torched Boston's hopes when New York filled the bases in the 11th.

But Leskanic came through, getting Williams to fly out.

In the bottom of the 12th, with journeyman Paul Quantrill on the mound, Big Papi sent the ball rocketing into the stands for a spectacular 6-4 Red Sox win.

"It certainly is disappointing," Torre said. "We're so used to Mo going out there and getting people out, which he did tonight. It's just that the walk and stolen base was the difference in that ninth inning."

It was one of the most emotional victories of the year—of many years—for the Red Sox.

Maybe those emotions stemmed from the desire not to be swept by their archenemies. Maybe they felt relieved as well as triumphant.

Regardless, the Red Sox temporarily had held off the Bambino's jinx.

"It was hard to say that it was a turning point," Fitzpatrick recalled. "No team had come back from 3-0 before, but you knew with that rivalry the way it was and is, if the Red Sox were ever able to open the door a little bit, they might never let it get shut again. You thought, 'That may turn out to be their best chance to do something; if they ever were able to pull that thing out, we might have a series.'"

After yet another marathon game, this one lasting just over five hours, both sides could have used a respite from each other and the pressures of performing in such a glaring spotlight. Instead, they had a late-afternoon Game 5 at Fenway.

Mussina, who was so unhittable for six innings of the opener, would start against Martinez, and the prevailing opinion was that the Yankees actually had the edge in that matchup.

"I'm a firm believer in momentum in a short series," Torre said. "Momentum is easily changed in a short series. It will come down to who pitches the best. There's not much you can do but just make sure we don't go out to the next game with any baggage."

Ortiz seemed to be carrying plenty of baggage when he considered facing Mussina. He sounded as if he'd prefer to face Sandy Koufax, Bob Gibson, and Nolan Ryan combined.

"Mussina has like 20 different pitches," Ortiz said. "And he throws all of them for strikes. Out of the 20, you've got to go and pick one, and if he throws it, you don't want to miss it, because if you miss it, you're going have to deal with the other 19. Oh, man, you see Posada sometimes taking his glove off to give some signs. He (doesn't) have enough fingers on one hand."

Big Papi was joking—we think.

What was no joke was the Red Sox's resolve. They weren't feeling exactly frisky, but their enthusiasm had been rekindled. It was time to ratchet up the aggressiveness even more.

As both sides showed signs of exhaustion, this game went deep into the night again. Fourteen innings.

Again, the Yankees built an edge, this time on Derek Jeter's three-run double in the sixth off Martinez. Up 4-2, New York couldn't hold it, and again Rivera blew the save, for only the fifth time in 37 postseason opportunities, but the second time in as many nights.

Ortiz's leadoff homer off Gordon in the eighth and Jason Varitek's sacrifice fly off Rivera later in the inning tied it 4-4.

Rivera pitched well this night, retiring Boston in the ninth to force extra innings. But that was as far as Torre dare let his ace go—no matter what that ace said.

"I don't get tired at all," Rivera insisted. "We're in the playoffs, trying to win a game to go to the World Series. There's no time for rest right now."

The rest of the game was a tense classic. The Yankees threatened, but couldn't score. Ditto the Sox. Now beyond the point of exhaustion, the Sox and Yanks were showcasing exactly what Damon referred to before Game 4: their professionalism.

In the 13th, with knuckleballer Wakefield on the mound—the same Wakefield who yielded the homer to Boone a year ago—Sheffield fanned. But Varitek couldn't handle the dancing pitch and Sheffield got to first base.

Twice more in the inning, Varitek would not be able to block

Wakefield's deliveries, and New York wound up with runners on second and third with two outs.

Wouldn't it be in perfect keeping with the Curse for Varitek to botch yet another pitch and have the pennant-clinching run stride home on a fourth passed ball of the inning? It was almost as if the Bambino himself was hog-tying the catcher so he couldn't field the knuckleballs.

Sure enough, another pitch got away—but only a foot or so and the runners held. Strange.

Even stranger was Ruben Sierra fanning on a knuckler that reached a maximum speed of 70 mph.

At that point, it was clear anything could and probably would happen in this series.

One predictable occurrence was who would win this game for Boston: Big Papi.

Torre was down to Esteban Loaiza, who lost his spot as a starter after pitching poorly once he was acquired from the White Sox. And Loaiza was coming through, hurling three strong innings.

But he walked Damon with one out in the 14th and walked Ramirez with two outs. Ortiz fouled off six pitches before poking a lazy single into center field.

Hardly the drama of the previous night, but just as effective. And just as emotional.

The Sox stormed out of their dugout, either mobbing Damon at home plate or Ortiz past first base. The fatigued fans found enough energy to leap out of their seats, hug, clap, scream, dance—and, of course, hope for more.

"This team has done something the last two days that will go down in history as an incredible accomplishment," Boston's Gabe Kapler said.

"The last two nights shows the depth, the character, the heart, the guts of our ballclub," Wakefield added. "It took every ounce of whatever we had left to win tonight's game and to win last night's game."

Game 5 took 5 hours, 49 minutes. For the first time in their flag-filled history, the Yankees were beaten in consecutive postseason extra-inning contests. Three games in Boston included 1,298 pitches, 82 hits, and 29 pitching changes over 35 innings.

"I think it will be good to go back home and gain some energy from the home crowd," Rodriguez said. "Three days here, it feels like we've been here a month."

‿

As if this series needed any more juice or volatility, Schilling planned to start Game 6. And while his ankle was not in optimum shape, his mouth was.

So was his confidence. Indeed, all of the Sox were brimming with surety.

"It's a chance to get us one step closer to the World Series, a chance to make up for Game 1, a chance to pick my teammates up," Schilling said. "They have been picking each other up for the last couple of days. There's just so many things that go into this. I couldn't ask for anything more.

"I'm just so proud to be a part of this team. This was just a phenomenal two nights . . . like Round 13 of a 15-round prize fight right now, two heavyweights, unbelievable."

Still, Francona was making a chancy move. For one, Schilling was awful in his previous appearance in the ALCS. And he wasn't exactly a picture of health.

But Francona felt his best option was to go with the gutsy right-hander who, if even close to his best, was better than anyone else on the staff.

The Yankees had the comfort zone of being back in the Bronx, and when they burst out of the dugout just before the first pitch, the crowd's roar could have been heard back in Boston. Sure, they had lost two very tough games when the pennant was within grasp. But just as surely, they would handle the Sox on this night as they always had handled the Sox in critical situations.

Then it would be on to yet another World Series appearance.

Torre, to his credit, recognized that such thinking was preposterous.

"You know, we have a lot of intensity on both sides of this thing, and you know, it takes on a life of its own," he noted. "As I said, each game is a series in itself, and I think obviously, these last two games have proven that. These ballclubs both want it badly, and, yeah, they are going to keep battling right until somebody winds up going beyond."

In Game 6, that someone would be Schilling. And Mark Bellhorn. And Keith Foulke, as the Red Sox became the first major league team to rally from 0-3 and tie a postseason series.

The night was filled with drama, theatrics, blown umpiring calls, nasty behavior from the fans, and lots of Red Sox heroics.

Schilling, his ankle stitched together, blood soaking his sock— yes, a true red sock—held the Yanks to four hits and one run in seven innings, leaving on top 4-1.

"This guy did everything he could to go back on the mound, and we did everything we could to get him there," Millar said. "When I saw blood dripping though the sock and he's giving us seven innings in Yankee Stadium, that was storybook."

What wasn't storybook in this game?

Just getting Schilling to the mound was a minor miracle.

"This training staff was just phenomenal—the things they did for me over the last four, five, six days," he said. "To avoid having it popping in and out, they sutured the skin down to something in between the two tendons to keep the tendon out. It worked."

While Schilling was an unexpected star because of his health situation, Bellhorn was a shocking headliner because, well, he might have been Boston's least effective performer thus far. He dropped from second to ninth in the lineup for the fourth game and his .129 batting average was the lowest in the postseason among the Sox.

In the fourth inning, with Boston up 1-0, the struggling Bellhorn hit a shot to left field off Lieber that went over the wall. Umpire Jim Joyce ruled it a ground-rule double, then changed it to a three-run homer after the other five umpires all said the ball cleared the fence on a fly.

Bellhorn had been in a 4-for-32 postseason slump.

"I kind of surprised myself that it went out," he said.

So what do you think it did to the Yankees and their followers, Mark?

"You know, any time you don't get hits or you're not putting good at-bats together, I think you lose a little bit of confidence," he said. "But that shows a lot about this team where everybody was on my side and kept telling me I'm going to come through for this team."

Foulke, the Sox's closer, also came through, but not without some of the usual excitement that always accompanies this rivalry.

Before Foulke came on, Arroyo was pitching the eighth with a

4-1 lead. Jeter's RBI single made it closer, and then A-Rod scuffed a ball between the mound and first base. As Arroyo fielded the squibber and ran toward first, Rodriguez slapped the ball away at the base line.

Jeter scored as the Sox chased the ball down the right-field line. A livid Francona stormed from the dugout to protest.

Again, the umpires needed a confab before ruling Rodriguez out for interference and sending Jeter all the way back to first.

"That's against the rules," Millar said of A-Rod's actions. "If you want to play football, strap on some pads and go play for the Green Bay Packers."

Rodriguez, everyone else in pinstripes, and Yankees nation couldn't believe the call, even if it was the correct one. This didn't happen to them when they played the Red Sox; it always happened to Boston, and destroyed whatever chance of winning the Sox had.

"I know that line belongs to me and he was coming at me," he said. "Once I reached out and tried to knock the ball, the call went against me. I should have just run over him."

Now the mood in Yankee Stadium had turned ugly. Fans tossed all sorts of items on the field as Torre argued the decision. For 10 minutes, play was held up, and when it began again, Sheffield ended the inning by fouling out.

Helmeted police kneeled in foul territory along the stands on both sides in the ninth inning.

Even then, most New Yorkers felt assured the Yanks would rally and end all of this nonsense, especially after Foulke issued two walks. But Tony Clark fanned for the final out, and Boston's players surged out of the dugout—for the third night in a row.

The series was even, 3-3. The Red Sox had done the unimaginable by coming back from a 0-3 deficit.

But all it had gotten them was a showdown seventh game, in Yankee Stadium. And history told everyone how that always came out—not in Boston's favor.

"For the last three days, we kept showing up saying we had to win today," Francona said, his voice brimming with the confidence inspired by seeing the Red Sox do exactly what was needed. "And because of that, we'll show up for the seventh game and say the same thing. Come to the ballpark and it's the most important game of the day. Carries a little extra weight."

Ah, but all of the weight was now being carried by the Yankees, whose pinstripes must have felt like iron shackles. Not only did the Yanks face the challenge of beating a surging opponent that was almost counted out twice, but they were very cognizant that a fourth straight loss would constitute the greatest collapse in baseball history.

And against their archrival, no less.

Not that the media and the public—not to mention, perhaps, their families and friends—were mentioning how this ALCS had gone. Oh, no.

Who would dare have brought up the fact the Yanks had routed Schilling and Martinez, and then won Game 3 19-8? Or that they had the best reliever in the game, Rivera, on the mound not once, but twice, to protect a lead and get them to the World Series?

Or that of the previous 25 teams down 0-3 in a postseason baseball series, none had gotten it to seven games.

Still, this was Yankees-Red Sox, and the mood through much of the nation (forgetting New England, of course) was of resignation: The Yankees would find a way to win.

"With some of these series, you sense this could happen, a big turnaround," said longtime baseball writer Ben Walker, who was covering the National League series the St. Louis Cardinals won. "Not this one. There was never any real thought of 'The tide has turned.' Most comebacks, you see a foundation laid for it. But there was nothing to indicate the Red Sox were going to win it.

"Even when they won Game 6 and got that call on A-Rod, you thought for a second, 'Did the baseball world tilt on its axis?' But then you realized all that made it was 50-50 who would win the seventh game. And the Yankees always won those games against the Red Sox."

Neither team's pitching staff seemed prepared for a Game 7. Boston would send Lowe to the mound, and while he was well rested, his lifetime stats at Yankee Stadium (3-5, 6.02 ERA) weren't encouraging. In his most recent start there, Lowe was awful, yielding seven runs and four hits in one-plus inning before leaving with a bruised shin.

The Yanks had the veteran Brown, who had been through the difficult postseason rigors many times with several teams, often successfully. But he'd pitched poorly in Game 3.

Regardless, the feeling among those who attended all six games was pretty clear: somehow, the Yankees would survive.

Some nervous Yankees fans figured they could find an edge outside the Bronx. Outside the city, in fact.

Make that outside reality.

In Hawthorne, New York, about 20 miles north of the Stadium, lies the grave of the great Bambino. And on this day, sensing the need for extra help, dozens of fans dressed in pinstripe jerseys and NY hats visited the Gate of Heaven Cemetery.

"I just came by to ask the Babe for help," Jeff Loughlin, a 52-year-old longtime fan, told the Associated Press. "I'm going to the game tonight, and you know, it's the most majestic feeling when they win a game like this. You can tell it's more than meets the eye."

The fans left small tokens of their devotion to the team and its greatest player: coins, cigars, pumpkins.

"We came before the seventh game (in 2003) and left a 1986 penny and a 1978 penny, because those were bad years for the Red Sox," said Carol Monaghan, who had two-year-old daughter Emma with her. "This year we left an '86, a '78 and a 2003, because it worked last year."

One man, Phil DeGasperis, wore a New York Rangers shirt, explaining it would create bad karma to wear Yankees gear to the cemetery.

"I try to stop by every year, especially when we're playing the Red Sox, to say a couple of prayers, make sure Babe and his buddies get to Yankee Stadium tonight," he said before looking at the gravesite and adding: "We want you to do your thing, Babe! Wake up Lou and Joe and Mickey."

If the Red Sox were paying attention to history, they would have expected Gehrig, DiMaggio, and Mantle to show up in uniform and in their primes. Yogi Berra, Whitey Ford, Reggie Jackson, and Ron Guidry, too.

No such thoughts infiltrated their preparation. This was a loose, uninhibited squad: Damon's Idiots.

And the Idiots were performing like Geniuses.

Still.

"At no point until late in Game 7 did I think the Red Sox would win," said the AP's Fitzpatrick. "The year before, they were coming off having Pedro on the mound with a three-run lead in the eighth inning—and the Yankees still won. So you never thought of them actually doing it."

There would be no more demons for the Sox on this magical night, however. There would be lots of Damon.

And Big Papi, as Ortiz slammed a two-run homer off the ineffective Brown in the first inning. Brown wasn't even around in the second when Javier Vazquez served up a grand slam to Damon, making it 6-0.

Damon hit another two-run shot to make it 8-1. Lowe gave up one hit in six innings.

Was the Babe turning over in his Westchester grave?

But wait. Francona made the odd decision of bringing in Martinez to pitch the seventh inning, the ace's first relief appearance in five years. That woke up the Yankees fans, who chanted "Who's Your Daddy?" and figured the miracle in this series would be their club's comeback from seven runs behind in Game 7.

And it looked like they were on to something as the Yanks got three hits and two runs.

"The only thought that keeps going through my head is, how much is it going to hurt when they blow this one?" said Red Sox fan Lee Gregory.

Memories of Johnny Pesky holding the ball in the 1946 Series as the Cardinals scored the winning run flashed through the minds of those anxious aficionados. Of Bill Buckner allowing a simple ground ball to slip through his legs in 1986. Of Bucky Dent. Of Aaron Boone.

Nightmares all. Horror shows.

And history all. There would be no flop this time.

"All empires fall sooner or later," Lucchino said after the 10-3 romp smashed the Curse—and the Yankees.

"All the fans and all the players all those years couldn't get a chance to go to the World Series because the Yankees were in the way. Now we're in their way," general manager Theo Epstein said. "That's for the '03 team, just like it's for the '78 and the '49 team. I hope Ted Williams is having a cocktail upstairs."

If he was, it was certainly at the expense of all those hallowed Yankees. The long, long run of dominance had ended.

But to fall like this? As victims of the most sensational comeback in baseball, if not sports history? As wildly as the Sox would celebrate—now and after their incredible run carried them right through four straight victories in the World Series over St. Louis—the Yankees would wonder.

"I wish my eyes were closed and I could open them now," Gordon said. "It could have been over in four. It's a tough one to bite."

"History would have told them to give up. It didn't matter to them. They didn't just fold the tent."

The toughest part for the hosts came when the Sox stormed out of their dugout after securing the final out of their incredible comeback. Other than the yelps and screams of the winners, Yankee Stadium was silent.

"I'm embarrassed right now," said Rodriguez, who went 2 for 17 in the final four games, which was better than Sheffield's 1 for 17. "Obviously that hurts—watching them on our field celebrating."

And celebrating not just this victory, but how they'd doused the evil spirits that haunted them for years and years, decades and decades.

"Last year, I remember we had a bad memory," said Ortiz, the ALCS MVP. "A lot of my teammates were just destroyed, because we played a pretty good game and we lost and it was a big-time opportunity to step to the World Series.

"We saw a lot of fans crying and feeling hurt and I think myself and all of my teammates, we were worried about it and kept that for ourselves. And that's one of the big reasons for us to come to the field and represent the way we did the last four games."

To represent the way nobody ever had. And might not again.

3

THE MIRACLE AT COOGAN'S BLUFF

Bobby Thomson's Homer, 1951

"The Giants win the pennant, the Giants win the pennant, the Giants win the pennant! I don't believe it, I don't believe it, I don't believe it!"

Russ Hodges's incredulous voice filled the radio airwaves, accompanied by the mighty roar of fans at the Polo Grounds in New York.

They had just seen a miracle, or the closest thing to it.

Bobby Thomson hit the "wrong" pitch into the right place in the left-field stands. The game-winning home run completed an incredible storybook pennant race for the New York Giants in 1951.

If a screenwriter had tried to sell the story to Hollywood, it would have been dismissed: too unbelievable.

Thomson was the hero and Ralph Branca, the pitcher who served up the historic homer, the goat—but hardly the only featured characters in this stirring baseball melodrama known as the Miracle at Coogan's Bluff.

Like all great productions, this one had a compelling group of leading men.

Start with the director of the Giants' remarkable story, Leo Durocher, the hot-tempered manager whose aggressive tactics had ignited a beanball war and king-sized feud with the Dodgers. The same Durocher who had once managed the Dodgers and joined the hated archrival Giants in the middle of the 1948 season after a fallout with Dodgers general manager Branch Rickey.

Mix in the combustible elements of Brooklyn's Carl Furillo and Jackie Robinson, who became Durocher's sworn enemies as the 1951 season drama unfolded. An interesting twist to this story: When Robinson broke baseball's color line in 1947, Durocher had squashed a rebellion by his players protesting Robinson's presence and helped to ease his way into the big leagues.

Baseball made strange bedfellows. Durocher had been Robinson's friend then, but now he was his foe.

The 1951 season also featured the emergence of a player by the name of Willie Mays—a Durocher prodigy and future Hall-of-Famer.

Durocher himself was voted into the Hall of Fame after five decades as a player, manager, coach, and broadcaster. He was also credited as the author of a line (loosely translated from the original) that became a fixture of the English language:

Nice guys finish last.

Durocher, who once gave New York Yankees teammate Babe Ruth a black eye, was admittedly anything but a nice guy on a baseball field. As Durocher would explain his philosophy in an interview with the *New York Times*:

> Look, I'm playing third base. My grandmother's on second. The ball's hit out to short center. As she goes by me on the way to third, I'll accidentally trip her up. I'll help her up, brush her off, tell her I'm sorry. But she doesn't get to third. That's just an exaggeration, but it's an explanation of what I mean. I want to win all the time.

The argumentative "Leo the Lip" was in his mid-40s in the 1951 season and had been around baseball just about all his life. A slick defensive shortstop, Durocher started for the Yankees and Cincinnati Reds and captained the famed St. Louis Cardinals

"Gashouse Gang" of the 1930s before he was traded to the Dodgers.

In 1940, he took over as player-manager of the Dodgers. By 1941, he had turned Brooklyn into a pennant winner and kept the Dodgers competing for the top spot through most of the '40s. Durocher battled umpires, players, and fans through these tumultuous years in Brooklyn and feuded with Rickey, the Dodgers' legendary leader who had opened the door for blacks in the big leagues.

Durocher's greatest moment might have occurred off the field when he defended Robinson's right to be in the major leagues. In a bizarre turn of events, the very year that Robinson broke the color line, Durocher was suspended for his alleged involvement with gamblers. Burt Shotton was hired by Rickey and promptly led the Dodgers to the pennant, with Robinson playing a key role as an out-of-position rookie first baseman.

Like many baseball managers, Durocher was highly superstitious. During one winning streak in the 1941 season, Durocher wore the same blue sport jacket, blue tie, gray slacks, and black shoes for nearly four weeks. "Naturally, I changed my shirt, socks, and shorts," he pointed out to a reporter.

Durocher was almost as famous for his marriage to movie star Lorraine Day, who did a daily baseball TV show during the season and loved the game.

Although Durocher credited the actress for introducing him to the more cultured things in life, such as painting and antiques, it didn't change the way he dealt with umpires or baseball in general. His battle with umpire Lon Warneke during the 1951 season was typical Leo.

Durocher was fined $100 for using "vile and abusive language" to Warneke. It happened when the Dodgers were playing the Cardinals in St. Louis. In the eighth inning, the Giants' Whitey Lockman was ruled safe at second on what became a double steal. The play triggered a long and vehement protest from Cardinals second baseman Red Schoendienst.

Durocher thought Schoendienst should have been thrown out of the game. After all, his own second baseman, Eddie Stanky, was ejected earlier for heckling umpire Dusty Boggess.

"He waylaid me under the dugout and made as if he wanted to

fight me," Warneke said of Durocher. "He called me all sorts of names."

Durocher, who had a volatile history with Warneke, defended himself in the postgame dispute.

"I didn't throw any punch. Neither did Warneke. I did tell him he had no guts, was a lousy umpire, and that everything I said about him in New York still goes."

If there was a storm in baseball during the 1951 season, Durocher was very often at the center of it—especially if it involved the Dodgers and Giants.

Midway through that season, Dodgers outfielder Furillo refused to appear on Day's television show at the Polo Grounds. The reason, Furillo said, was that Durocher had ordered his pitchers to throw at Furillo's head.

"No one else in the league does it," Furillo said. "One day last year he told me he was going to throw at me, and the same day I got hit on the head. If it happens again, I'll get him. For every day I spend in the hospital, he'll spend two."

These "beanballs" only fueled the feud between the Dodgers and Giants, which had been going on for many years, but which really intensified during the '51 season. Pointing the finger at his former manager and friend, Robinson said Durocher was to blame for the bad blood with his beanball philosophy.

"Some of (Leo's) pitchers, like Larry Jansen, don't want to do it, but they have to," Robinson said in an interview for *Look* magazine.

Giants right-hander Sal Maglie didn't seem to mind. But when he threw at Robinson, the Brooklyn second baseman retaliated. On one play, Robinson bunted down the first-base line, forcing Maglie to come over and field the ball. When he did, Robinson bumped him with a hard hip check.

Durocher called Robinson a "busher" for that type of tactic. Robinson's reaction to Durocher:

"Then you're a bush league manager because you taught me to do things like that."

Durocher was doing his best to unsettle one of the most powerful Brooklyn teams in history. Having managed in Brooklyn, Durocher knew this team inside and out. With Robinson, Furillo, Roy Campanella, Gil Hodges, Duke Snider, Pee Wee Reese, and Andy Pafko, the Dodgers had all-stars at just about every position.

And with Billy Cox at third, Brooklyn boasted the best glove man in the league at that position.

The year before, the Dodgers staged a late rally to nearly snatch the National League pennant away from the Philadelphia Phillies. On the final day of the 1950 season, the Dodgers trailed the Phillies by one game when the teams collided at Ebbets Field in Brooklyn. A Dodgers victory would force a playoff.

The game featured a strong pitching duel between each team's ace: Robin Roberts of the Phillies and Don Newcombe of the Dodgers. With the score tied 1-1 in the bottom of the ninth, the Dodgers put their first two runners on base. Snider, the Dodgers' slugging center fielder, hit a line drive single to center. Cal Abrams raced from second base, tore around third, and headed home with the apparent winning run. But a strong throw by Phillies center fielder Richie Ashburn cut down the runner by a large margin. The Dodgers later loaded the bases, but were unable to punch home the winning run.

In the top of the 10th, Dick Sisler hit a three-run homer into the left field seats for a 4-1 Phillies victory.

Another home run into the left field seats just one year later would again be costly—indeed, historic—to the luckless Dodgers.

As the 1951 season got underway, the Associated Press sized up the National League pennant race as a three-team affair.

"Beginning April 17," the AP said, "it is going to be a dog-eat-dog with the Giants, Brooklyn Dodgers and defending champion Philadelphia Phillies doing most of the clawing and biting."

The Giants had a formidable team, most notable for a strong pitching staff, which included Jansen, Maglie, and Jim Hearn.

There were good hitters up and down the Giants' lineup, with Thomson, Lockman, Eddie Stanky, Alvin Dark, Monte Irvin, Don Mueller, Henry Thompson, Wes Westrum, and a high-spirited kid named Mays.

When Mays joined the Giants in late May, he went directly to center field and forced a realignment of the outfield. Thomson, the center fielder, was moved to left field. That lasted until he was switched to third base in July.

Thomson said he played the infield in self-defense.

"I realized from the start that I was no third-sacker," he said. "So I concentrated so much on trying to keep from being killed at third base that I never had time to think about hitting until I was up at the plate."

Hitting came more naturally to Thomson.

As a rookie in 1947, Thomson hit 29 home runs, the first of eight seasons in which he would surpass the 20 mark.

Born in Scotland, Thomson came to the United States as a boy and grew up in Staten Island, New York. He signed a contract with the Giants in 1942, but wartime put his baseball plans on hold. When he returned from the service, Thomson was almost an instant success with the Giants. By 1948 and '49 he was part of an up-and-coming Giants team and playing in all-star games.

In 1951, Durocher was happy with his team when it left training camp, not so happy with the way the Giants played early on. They lost 11 straight games in April, including a three-game sweep by the Dodgers in their first meeting at the Polo Grounds.

The Giants continued to have trouble with the Dodgers into the summer. On July 4, the first-place Dodgers swept a doubleheader to open their lead to six and a half games over New York.

The second game of the twin bill, won 4-2 by the Dodgers, was filled with controversy. So what was new? It was a Dodger-Giant game, after all.

The Giants had runners on first and third with one out in the ninth inning when pinch-hitter Earl Rapp grounded to Robinson at second base.

On his way to second, Han Schenz avoided the tag of Robinson, who threw to first to retire Rapp. Umpire Ralph Pinelli ruled it a game-ending double play because he determined that Schenz had run out of the baseline.

"Durocher and Eddie Stanky ganged up on base umpire Ralph Pinelli in a rage . . . ," the Associated Press reported. "Pinelli stalked off the field with practically all the Giants hanging onto his shirt tail."

It wasn't the only time Durocher was enraged that day. He filed a protest, claiming Dodgers manager Charlie Dressen was coaching his team from the stands following his ejection earlier in the second game.

Durocher was even unhappier the next day when the Dodgers whipped the Giants 8-4 with a 13-hit attack led by Hodges's 27th home run and Pafko's 17th. The three-game sweep boosted the Dodgers' lead to seven and a half games.

Looking ahead to the second half of the season after the All-Star break, the *New York Times* was confident of the Dodgers' chances.

"If the Dodgers even approach their excellent first-half form—and there is no reason why they shouldn't—the battle in the National League from now on will be strictly for second place," the *Times* said.

That prediction looked pretty good when the Dodgers swept a three-game series from the Giants in early August to go up 12½ games on New York. And even better when the Dodgers improved their lead to 13½ games on August 11.

The Giants were seemingly not only knocked out of pennant contention by the Dodgers, they were in danger of losing their grip on second place to the fast-coming Phillies.

Not so fast, Brooklyn.

The Giants started slicing away at the Dodgers' huge lead with the help of a three-game series sweep of Brooklyn in the Polo Grounds. When the Dodgers left town, their lead had been reduced to nine and a half games and the *Times* reported, "Maybe the National League is going to have a pennant race after all."

Mays continued to amaze people with his play in center field, a foreshadowing of great things to come. In a 3-1 triumph over the Dodgers, Mays chased down Furillo's long fly ball, then doubled Cox at home as the Brooklyn third baseman attempted to tag up and score.

Suddenly, the Giants were hot. When they won their ninth straight with a 5-4 victory over the Phillies on August 19, they pulled within eight games of Brooklyn. It was still a big gap, but the Giants had cut five and a half games off the Dodgers' lead in a matter of merely eight days.

The Dodgers had a history of blowing big leads. In 1942, they lost a 10-game lead as the St. Louis Cardinals staged a late rally to win the pennant. Durocher happened to be managing the Dodgers at the time.

"The Dodgers are beginning to look nervously over their shoulders to see who that guy is that's following them," Arthur Daley wrote in the *Times*.

The victories mounted for the Giants: 10 in a row, 11, 12, 13, and 14. That's where it looked like the streak was going to end, in the first game of a doubleheader with the Chicago Cubs.

In a tingling back-and-forth game, the Cubs had taken a 4-3 lead in the top of the 12th. On the mound for Chicago was Dutch Leonard, a tricky knuckleballer who had worked out of a bases-loaded jam in the eighth.

In the 12th, the Giants loaded the bases with one out. Lockman singled in the tying run and pinch-hitter Bill Rigney drove in the game-winner with a sacrifice fly for a dramatic 5-4 New York victory. It kept the Giants' winning steak alive, and they went on to win the second game 6-3 for their 16th straight—longest in the NL since Chicago's 21-game streak in 1935.

Now the Dodgers' lead was down to five games.

It was a classic team effort for the Giants. They were getting help from everyone, including two players who had been in the minors the year before—Mays and pitcher Al Corwin. Also George Spencer, a forgotten man in the bullpen, was contributing. By the final week of August, Corwin and Spencer had already combined for 15 victories while losing only four times.

However, the Giants' cause seemed hopeless when the Dodgers beat St. Louis 4-3 on September 20 to virtually wrap up the pennant. At this point, the Giants' biggest foe was not the Dodgers, but time. With 10 games left, Brooklyn held a 4½-game lead. And even when New York shaved Brooklyn's advantage to 2½ games in the last week of the season, it seemed only a miracle could save the Giants.

Maybe more than one miracle, in fact.

In order just to tie, the Giants had to win their last four games with Philadelphia and Boston, two of the tougher teams in the league, while the Dodgers had to lose four of their last seven.

The Giants continued to do their part, and the Dodgers did theirs, running into all sorts of problems in Boston. "It couldn't happen to a nicer bunch of guys," Durocher said sarcastically after hearing of Brooklyn's doubleheader defeat by the Braves while his Giants were beating Philadelphia 5-1 with the help of stout relief pitching by Maglie.

The Boston-Brooklyn series featured a flare-up by the Dodgers that made headlines. Following the Braves' 4-3 victory on a disputed call at home, the door to the umpires' dressing room was kicked in. Robinson and Campanella were fined $100 each and Dodgers pitcher Preacher Roe $50 by National League president Ford Frick. Frick fined the players "for the scenes they put on in the runways and in front of the umpires' dressing room in the presence of fans and opposing ballplayers."

There were reports that Robinson had done the damage to the umpire's door, but he protested his innocence. "I know who did it, and it wasn't me," Robinson said. "But I won't tell who did it."

Were the Dodgers unraveling?

After losing three of four in Boston, their lead had shrunk to mere percentage points as they pulled into Philadelphia for a three-game series. The task for the Dodgers was simple: Sweep the series from the Phillies and the pennant was theirs, no matter what the Giants did in their two games in Boston.

Easier said than done. When Brooklyn lost the opener to fall into a tie with idle New York, the Giants' players rocked their hotel headquarters in Boston with shrieks and yells. While his players celebrated noisily, Durocher did so quietly.

"I can't get up," Durocher said as he sat in an easy chair. "If I make a move, I'll explode with happiness."

Had anyone noticed that the New York Yankees had clinched their third straight pennant in the American League? Or that another Subway Series was guaranteed?

That was overshadowed by one of the greatest pennant races in baseball history.

On Saturday, both the Dodgers and Giants won. The *Los Angeles Times* headline said it all:

"Giants, Bums in Last-Day Tie."

For a while, it looked like Sunday was going to be the "Bums'" last day of the season. The Dodgers trailed the Phillies 6-1 before rallying to tie 8-8 in the eighth inning.

The game went into extra innings, with extra pressure on the Dodgers: The scoreboard showed them that the Giants had already won their game with the Braves.

Enter Jackie Robinson.

In the bottom of the 12th, the Phillies loaded the bases with two out. Eddie Waitkus hit a line drive up the middle. Robinson raced to his right and made a diving catch as he tumbled hard on the ground, saving the game—and the Dodgers' shot at the pennant.

Robinson was injured on the play, but stayed in the game after some medical attention. Good thing for Brooklyn he did.

In the top of the 14th, Robinson whacked a home run to give the Dodgers a nerve-grinding 9-8 victory.

Result: a tie for first place between the Giants and Dodgers and only the second two-out-of-three-games playoff in the 75-year history of the National League.

For the Dodgers, a great relief. For the Giants, a great joy.

"My boys here did it when everybody claimed it was an impossibility," Durocher said. "Words can't describe the happiness I feel."

What the Giants did certainly seemed like an impossibility. In the last seven weeks of the season, they won 37 of 44 games, an extraordinary .841 clip.

Hearn, one of the key pitchers for the Giants in that stretch, was chosen by Durocher to start the playoff opener at Ebbets Field. The Dodgers countered with Ralph Branca.

Branca was making his second start in a playoff opener. In 1946, he had been tapped to start the first playoff in National League history. He lost to St. Louis, and the Cardinals went on to beat the Dodgers in two straight to advance to the World Series.

Branca, a native of Mount Vernon, New York, had played basketball at New York University before starting a baseball career with a Dodgers farm team in 1943. In 1944, he made his debut in the big leagues as an 18-year-old rookie, and was mostly used as a relief pitcher. It wasn't until the 1947 season, when Branca won 21 games, that he started to fulfill his promise. He followed that by winning 27 games in the next two seasons and appearing in two all-star games.

Branca struggled over the next two years, but eventually made his way back into the rotation in 1951 as one of the Dodgers' top three pitchers, along with Newcombe and Roe.

A crowd of 30,707 turned out at the Dodgers' Ebbets Field bandbox to watch the first game of the 1951 NL playoffs on October 1. The faithful went home disappointed as Thomson and Irvin hit home runs to offset one by Pafko in a 3-1 Giants victory.

"It's all like a dream," the tanned and stubble-faced Hearns said in a jubilant Giants locker room after New York beat Brooklyn for the seventh time in their last eight meetings. "Here we were in last place. And now we've won the first game of the playoff."

A *New York Times* writer called the steamrolling Giants "The Polo Grounds Express."

But the "Express" came to a sudden halt the next day. The Dodgers won the second game 10-0 with a four-homer attack and the hurling of young Clem Labine, who was thrust into action only because Dressen had no other rested pitchers.

For most of the next game, the deciding game, it looked like the Dodgers would head into the World Series.

Newcombe was outpitching Maglie, who had been a thorn in the Dodgers' side all season. Brooklyn's ace had allowed only four hits in the first eight innings and went into the ninth holding a 4-1 lead. The way he was pitching, Newcombe looked unbeatable. And his fastball looked faster in the gathering darkness of late afternoon. All he needed was three more outs and the Dodgers owned the pennant.

On the Giants' bench, Durocher told his team: "We have three big outs left. You haven't given up all year, so don't give up now. Let's get some runs."

The Giants replied almost in chorus: "We'll get the Bums!"

Alvin Dark singled to lead off the Giants' ninth, and Mueller sent the New York shortstop to third with another single.

After Newcombe retired Irvin on a foul popup, Lockman doubled to drive in Dark and send Mueller sliding into third. Mueller was injured on the play and the Giants, now trailing 4-2, sent in Clint Hartung as a pinch-runner.

The Dodgers held a conference on the mound. Suddenly, Newcombe, the strong-armed Brooklyn ace who had once started both ends of a doubleheader, began walking toward the Dodgers' center field dressing room at the Polo Grounds.

In came Branca to face Thomson.

"When I came in to relieve Newcombe, I just kept thinking, 'Get these two guys out and we're in the Series,'" Branca said.

Labine and Carl Erskine were also warming up in the bullpen. But Dressen had already decided on Branca, according to bullpen catcher Rube Walker. He never asked Walker for an opinion. "He had his mind made up, and that was it," Walker said.

As Branca warmed up on the mound, Thomson huddled with Durocher up the third base line.

"Bobby, if you've ever hit one, hit it now," Durocher told Thomson, who had hit 31 homers for the Giants, including one earlier in the playoff series against Branca.

Up to that point, Thomson had been the goat of the third game with a base-running blunder that had run the Giants out of a rally. Now was the time to make up for that.

Branca's first pitch came in right over the plate. Strike one.

"When he took it for a strike, my heart sank," said Lockman, who had a good view of the pitch while leading off second base. "It was a perfect pitch for him. *That* was the pitch he should have swung at."

The next one was high and tight.

"I saw Branca let loose with his fast pitch and I was all set," Thomson said.

So was Russ Hodges—for the call of his life.

A swing. A crack of the bat. Pafko turns toward the wall and watches the ball sail over his head into the left field seats at the 315-foot mark.

Home run!

Giants win the pennant! Giants win the pennant! Giants win the pennant!

"When it passed over my head, the whole thing became a terrible blur," Pafko said after Thomson's homer gave the Giants a 5-4 victory and launched them into the World Series.

It was a blur for Thomson, too.

"When I saw it go into the stands," he said, "I don't think I touched the ground the remainder of the way. I just floated around. It was that kind of a feeling."

Robinson, ever the professional, stood grimly behind second, hands on hips, to make sure that Thomson touched every base.

Thomson did, of course—he wasn't floating quite that high—and then was greeted by a mob of teammates at home plate.

"The Giants, lined up at home plate, fairly mobbed the Hawk as he completed the last few strides to the plate," the *New York Times* reported. "Jubilant Giant fans, fairly beside themselves, eluded guards and swarmed on the field to join the melee."

There was pandemonium in the Giants' sweltering dressing room, too—"such confusion," said the Associated Press, "that hardly anyone could get in a word."

The crowd in the dressing room included Dodgers president Walter O'Malley and Dressen, who had come in to congratulate Durocher. Robinson later came by.

"I told you we'd finish one, two," Dressen said as he shook hands with Durocher. "I was right, only we were second."

© *Sports Illustrated.*

Bobby Thomson and Manager Leo Durocher celebrate "the shot heard around the world" on October 1, 1951. Photo by Jerry Cooke.

The Dodgers' dressing room was like a tomb.

AP reporter Ted Meier was one of the first newsmen on the scene there. Meier recalled that Branca was sitting on a stairway with his head down in his arms, hardly able to speak.

In later years, Meier recalled that Branca told him, finally, "If you're lucky in love, I guess you can't be lucky in baseball, too."

Branca was 17 days away from marrying his sweetheart, Ann Mulvey.

As Branca dressed quietly in front of his locker, he told reporters: "I guess we weren't meant to win it. The ball was high and inside, not a good pitch, and it only cleared the wall by that much," spreading his arms to indicate a matter of inches.

Durocher was expecting to have a big homecoming party in California for him and his wife at the end of the season. Lorraine Day's brother had printed the invitations in the shape of a baseball. But after the Giants won the pennant, he reprinted them with a big red "X" through the date. The revised card said, "Postponed by Bobby Thomson."

In subsequent years, Branca and Thomson would become an inseparable pair on the baseball memorabilia circuit. Branca often kidded that he was married to Thomson longer than he was married to his own wife.

The Giants went on to lose the World Series to the Yankees. It was almost anticlimactic. After all, one miracle was enough for the season.

4

THE SAINTS COME MARCHING BACK

2005–2006 New Orleans Saints

Who dat? Who dat gonna keep our Saints from Nawlins?

Not even the most devastating storm in American history could keep the New Orleans Saints from going home again.

Hurricane Katrina leveled much of the Gulf Coast, with New Orleans suffering unimaginable destruction. The plight of the local NFL team might seem trivial in comparison to levees breaking, floodwaters tearing through homes, thousands of lives lost. And for a while, yes, the Saints' travails paled—except for their personal stories of loss and carnage.

But the perseverance displayed by the organization not only is enlightening, it's uplifting. This was a comeback of a totally different kind, a story of caring and courage, one that, in the end, paid tribute to the human ability to adapt, to endure, indeed to survive, while never letting the ultimate goal fade from sight.

This is a comeback not on the scoreboard or the field. This is, well, a revelation for everyone involved with the New Orleans Saints: players, executives, aides, relatives, and fans.

And on September 25, 2006, the Big Easy put on the kind of show for which it is famed, as best explained by a native son from another sport, Dallas Mavericks coach Avery Johnson.

"Obviously, a football game is not going to solve all of our problems or take away the misery or the hurt from all that has gone on here," Johnson said. "But if it is just for three hours, you never know how that can reenergize somebody and bring them some joy and hope."

The warnings began while Katrina was still gathering up its deadly force in the Caribbean. For decades, New Orleans and the Louisiana Bayou always escaped the most serious damage from such storms. This one, though, was headed directly toward the area, with winds capable of, well, the unthinkable.

Just a year earlier, when Hurricane Ivan threatened to make landfall in the New Orleans area, the Saints practiced in San Antonio. This time, with a preseason game scheduled for Oakland on Thursday, September 1, the team headed to California.

"We decided to leave as late as possible on Sunday to give everyone enough time to take care of their personal situations and to ensure that everyone's family was out of harm's way," team spokesman Greg Bensel said.

It was not an easy trip for the Saints. While they would practice for three days at San Jose State—eventually purchasing $5,000 worth of tickets to the school's first game of the season in thanks for its hospitality—many Saints had friends, family, and property back home, in the midst of a bull's-eye that Katrina was bearing directly toward.

"We're professionals and we're supposed to have our minds only on the job at hand," star receiver Joe Horn said. "But of course that's hard, it's almost impossible, when you know what might be happening back home."

What was happening was something Ray Bradbury or Rod Serling might have conjured. Except this wasn't science fiction, wasn't some grade-B horror movie.

This was real and pure devastation.

Members of the Saints watched on television from more than 2,000 miles away as Katrina's winds ripped through anything in her path—much of which was not designed to withstand anything close to such a hurricane. Levees leaked, then collapsed. Houses were washed down waterways that once were avenues for automobiles.

For those without the means to leave or with nowhere else to go, the evacuation process failed almost as horribly as the roofs and walls that Katrina laid flat. Thankfully, a vast majority of the Saints had the wherewithal to get their loved ones to safety.

That was about the only relief the players felt.

"This has been on everybody's mind," said cornerback Jimmy Williams, who had a comfort zone while in San Jose because he formerly played for the San Francisco 49ers. "From where did they leave their car parked because it's probably going to be underwater because of the flood, to alligators in your house. I never had to worry about that stuff when I played in San Francisco."

Williams brought his wife, Chandra, with him to California. Other Saints made sure their families had relocated.

Still, none of them was prepared for those television pictures. Calling home was fruitless. All they could do was watch, wait, and hope.

"I slept for only about an hour, if that," said receiver and kick returner Michael Lewis, a New Orleans native. "I watched about everything I could on TV. I had the Weather Channel on all night."

"This is just a nightmare for anyone," added quarterback Aaron Brooks. "You never want to wish this on anyone. This is ludicrous, it's crazy. You have to overcome it. It's tough because there are going to be a lot of lives lost. There are going to be a lot of hard feelings from it all, but you've got to have faith and you've got to be strong."

The strength the Saints would have to muster, the resolve they would need to gather, was immeasurable. Their nomadic existence had only just begun.

A preseason football game barely registered on the scale of significance in light of the woes back in the Gulf Coast. The Saints managed a few hours of concentration on football, but fell 13-6 to the Raiders. They immediately turned their attention back to the plight of the folks back home—a home that would never be the same.

"You have people who are trying to survive and unrealistic looters who are trying to get sneakers and shirts to put on because it's wet out there," Horn said after watching TV accounts of looting in New Orleans. "I'm not upset by people breaking in and getting things. To take things like DVD players, TVs and things like that, that's just crazy. But I would be doing the same thing if I were in New Orleans and my children needed to eat or I had to go to the mall to get a shirt for them to wear.

"Guess what, you'd be calling Joe Horn 'looter.' The businesses there aren't going to sell anything, because it's all going to be under water. If I owned a business, I'd be telling the people to come get it."

Horn, known as much for his outlandish cell phone touchdown celebration that cost him a $30,000 fine two years previous, would become something of a spokesman for the nomadic Saints. No player, coach, or executive with the team would display more civic responsibility, more compassion, indeed, more humanity than Horn.

After the preseason concluded, Horn made a trip to the Houston Astrodome to meet with hundreds of Katrina survivors who now were refugees.

Chatting, holding infants, staging impromptu little football games with youngsters and signing dozens of autographs, Horn spent more than three hours in the dome.

"Anybody can throw money around at these people, but they need love," he told the Associated Press. They need to be able to feel me. So when I leave, I hope they feel a little better.

"Right now money doesn't matter. Who you are or where you're from doesn't matter. Getting to come out here and give a child a hug or give someone a hug who knows that their house and everything that they have is gone is what's important."

The players wanted to get home or back to their families to help in any way they could. Their children needed to be registered in new schools. Temporary living quarters had to be found, transportation provided. Nothing was structured anymore.

But they also had their jobs to consider, as trivial as football might have seemed with so much chaos and consternation filling their lives.

"I've given everything a lot of thought," said Lewis. "I sat down with a couple of guys. You can't do much right now until the water comes out. But, when we can, we're talking about doing something in the parks to give the kids something."

Coach Jim Haslett faced perhaps the most difficult challenge: How could he keep his team focused on the season opener at Carolina when, as Lewis indicated, their hearts were back on the Bayou, their minds were filled with nonfootball thoughts.

As a professional linebacker, Haslett was an intense competitor some might have dubbed an overachiever. Rarely was he the most skilled player on the field. Yet, often, he was among the most successful.

As a coach, Haslett maintained that intensity, which his players identified with and which helped him become 2000 NFL Coach of the Year. But he also knew how to deal with each Saint on a personal level. It was the kind of approach he appreciated when he was on the field, and it never was more important than in the immediate days after Katrina struck.

In San Antonio, where they set up a temporary home, the Saints held their meetings in office buildings and had training facilities in hotel ballrooms. If they were lucky, the Alamodome was not occupied by a convention or a rodeo and they could practice there. Otherwise, they worked on high school fields.

"I would love to get in the hot tub right now and get in the cold tub and get my legs back," Horn said. "But I'm sure there's a lot of people that would love to have their homes. They'd love to see their little brother walk through the door. What the New Orleans Saints are going through right now is a cakewalk."

Not quite, but certainly not close to the hell so many people's lives had been plunged into back home.

"I think when you feel sorry for yourselves, you go upstairs and watch TV and that kind of goes away," Haslett said. "We're kind of crammed into some quarters. We're short a copying machine and I've got a couple of coaches sleeping at the Alamodome. But we're not behind at all in our preparations. It's not going to hurt us one way or another being here at all."

Haslett tried to insist the players could find a sense of normalcy, but he was pushing it when he said: "The players want an automobile and a place to live. Once they get that, they have a place where you can drive over to work and go home and lay down. That's all you really need in this business."

The business of their season schedule also was in turmoil. As were, of course, the lives of their relatives and friends.

"But we're not going to let them make excuses," Haslett said of his players. "If we have to play every game on the road, we'll make our adjustments. If the NFL wants us to play every game on the road, we'll do it."

The league itself was uncertain how to handle that dilemma. Dozens of scenarios were presented, but commissioner Paul Tagliabue's main objective was to get the Saints back into the area in some fashion during the 2005 season.

So playing nothing but road games, a ridiculous competitive disadvantage, never truly was considered. Relocating the Saints to Baton Rouge to play their schedule at Louisiana State University was the primary objective, but it proved unmanageable for several reasons—not the least of which was the strain already placed on the state capital by the relocation of thousands of homeless people from New Orleans.

LSU, of course, had its own home schedule, and the challenge of staging an NFL contest with lengthy advance notice is difficult enough. So eight home games at LSU could not happen.

While Tagliabue and the schedule makers were devising a plan, the Saints knew exactly where they had to be on September 11, 2006: in Charlotte.

"I don't expect on Sunday for the Carolina Panthers to feel sorry for us," Horn said. "In their heart, I'm sure they will. But once that clock starts, I'm not going to run around and catch a ball and not expect Julius Peppers to knock my head off."

The Panthers donated 350 tickets to the game to Hurricane Katrina evacuees who were registered with the Red Cross at the Charlotte Coliseum, along with $10 food vouchers for each of those fans to use at the game. The tickets came from the players' allotments.

And, just as at every stadium throughout the season, hurricane relief fund stations were set up to accept donations. A total of $176,000 was raised outside the Panthers' ballpark on opening day.

By all rights, the Panthers should have run right through the distracted Saints. Carolina was a playoff contender, a team that eventually would make the 2005 NFC championship game. It was at home and, coming off a year in which injuries had ruined any chance of getting back to the Super Bowl—where the Panthers lost to New England after the 2003 campaign—Carolina's resolve to turn things around was unquestioned.

But so was the resolve of the Saints. Yes, they were going through unparalleled turmoil and anguish for a pro sports franchise. They were NFL nomads, which observers seemed to translate into NFL no-chances.

They also had learned something about togetherness. And resourcefulness.

"Ever since I was a kid, when you raise your child, you want to get them in a routine. I think it's the same for a football player," Haslett said. "We haven't been in a normal routine. Our guys are really resilient and they adapt real well. They don't complain. They do it."

What they did that Sunday was remarkable.

Deuce McAllister ran for two touchdowns and one minute after Carolina tied it, longtime Saints kicker John Carney nailed a 47-yard field goal with three seconds on the clock, giving New Orleans a 23-20 victory. This was their answer to all those displaced fans who, upon meeting or speaking with the players in shelters throughout the South and Southwest, said they would be watching and rooting for their team. They asked for a win, and the Saints delivered—dramatically and unforgettably.

"In the back of our minds, we know we have to give them one tiny bit of hope," Brooks said. "We have complete faith in what we are doing, because every time we go out there, it is our job to give them hope that every day will be a better day."

The players were inspired by a letter Haslett read the previous night in which New Orleans mayor C. Ray Nagin described the scene during and after Katrina struck.

"He talked about the things he had seen, babies dying," Horn said. "You would only see it in a horror story. People were crying on his shoulder, saying they don't know where their son is, where their daughter is.

"I can't speak enough about how our heart goes out to them. The letter had an impact. We respect and acknowledge what everyone has gone through."

Moments after they rushed onto the field to mob Carney following his winning kick, the Saints handed out two game balls: to Nagin, and to the victims of Katrina.

Stunningly, the Saints were 1-0. They'd conquered their first big football test.

There would be many more.

Particularly the schedule, which the NFL finally had formalized. The "home opener" would be played in Giants Stadium, the true home of the Saints' opponent—yet another competitive drawback for everyone but the Giants—on Monday night, September 19.

Haslett immediately questioned such a move, while the silence of team owner Tom Benson was almost deafening.

But Haslett prepared the Saints for the trip to New Jersey, where the NFL planned to stage tributes to New Orleans, the Saints, and to those victimized by the hurricane and its aftermath. About 600 displaced New Orleans residents were flown to relief agencies in the area, and many were provided tickets to the game. New Orleans police chief Eddie Compass and former president George Bush were asked to take part in the coin toss. Bunting around the stadium and in one of the end zones would be in Saints gold and black.

New Orleans natives Harry Connick Jr. and Branford Marsalis would perform the national anthem on piano and saxophone, and New Orleans jazz trumpeter Irvin Mayfield would play "America the Beautiful."

The league held a telethon for the relief effort. The Red Cross set up booths to collect donations inside Giants Stadium, and the Giants pledged to match the amount in donations.

Saints season ticket holders and anyone with tickets for the game originally scheduled for the Superdome were given first shot at tickets for the Meadowlands. Not many took advantage, so the rest of the seats were filled with, naturally, Giants fans.

"Everybody can put sheepskin over their eyes and act like it's not a home game for the Giants, but we all know," Horn said. "I'm sure the fans and the New York Giants football club care about what happens and their heart goes out to us. We will appreciate that, but we're also not crazy and thinking it's a home game."

And the Giants weren't ignoring their role: There's no feeling sorry in football.

"We're sympathetic, but once you step on the field, football's football," said Giants star defensive end Michael Strahan. "That guy across from me is not trying to be my friend once we're out there, and I'm not trying to be his, either. We have to play our hardest. We're playing to win, we're not going out there to put on a show and let these guys win the game."

They didn't. The Saints lost 27-10 in a sloppy contest punctuated by six turnovers and 13 penalties. The game, while memorable for its uniqueness, was barely noteworthy otherwise.

The next day, when the Saints were back in San Antonio, Haslett let loose on the NFL and, through inference, on Benson.

"They could have done that anywhere," Haslett said of the game site. "They could have played that game in Baton Rouge. They could have played it in San Antonio and could have done the same thing.

"To play it in Giants Stadium, to give them another home game and to put us in a situation where we couldn't hear. . . . It wasn't why we lost that game, but . . .

"It wasn't a home game. I look up at the scoreboard and there are signs, 'Let's Go Giants.' The referees, when they flipped the coin, they asked us if we wanted heads or tails. They had no idea who the home team was and who was away. The crowd noise we had to deal with, we never had to do a silent count at home."

Worse, according to Brooks, was the entire atmosphere the NFL created.

"They made this seem like the Super Bowl," he said. "We played a team that outplayed us, but it was way overdone. Setting up a stage, traveling out here, was uncalled for.

"Try not to patronize us next time, traveling us to New York, saying we're playing a home game."

There wouldn't be a "home game" for another two weeks. But at least there was a plan.

The Saints would play three games in the Alamodome, against Buffalo, Atlanta, and Detroit, and four in Baton Rouge, facing Miami, Chicago, Tampa Bay, and Carolina. None of the games would be blacked out in San Antonio or Baton Rouge, regardless of crowd size.

Haslett and his players seemed satisfied with such a schedule. No more home games in the opponent's ballpark. No shuttling to Shreveport or Austin or Houston or Jackson, Mississippi. They could establish some sort of a routine.

"It's more of a travel issue," the coach said. "I know what their agenda was, to play as many games as possible in our home state. Our players like that, too."

With the revised schedule came questions and concerns in New Orleans. It was clear that San Antonio, which in the late

1980s and early 1990s courted the NFL and built the Alamodome to pro football specifications, was a challenger for the Saints. And with Benson making no definitive statements about a return to the Bayou, there were fears throughout Louisiana that Katrina had also carried away New Orleans' proudest sporting possession. For good.

And while so many were denying such a scenario existed, Saints fans wondered—particularly after Benson urged San Antonians to rally around his team.

"It's most important for there to be capacity crowds to attend every game we have here," Benson said. "It could make me proud, not only of our football team, but show what kind of city you have here."

Benson, of course, owns a home in the San Antonio area, where he made his fortune with auto dealerships.

Only one of the three games in the Texas city would sell out. And none came close to doing so in Baton Rouge, where Tiger Stadium was more than half empty for three of the four contests.

The Saints exhibited their fortitude once more when they beat Buffalo 19-7 in their Alamodome debut. At one point, the crowd of 58,688 was so loud it caused the Bills to waste a timeout and also take a delay-of-game penalty.

And when, to raucous chants of "DE-FENSE," the Saints stopped Bills running back Willie McGahee on a fourth-and-inches run, well, it almost felt like home.

"We're still the New Orleans Saints," receiver Donte' Stallworth said. "New Orleans is still cheering for us and we have San Antonio on our side as well."

They wouldn't have much winning on their side the next two months. The Saints dropped six straight before a return trip to the Meadowlands. This time, they played the Jets. This time, they were officially the visitors. And this time, they won, 21-19.

It would be the final victory of the season. The Saints lost their last five contests, went 0-4 in Baton Rouge, and finished 3-13.

Just before their final "home" game, in San Antonio against the Lions on Christmas Eve, many of the Saints reflected on their season of wandering—and wondering about what lay ahead for the franchise and the city where it belonged.

"This is how it really feels like for a home game," running back Aaron Stecker said. "We don't have to get on a plane, go and stay in a hotel. After the game we jump in the car and head right home in a few minutes, spend the rest of Christmas Eve and Christmas Day with our families. It's real nice."

But it was not in New Orleans. When would they be back in New Orleans?

⌒

One thing was certain: Haslett would not be going back to New Orleans. Given an impossible task, he coached "with all I had, but I guess it wasn't enough."

Just after the season ended with a 27-13 loss at Tampa, Benson and GM Mickey Loomis fired Haslett and his staff. Could Vince Lombardi, Don Shula, or any other Hall of Fame coach have won under the circumstances Haslett and the Saints faced? Not likely.

Such is the nature of pro football, however, that the numbers on the scoreboard and in the standings too often stand alone, regardless of situation. Haslett became a victim of that approach.

"I think Jim performed really well under some adverse conditions, unprecedented conditions," Loomis said. "But unfortunately we haven't had the results the past five seasons that you come to expect in this league. It wasn't based just on this season."

Added Stallworth: "It was tough under these conditions for Jim and the team to win games. But this business is about wins and losses."

Which, in this case, was a shame.

So the Saints had to move on, just like their city, which was making the arduous recovery journey.

By the end of 2005, New Orleans at last had its commitment from Benson that the Saints were coming back. Urged by Tagliabue, whose role in the franchise's return to the Crescent City never should be underestimated, Benson lukewarmly pledged his loyalty to Louisiana.

But would they be back to stay? Benson had an out: a clause in the Superdome lease allowing him to pay $81 million to leave.

That led to skepticism throughout the community, a community that should have had more important matters on its agenda.

"If there's a change in attitude by the franchise toward the community, with the proper articulation of commitment to New Orleans, then the fan base will forgive some of their frustrations and will rally around the team as a symbol of the rebuilding of

New Orleans," said New Orleans Convention and Visitor's Bureau president Steve Perry. "In a recovery, certain things provide a very powerful symbolic impact. And with the right message and the return of our tourism and hospitality industries, you're going to see a rallying behind the team, the new coach and No. 2 draft pick."

Tagliabue, more than anyone, recognized the necessity of bringing back the franchise on a permanent basis—even if that meant forcing Benson's hand, or forcing him to sell the team so it could remain in New Orleans.

"It would be extremely damaging to the NFL as a brand to move this franchise, because you're going to see over the next year the recovery of New Orleans become equated with American patriotism," Perry said. "And there are too many small markets like Green Bay and Jacksonville where the NFL has worked and had a tremendous impact on those communities to have the league give up on New Orleans, especially with New Orleans' (football) history."

Still, with all the rhetoric, all the promises, getting the Saints back was not a done deal. There was one major chore ahead: turning the Superdome back into, well, the Superdome.

It was impossible to ignore the attention—and expense—applied to rebuilding the dome.

The stadium became a focal point stretching far beyond punts, blitzes, and touchdowns. Was it really wise or necessary to concentrate so much effort and so much funding ($185 million, of which about $120 million came from FEMA) on renovating the facility? With homes and businesses destroyed, the entire infrastructure of the city severely damaged, and the population being cut nearly in half, should that money have gone elsewhere?

That argument was made often within the parishes of New Orleans and its outskirts. For many, the dome no longer was considered a grand emblem of the city. It was a reminder that more than 18,000 residents sweltered there in the rankest conditions following Katrina. It was a reminder of the death and destruction brought by the storm.

But there were equally strong arguments for saving the facility, for replacing the 9.7-acre roof, of which 70 percent was ruined. And for laying 1.6 million square feet of carpeting, 650,000 square feet of wall board, and 500,000 square feet of ceiling tiles.

Nearly 4,000 tons of trash and debris were removed from the facility.

Much of the upholstered furniture was damaged by water and mold, including everything in the suites. In the stadium bowl itself, more than one-third of the seats had water damage. The turf was damaged by contaminated water.

Eleven of the 38 escalators and 6 of the 15 elevators had to be replaced, as did four scoreboards. The communications system within the building, as well as the telephone lines, had to be redone.

"It's an unprecedented situation in American stadium history," said Doug Thornton, regional vice president of SMG, the company that manages the Superdome. "There's no other stadium that's been destroyed by a natural disaster like this that you can look to for guidance. We've had to kind of start from scratch."

There was more at stake, though, than simply reconstructing a stadium. In an odd, perhaps morbid way, a revitalized Superdome would be as meaningful to the natives of the Big Easy as the rebuilding on the site of the World Trade Center in New York will be to the people in the Big Apple.

"The Superdome has become the most recognizable symbol of New Orleans," said Tim Coulon, chairman of the Louisiana Stadium and Exposition Board. "The rebuilding of the Superdome will represent the rebuilding of the city."

As would the Saints coming back represent a renewal of a way of life. Despite their checkered record, the years upon years of being an NFL laughingstock, the Saints were so very special to New Orleans, to Louisiana, to the entire Gulf Coast. They were proof that the city and the region belonged in the big time.

The fans would flock back. They did so during the days of the "Aints," when some of the folks in the stands wore paper bags over their heads. There wasn't much to be proud about on the field, where even such great players as Archie Manning and Earl Campbell, Rickey Jackson and Pat Swilling and Willie Roaf couldn't bring a championship. But there was pride in having a pro football team calling Nawlins home.

Nearly everyone was certain that Katrina hadn't erased that sense of pride, and that the support for the team remained strong within the community.

"In terms of the Saints' future, we've got a ways to go," Thornton said. "There's no doubt the public will support the team. But there's always that issue of the economic base, the corporate base."

Indeed, that was a major concern. While the NFL had provided financial aid, verbal encouragement, and not a small amount of lobbying and pressure on local politicians, how would the ravaged businesses in the area respond to an emphasis on bringing back the Saints?

They would respond wholeheartedly in favor, and for obvious reasons.

Losing the Saints would emphasize the doubts about revitalizing New Orleans itself. If America's most popular sport wasn't returning, why should conventioneers consider the city? Tourists? The music industry: Could the jazz really be silenced in the Big Easy?

So while season tickets sold at an unprecedented rate—a week before the first home game, every seat in the Superdome for the remainder of the season was snatched up by fans—corporations were boosting the Saints, too.

"There are so many negative stories one year after Katrina, so I felt compelled to come out and talk about a positive story," Benson said at the team's suburban headquarters just before the 2006 season. "We have spoken so often about the return of football in the Superdome and what that symbolizes. You do not need to look any further than the resolve of fans and businesses and the way they have rallied around our team.

"We're now competing on that basis with places like New York, San Francisco, Chicago, and other major cities. This is just tremendous. People in New York and other places can't hardly believe what you all have done and people in this whole area have done."

⌒

Such positive response needed to be reinforced by the team, of course. Loomis had a busy off-season in which he hired a new coach, Sean Payton, and then lucked into the most mercurial star in the college football galaxy, Southern California running back Reggie Bush, the Heisman Trophy winner.

Payton, 42, had served several teams as an offensive coordinator and was hired away from the Dallas Cowboys just 17 days after the 2005 season concluded. While he had no idea that Bush would fall into the Saints' laps after Houston would take North Carolina State defensive end Mario Williams with the top overall draft choice, Loomis understood he needed to bring attractive and disciplined football back to the Big Easy. The GM felt Payton had just the right touch to achieve that.

"Obviously 2005 was a traumatic year for this area, it was a tough time for this team," Payton said. "I hope that in some small way the effort of this team in 2006 and beyond will represent this city and this region well.

"Some people would say: 'Stay in Dallas. The situation there is good.' We're three-quarters of the way through building a brand new house in Dallas. Hopefully I'm not viewed as a young, naive coach coming into a situation here. I'm excited about this opportunity. I know it's a challenge and we're going to roll our sleeves up.

"We can impact people's lives in a positive way as they go through this transition. I think this area, this community, this region is tough, and our team better reflect that, too."

Much as New Orleans was laying a new foundation in its rebuilding efforts, Payton and Loomis immediately set out to find a cornerstone for the Saints' turnaround. Two months later, when free agency began, they plucked one of the jewels—albeit a somewhat tarnished gem—in quarterback Drew Brees.

Brees had been targeted by several other teams, most notably Miami, but the Dolphins were worried a shoulder injury that abruptly ended Brees's 2005 season in December would have a long-term effect.

The Saints had some concerns, but Brees quickly convinced them he was healthy. They already knew he was a winner.

Brees signed a six-year deal worth nearly $60 million to leave San Diego for New Orleans. He couldn't wait to get started in his new home.

"You still see the city is very alive and you've got a lot of great citizens of New Orleans committed to rebuilding this city that are just so excited about Saints football," Brees said. "In times of tragedy, in times like this, people look to whatever they can to try to lift their spirits, and I think for a lot of people that is Saints football. . . . What a great opportunity it was for me to be here as quarterback, but not only that, but as a person in this community."

Six weeks later, he would be joined by Bush, the most dynamic prospect to enter the NFL in years.

Payton was eating dinner at one of celebrity chef Emeril Legasse's New Orleans restaurants—Legasse has been a key figure in the rebuilding of the city, too—when he was interrupted by a phone call.

Not many such calls could make Emeril's food taste even better, but this one did: Bush was not going to the Texans the next day.

Somewhere between the soup and the main course, Payton had already come up with plays in his offense that would feature Bush. And Emeril was plotting a new menu feature in honor of Bush.

The next morning as the Saints were on the clock, a thousand fans at their suburban training headquarters—which, amazingly, had survived Katrina in good shape—gathered in a tent and shouted "REG-GIE, REG-GIE" even before Tagliabue announced the pick.

Like Brees, Bush embraced the challenge of making the Saints into a winner and revitalizing New Orleans.

"It's a blessing to be here. I think I can do a lot for not only this organization, but the city itself, which obviously had some adversity within this last year or so," Bush said. "We're going to turn this program around and bring something special to this city. Get ready."

⌒

New Orleans definitely was ready. The schedule called for a Monday night opener in the third week of the season, a national TV showcase of the Big Easy's bounce-back.

What the team itself had done on the field in the first two weeks made the Monday-nighter even more attractive. The Saints won at Cleveland and at Green Bay, their first 2-0 road start ever. Making the matchup with the Falcons even juicier: New Orleans' archrival from Atlanta also was 2-0.

So, in week three of the 2006 NFL season—not usually a showcase time for America's favorite sport—the spotlight was on New Orleans. And, thankfully, for some very positive reasons.

"We're seeing demand for rooms is up and it peaks on Monday night," said Bill Langkopp, executive director of the Greater New Orleans Hotel and Lodging Association. "That's very rare, but that's what's happening, so it must be people coming to town for the game."

Those people helped the native Louisianans turn the Saints' homecoming into Mardi Gras, July 4th, and New Year's Eve, all packed into one weekend. Folks were smiling again. They had something grand to concentrate on for a few days—and they'd certainly earned the right to focus on football as a relief from the daily grind.

Their passion for the Saints had survived decades of on-field disappointment; that passion couldn't be drowned by Katrina, either.

On the streets of the French Quarter and surrounding the stadium, music played. Scalpers hawked tickets. Parking was so impossible that Brees nearly had to abandon his car on the street before someone showed him the way to temporary parking for the players.

Black and gold was the color of the day, punctuated, of course, by the fleur-de-lis. There seemed to be as many number-25 Reggie Bush jerseys sported by fans as there were beignets and crawfish on restaurant menus.

Although several buildings surrounding the Superdome remained barricaded and a shopping mall nearby was shuttered, the streets were filled hours before kickoff. Music—jazz, gospel, country, rock—filtered up and down every block.

Nearly an hour before kickoff, the dome was full.

"The word *homecoming* has a real meaning in college and professional sports," Tagliabue said, "but tonight the word *homecoming* will take on a new meaning and will forever be redefined by what is happening here in the Superdome."

Added Saints defensive end Will Smith: "It's the loudest I've ever heard it in pregame warm-ups. I don't think anyone went to work today."

What was happening was more than football, of course. Green Day took the stage, followed by Bono and The Edge and U2. A building that was chaos central one year earlier now was rocked out by the heavyweights of the music world. To be followed by, at least on September 25, 2006, two heavyweights of the NFL.

"We still face challenges in rebuilding our homes and businesses, but this game . . . is proof of what we can accomplish if we work together," said Rita Benson LeBlanc, the Saints' executive vice president. "The Saints have been a unifying force in this community for 40 years now, and we are proud to use this occasion to announce to the world that New Orleans is open for business."

The Saints' on-field response was magnificent. From the outset, they dominated the Falcons. Indeed, it wouldn't have mattered who the opponent was on this magical night. *Perhaps* not even the Steel Curtain teams of the 1970s or the Bears' Monsters of the Midway of 1985 would have measured up this time.

It was, well, destiny.

"I wish we could have had the entire population inside this dome," said Steve Gleason, who blocked a punt that was recovered by teammate Curtis DeLoatch in the end zone with just 1:30 gone in the game. "That's who we were playing for. I was out there playing my butt off for the people of this city . . . infinite joy."

And if any city deserved such joy, it was New Orleans. For a few hours, the headaches, hardships, and horrors of Katrina weren't prominent in the minds of the survivors. Their Saints were back—and they were playing like champions.

© *Sports Illustrated.*

Reggie Bush (25) and Terrance Copper (18) storm into the New Orleans Superdome on September 25, 2006, marking the return of the Saints to the city after a thirteen-month absence. Photo by Bob Rosato.

"When Steve Gleason blocked that punt and the crowd erupted, I remember just looking and going, 'This is awesome,'" Brees said. "Just that feeling that we're going to win this game, we're going to win it for this city, and we're going to ride this wave for as long as we can. It was kind of those feelings like we're back. This city is back.

"From the moment I signed with the Saints, I was looking forward to this. It was a great night. It's something we'll never forget."

Nor should anyone in New Orleans ever forget it.

"We need this team," said Dawn Murray, a fan dressed in Saints colors from head to toe—including gold shoes. "It crosses all lines. It's not Democrat or Republican. It's not rich or poor. It's not black or white. It's black and gold."

Added Payton, "There is going to be an ebb and flow to your season, peaks and valleys, and you hope that you can get them back mentally as well as physically sharp enough the next week. That's part of the challenge. It's something that we're not the only ones faced with that all the time. Monday night was different, obviously. There was a lot of emotions in that game."

Even opposing coach Jim Mora, who worked for his father, also named Jim, when the elder Mora coached the Saints, paid tribute to the locals.

"These people are special," he said. "And resilient and tough and proud of their city, proud of their football team. It really showed."

It was a transcendent evening, carrying to dizzying heights a region in need of an emotional lift. Sure, the next day would bring a return to the harsh reality of broken homes, unpaved streets, struggling businesses.

Maybe the Saints' 23-3 romp wouldn't provide a full catharsis, but the temporary relief it provided—and the hope for the future—was essential.

"When you see that teeming mass of people absolutely enjoying themselves, it sends the message that, yes, the people are alive and coming back," said Mary Beth Romig of the New Orleans Metropolitan Convention and Visitors Bureau. "This weekend is affording us the kind of exposure we couldn't have gotten otherwise.

"If there's a meeting planner on the fence about 2010 and they watched last night, they'll say, 'Why am I on the fence?'"

Indeed, the big show at the Superdome could be used to emphasize the "normality" in some areas of the Big Easy. Hey, the city and its people were saying, the French Quarter suffered less damage than nearly all of its surroundings, and the unique hospitality of Nawlins remained intact.

During the summer of 2006, barely more than half of the 28,000 available hotel rooms were occupied as FEMA employees and others working to rebuild the area departed. The Saints' return boosted that number, at least leading up to the Falcons game, to 80 percent occupancy.

"But we need more than one big weekend," said Jerry Amato, chef at the famed Mothers Restaurant. "We need people to move back to town to live. We need more tourist business, more weekend visitors, big conventions, all the things we used to have."

Although New Orleans might never be like it once was, the Saints coming back certainly served as a shining beacon for a community needing more than just a ray of light.

"There are more questions than there are answers right now toward the community," said new NFL commissioner Roger Goodell, who succeeded Tagliabue. "From our standpoint, the reaction that we've had in returning the Saints has been very, very positive."

Weeks later, the cruise ship industry, a staple of tourism and business in the area, returned to the New Orleans docks. Hotels, casinos, riverboats, and restaurants all got into full swing during the NFL season.

"What they have done is what New Orleans does best: recreate the party atmosphere that always surrounds a big event in this city," said University of New Orleans chancellor and economist Tim Ryan. "Big events can be held anywhere, but no one throws that party better than we do. This will show the world we are ready to do it again."

And ready for a Saints team to achieve far more than any had done. The team not only won the NFC South with a 10-6 record, it earned a first-round playoff bye for the first time in its four decades of life. Then the Saints made their first NFC championship game by beating the Eagles in a home contest that, for party atmosphere, rivaled the September 25 jubilee.

The feel-good saga ended with a title game loss at Chicago. But the comeback karma never faded.

5

CLIPPING THE RED WINGS

1941–1942 Toronto Maple Leafs

Everybody in pro hockey knows about 1942. About the Stanley Cup finals. About the Toronto Maple Leafs and Detroit Red Wings.

Even the foreign-born contingent of NHL players is aware of what happened in hockey's crucible, where every shift and every shot, every pass and every save, can be critical.

Yes, they all are cognizant that the Leafs lost the first three games of the best-of-seven championship series, then stormed back to win the Cup.

Why are they so well-educated on a piece of history that happened generations ago, in a watered-down National Hockey League in wartime?

Because the players and coaches and fans are reminded about it every time a team falls into a 0-3 hole in the finals. You know, "Hey, it's happened before, so it can happen again, and we can do it."

Well, in theory perhaps those teams can replicate Toronto's stunner. But no hockey team has won a title by coming back from such a deficit since—the New York Islanders managed to win a second-round series in 1975 after dropping the opening three contests—and few even force a sixth game, let alone a seventh.

Yet, year after year, regardless if it's the opening round or for the championship, someone cites the '42 Leafs.

Such as Washington Capitals coach Ron Wilson in 1998 when his team trailed the Red Wings 3-0.

"Hey, remember 1942 and the Toronto Maple Leafs," he said.

Or Philadelphia Flyers coach Terry Murray the previous year, again vs. Detroit.

"I don't have a crystal ball and I think I would be (lying) if I came out and said: 'Sure we can,'" he said. "But it's been done. Toronto did it back in 1942.

"We want one win right now. We have to come into the (fourth) game with our heads on straight and play smarter. If we can get one win, we'll look at the next one after that."

Neither the Capitals nor Flyers ever got a look at a next game; both were swept by the Wings.

And it certainly looked like Detroit would be sweeping past Toronto in '42.

The Wings had been clipped easily by Boston in the previous year's final, losing four straight games. It was imperative that they get off to a quick start against Toronto, which knocked off the regular season's top club, the New York Rangers, to make the Cup finals.

"We know the Leafs will be considered the team to beat," Red Wings coach–general manager Jack Adams said. "We must show we can beat them right off the bat and get them thinking about our club's strengths."

The finals opened in Toronto's Maple Leaf Gardens, a raucous place where fans often stood for entire periods cheering on their Leafs. Those fans anticipated their heroes' first title in a decade, but they also knew not to be too optimistic. Why?

Simply because since beating the Rangers for the 1932 crown, the Leafs had made the finals six times—and lost all six. That included three in a row from 1938–40.

Toronto's rivalry with Detroit wasn't quite as fierce as when it faced Montreal for Canadian supremacy, but the Leafs and Wings were not exactly bosom buddies. Their GMs, Conn Smythe in Toronto and Adams in Detroit, always were trying to best each other, making for tense relationships before big matches.

And nothing could be bigger than this matchup.

Adams got precisely what he sought early in Game 1 when Don Grosso converted during a goalmouth scramble. Just 97 seconds into the final round, the Wings were ahead.

"A great boost and a wonderful goal," Adams said.

Five minutes later, the Leafs tied it thanks to Johnny Mc-Creedy, but the Wings shot back ahead on a brilliant goal by Sid Abel, a future Hall-of-Famer. Abel skated nearly the length of the ice, avoiding several checking attempts by the Leafs, before beating goalie Turk Broda (another future Hall member).

The celebrations were short-lived in Detroit, as was the lead. A mere 29 seconds later, Sweeney Schriner beat Johnny Mowers.

After one period, it was 2-2, and a shootout seemed at hand.

During intermission, both coaches, Adams and Hap Day of Toronto, expressed their displeasure at the lack of checking in the opening 20 minutes. Loudly. And each set of players paid heed, because the game turned physical and skating room came at a premium the rest of the way.

When the Leafs did get a strong scoring chance on a two-on-one break, Mowers made a spectacular pair of saves on Billy Taylor and Bob Goldham.

Deep into the second period, Detroit again took the lead when Grosso got his second of the night. He had been leveled moments before by Rudolph Kampman, who displayed why he was nicknamed "Bingo" with a precise hit on Grosso.

But the Red Wing got to his feet and put a high shot behind Broda. Bingo, indeed.

Detroit carried the 3-2 margin into the third session, when controversy struck—and not for the first time in these finals.

Toronto's Pete Langelle scored to tie it early in the third period, but referee King Clancy (yep, a future Hall-of-Famer) whistled the play dead. Clancy had called a major penalty on Detroit's Jimmy Orlando for cutting Bob Goldham with a high stick—and the whistle had blown before Langelle's tally.

With the crowd in an uproar, the Leafs went on a seven-minute power play. Mowers was more than equal to the challenge, though, even with four Toronto forwards on the ice for the power play. Detroit held on, breathlessly, for a 1-0 edge in the series.

"That was difficult going," Mowers said. "There were many

times when it looked like the Leafs had 10 players on the ice. But we held on and it's a big win to take the first game in Toronto."

Smythe, Day, and the Leafs felt they'd outplayed the Wings, but Mowers's goaltending and Grosso's two goals and an assist were the difference. The Leafs vowed to play physical hockey once again in Game 2—and to reverse the outcome.

"We lost only one game and you have to win four," Day reminded reporters. "We don't often lose at the Gardens."

Maybe not, but in this series, the Leafs hardly were invincible at their venerable building.

The Wings jumped in front 2-0 in the first period on goals by that man Grosso and by Mud Bruneteau. Grosso was on his knees when he poked in a rebound for his score.

With the crowd eerily quiet and the Wings outskating and outhitting the Leafs, Toronto managed its one moment of glory in the game. Schriner's backhander made it 2-1 heading into the final period.

But Grosso scored again, giving the Wings winger a torrid nine in the postseason, then an NHL record. Jerry Brown finished off the win with a deflection, and Mowers made 27 stops.

The Wings headed home, where they had not lost in 12 straight games, with a commanding lead.

"How has this happened?" Toronto's Lorne Carr wondered. "We haven't been playing badly. I guess the Red Wings are playing exceptionally well."

Still, the Leafs promised they would not hang their heads. They'd had some success on the road before, and in the playoffs, with the intensity ratcheted to immeasurable levels, they would not be flat for the third game, at Detroit's Olympia.

Carr was the catalyst, too. He scored twice in a span of 30 seconds late in the first period, boosting Toronto into a 2-0 lead.

"We thought it had turned for us," Carr said.

Instead, it turned out very badly for them. By the end of the opening session, the Wings had tied the score on goals by Brown and Jack Carveth.

Burly defenseman Eddie Bush, who set up both of those scores, then had assists on goals by Pat McReavy and Syd Howe for a 4-2 lead through two periods. And even though the Wings had lost Abel to a suspected broken jaw, they got a goal from Bush—his fifth point of the night—and 17 third-period saves from Mowers for a 5-2 win.

The Wings were one victory from the Stanley Cup. The Leafs? They looked tattered and battered.

"Don't worry about us. We'll beat 'em four straight," Taylor said with a smile and not a lot of conviction as the teams prepared for Game 4.

Day was frantically searching for some morsel of strategy that might spark a turnaround. What else could he do in such a desperate situation?

Often nowadays, a coach might make a goaltending change. Back in 1942, teams carried one netminder, so Day didn't have that option.

He also knew that the fans and media in Toronto, a hockey-mad city with no other major league team back then, were ready to, uh, call it a Day with him, particularly if the Leafs were ignominiously swept by the Wings.

Day couldn't sit still, so he benched Gordie Drillon, merely the Leafs' leading scorer, and defenseman Bucko McDonald. Into the lineup for speed (and hunger) Day inserted forwards Don Metz and Hank Goldup and defenseman Ernie Dickens, a rookie.

And Day took the psychological route by reading a letter from a young fan who wrote how disappointed she was in the Leafs' performance in the finals. Day hoped his players would draw inspiration from the letter.

But with the Stanley Cup itself sitting in the bowels of the Olympia and with their confidence soaring, the Wings continued to stymie the Leafs. Neither team scored in the first period, and then Detroit took a 2-0 edge on goals by Bruneteau and the courageous Abel despite his health issues. With half the game remaining, the Wings and their fans could taste the champagne that would sit in the Cup.

Out of this seemingly hopeless scenario, the Leafs staged a comeback for the ages, a rally that still motivates athletes today.

Bob Davidson and Carr scored in a span of less than a minute and a half to tie it heading into the third period.

"That was a big lift, getting back into a tie after being down by two," Carr said.

Even after Carl Liscombe's long shot eluded Broda early in the third session, giving Detroit a 3-2 lead, Toronto didn't wilt. The fresh legs provided by the young forwards helped, as did an awakening by Toronto's best player, Syl Apps (yet another future Hall of Fame inductee).

Apps tied it with his first goal of the finals and, for the first time in the series, overtime loomed.

The contest never got that far, and the ending of Game 4 was as wild as any in NHL annals.

Don Metz's brother Nick, assisted by Apps, scored with 7:15 remaining in regulation. Finally, the Maple Leafs had victory within their grasp.

A few minutes later, Detroit's Eddie Wares swore at referee Mel Harwood and was assessed a 10-minute misconduct penalty. But he refused to leave the ice immediately amid some arguments between players and coaches on the Detroit bench and Harwood.

When Wares was escorted to the penalty box and the puck was dropped, the discombobulated Wings had seven men on the ice. So Harwood handed them a minor penalty that Grosso was ordered to serve.

Taking one of Detroit's main weapons off the ice when the Wings desperately needed a goal sent the players and the Olympia fans into a frenzy. Grosso threw down his stick and gloves; he eventually drew a fine from the league for those actions.

And after the final buzzer, when the Leafs had avoided a sweep and perhaps seized some impetus, an enraged Adams stormed onto the ice after the referee, who also was being verbally assaulted again by Wares and Grosso. Adams took it even further, throwing punches. Even some fans in the stands tried to get into the action near the penalty box, throwing punches at the linesmen.

Harwood was escorted from the ice by policemen, and both he and league president Frank Calder required protection as they left the arena.

In terming the incident "a disgrace to the sport," Calder suspended Adams indefinitely. Adams would work no more behind the Detroit bench in the series, which headed back to Toronto sporting a figurative black eye.

It wasn't until Game 4 that Day looked like a brilliant strategist. But the Wings looked awfully foolish, and by losing their cool, they'd allowed the Leafs some life. Lots of life.

Toronto won the fifth game 9-3, jumping to a 7-0 lead. Don

Metz, whom Day placed in the lineup for Game 4, scored three times and set up two other goals. The revitalized Apps also had two goals and three assists.

The Wings, meanwhile, continued picking up senseless penalties. Toronto's first two goals, which set the tone for the game, if not the remainder of the series, were on power plays.

Grosso, perhaps still furious about the late penalty in the fourth game, slugged it out with Goldham, a battle that spilled into the penalty box, too. Referee Clancy struggled to keep matters under control late in the rout, but at least he didn't have to deal with Adams; Ebbie Goodfellow was handling the coaching chores.

"We were ready for an explosion like this," Day noted. "It was very good to see."

The Leafs also could see a Cup in their future. They'd rallied to win Game 4 in Detroit just when the prize seemed headed to the Motor City. And now they returned to Motown with momentum—one game away from tying the series.

It was evident from the opening face-off of Game 6 that the Wings were tight. No team had blown a 3-0 lead in an NHL series—indeed, no Stanley Cup final had ever gone to seven games before—and Detroit wanted no part of a return trip to Canada for a deciding contest. So the Wings were cautious and not nearly physical enough.

Still, the first period ended scoreless and was played cleanly, a tribute to the officiating skills of Bill Chadwick.

"I thought we'd settled down after that period," Goodfellow said. "The way they had come after us in the (fifth) game, it looked like a good thing for us to be 0-0."

It wasn't. Metz the Miracle Worker connected with a short shot past Mowers a mere 14 seconds into the second period. As a hush fell in the Olympia, the Leafs went into a defensive shell to protect that precious goal.

"We felt we could hold on until they made a mistake trying to tie it," Day said.

Again, he was spot-on. Detroit attacked furiously for minutes on end, but could not dent Broda, and the score remained 1-0 until deep into the third period.

Then Schriner broke free and hit Goldham with a perfect pass. His rare rush from a defensive position paid off as Goldham faked out Mowers and deposited the puck behind the Detroit goalie with 6:28 to go.

When Taylor was set up by Schriner only 32 seconds later, Toronto had its third successive victory.

Shockingly, the Stanley Cup finals were headed back to Maple Leaf Gardens for Game 7—a scenario nobody outside of the Leafs' locker room could truly have believed in just a week earlier.

Among the Red Wings, there was little composure and little confidence. The turning point, it seemed, had been Adams's tempestuous reaction at the end of the fourth game. Without their mentor, the Wings were a confused lot.

"It has been a struggle," Abel said, "but if we win this game, we have the Stanley Cup."

True enough. And the Wings actually took the lead early in the second period on Howe's goal. Then they attempted to do what the Leafs were so successful at in Game 6: protect a slim margin.

It worked into the third period, until Toronto went on a power play. Schriner, who like Don Metz and Apps had become a pivotal performer, made the rafters shake when he tied it.

"We knew the next goal would be the winner," Schriner said. "We wanted to get it quickly."

They did. Langelle, whose apparent goal in the opening game was disallowed and sent the Leafs into their early-series spiral, beat Mowers less than two minutes later.

Toronto led 2-1. Was there any doubt the Leafs would hold on?

Not after Taylor, who it seemed like ages ago had predicted his club would win four straight and make history, passed to Schriner. He scored the last goal of the greatest comeback hockey has seen.

To punctuate that comeback, the NHL's tradition of presenting the Stanley Cup to the winners on the ice seemed perfect. Every player, from the wily veterans to the fresh-faced kids, from Broda to the Metz brothers, from Apps to Schriner, from coach Day to manager Smythe, touched and kissed the chalice.

"We did it the hard way, harder than anyone ever has, I guess," Day said.

Before or since.

6

THE BRONX ZOO

1978 New York Yankees

The New York borough of The Bronx is famous for two landmarks: The Zoo and The Stadium. If you grew up in or lived in the Big Apple at any time, you didn't need to mention the location. Everyone knew it was the Bronx Zoo and Yankee Stadium.

In the late 1970s, the baseball team managed to pretty much combine both shrines. Thanks to the wildest collection of personalities east of Charles O. Finley's Oakland A's earlier in the decade, a trip to the Stadium meant a visit to the Zoo, too.

Not literally, of course. But with all the shenanigans carried out by the likes of Reggie Jackson, Thurman Munson, Billy Martin, Sparky Lyle, Lou Piniella, Mickey Rivers, Graig Nettles, and the zookeeper himself, George Steinbrenner, well, you entered the House That Ruth Built wondering what was next.

And there always was something next.

Steinbrenner was dubbed "The Boss" for the iron-fisted way he ran the ballclub. To his credit, he'd taken baseball's premier franchise from the gutter it fell into when CBS owned it and poured money, time, and effort into a quick rebuilding.

He also dominated the back pages—and sometimes the front pages—of the local tabloids with his pressurized approach and his off-field woes. He was suspended by baseball commissioner Bowie Kuhn in 1974 for two years for conspiring to make illegal contributions to the 1972 presidential reelection campaign of Richard Nixon. He later was suspended by commissioner Fay Vincent for his dealings with a shady gambler, Howard Spira.

Steinbrenner, who purchased the Yankees for a mere $8.7 million and turned them back into a gold mine now worth more than $1 billion, expected the maximum production out of each member of his organization, from bat boy to publicist—he went through those like pitchers do resin bags—to superstar outfielder to recalcitrant manager.

"If I go out and get the best hitters, the best pitchers, the best fielders, and I pay them as such," he said, "I expect them to perform better than anyone else. And I expect them to win."

From 1973, when the Cleveland shipbuilder took charge, until 1976, the talent base in the Bronx improved immeasurably. The Yankees' last pennant had come in 1964, when they lost the World Series to St. Louis. The succeeding 10 years included flops to the very bottom of the American League, a place where perhaps the Mariners or Indians belonged, but not the New York Yankees.

Steinbrenner, back from his first suspension, got a nice payback in '76, when the Yankees finally won another pennant. While they were swept by Cincinnati's Big Red Machine in the Series, it was clear that Steinbrenner had the Yanks on the right path.

And in 1977, under the volatile Martin and a collection of all-stars, they won the World Series for the first time in 15 years. Perhaps they won more out of fear of The Boss than because of overriding talent, although Steinbrenner always has claimed his image is misrepresented.

Steinbrenner's assessment of his personality? "I'm really 95 percent Mr. Rogers," he said, "and only 5 percent Oscar the Grouch."

There certainly were plenty of Oscars and not many Fred Rogers around the 1978 Yankees, who entered that season as overwhelming favorites in the American League. They had the sluggers in Nettles and Jackson, who was coming off an MVP performance in the World Series, including three home runs in the clinching Game 6 against the Los Angeles Dodgers.

They had the table-setters in Rivers and Roy White, and the clutch hitters in Munson and Piniella. Their defense was outstanding, particularly the double-play combo of shortstop Bucky Dent (remember that name) and second baseman Willie Randolph, and the incomparable glove work of Nettles at third base.

The pitching staff featured an emerging Ron Guidry, whose "Louisiana Lightning" would be unhittable nearly all season, and future Hall-of-Famer Catfish Hunter, backed by a solid rotation and a magnificent bullpen anchored by Lyle and Goose Gossage.

Oh, the personalities were combustible, beginning with Jackson vs. Munson, a running feud from the time Reggie proclaimed, "I'm the straw that stirs the drink" in the Bronx. And there was Jackson vs. Martin, who angrily confronted the outfielder on national television in the dugout of Fenway Park the previous year because the manager felt Reggie "dogged it" rather than chase a check-swing hit by Jim Rice.

But there also were calming influences, from team president Al Rosen to Chris Chambliss and White. There was the comic relief provided by Rivers and Lyle, whose penchant for sitting naked on birthday cakes brought a whole new meaning to clubhouse antics. There was the classiness of Hunter and Guidry.

It all worked in 1977, so why not in 1978?

Well, lots of reasons.

For one, Lyle was unhappy because of the addition of the fireballing Gossage. Lyle had won the Cy Young Award in '77, his slider dancing so confoundingly that even the best hitters flailed away at it. During spring training, Lyle showed up a week late and then confronted Steinbrenner, seeking a trade.

"George," Lyle told the owner, "there's never been a bullpen with enough room for two guys. You need to trade me."

Steinbrenner knew how important Lyle was in the locker room, even if he also sensed that Gossage would get the main closing assignments. But The Boss also knew how to placate Lyle, and he mentioned the attention the left-hander got in New York and how he was headed for the Hall of Fame if he remained a Yankee.

Oh, and Steinbrenner never promised more money. So Lyle fumed—and went public with his unhappiness.

Then there was Jackson, who while a media and fan magnet, was hardly the most popular player on the team. He might have had his candy bars and his awards and his high opinion of himself, but Jackson was something of an outcast among even this loosely connected conglomerate.

It certainly didn't help that the on-field leader of the Yankees, Munson, and the manager, Martin, had such little regard for Reggie. And both men had mean streaks as long as the line for tickets at games.

Add in Martin's unpredictability, injury problems, and the team the archrival Boston Red Sox were putting together and 1978 had its potential for disaster.

And disaster struck quickly. Dent and Randolph got hurt. Hunter spent a lengthy stay on the disabled list. Other than Guidry, in fact, the starting pitching was mediocre. Lyle still was unhappy about his supporting role.

Steinbrenner, who was allowing Rosen to run the front office while the owner tended to other business from his Tampa home, flew to New York and confronted Martin about all the negativity surrounding a club that wasn't playing badly, but wasn't playing like champions.

Martin and Steinbrenner had a screaming match over the makeup of the squad and what Martin perceived as Steinbrenner's meddling. Flash fires began breaking out everywhere.

As the mid-June trading deadline approached, the floundering Yankees were hearing requests to get out of town from all points. Ed Figueroa wanted to go to a team where he'd be one of the top three starters, with the accompanying certainty when he would be on the mound. Randolph asked Rosen why he was the lowest-paid regular on the club, even though the second baseman was among the most reliable performers.

"I go out and bust my butt," Randolph said, "and I want you to go out and bust your butt for me. I'm not trying to rouse things, but I feel I'm overlooked and not being respected."

Munson wasn't talking to the media and, at times, not even to his teammates. Rivers, known for his uninhibited spending, was having financial difficulties.

Both Steinbrenner and Rosen believed they'd given Martin the tools to not only defend the title, but do so impressively. Instead, the Yankees were chasing Boston.

"Billy, being a professional manager, knows what happens to managers who are supposed to win and don't win," Rosen said. "If you don't win the games you expect to win and don't put a 10-

game streak together . . . and you fall further behind, you have to do something to shake up the ballclub."

A month later, the Yankees hadn't gotten any closer to the Red Sox, and Steinbrenner let loose.

"Everybody says I should stay out, but I own the team and I need to get involved," he said. "If I don't, we're not going to get any better and this team should be doing a lot better. If I don't get involved, we're going to get worse.

"I'm not a miracle worker, but somebody has to step in and do something to get us going. We're halfway (through the season) and we haven't gone anywhere. I won't stand for what I'm seeing.

"We're playing awful."

Awful? Not really. The Yankees were better than everyone in the AL except the Red Sox. But they never looked dominant—except when the incredible Guidry was on the mound, going 13-1 through the All-Star break—and they rarely looked fully engaged.

Was the turmoil within robbing the players of their drive to win? Nettles said they needed a miracle to contend for the pennant, citing a "None for all and all for none" motto.

That attitude wasn't unique in pro sports—Finley's A's proved that, winning three straight World Series in the early '70s despite internal discord. But the Yankees refined the discord.

"It was sort of peculiar in that it didn't seem so much like a team as a bunch of guys who showed up for work at the same office every day," said Bill Shannon, a longtime official scorer and author who probably has seen more baseball games in New York than any media member. "It didn't have the team atmosphere expected in a big-league clubhouse. This was a bunch of guys who were considering themselves professionals and experienced performers at their jobs, and they did their work but didn't have a whole lot else in common, and then went their separate directions.

"You generally got the sense they didn't particularly care for each other as a group."

In mid-July, AL West power Kansas City came to the stadium, affording the floundering Yankees a chance to measure their chances for the second half of the season against a contender. The Royals swept the series, dropping the Yankees 14 games behind Boston. And in the final game, all hell broke loose.

Not surprisingly, Jackson was in the midst of it, now becoming the straw that broke the camel's back.

In the 10th inning of a tie game, Munson led off with a single and third base coach Dick Howser showed Jackson, the cleanup hitter, the bunt sign. Jackson couldn't remember the last time he got such an order, but he didn't disagree with it, considering the situation. If he could move the runner to second, the Yanks had two shots to get him home.

But the pitch was far out of the strike zone for a ball.

Martin then decided to have the slugger swing away, reasoning the next pitch would be hittable. But Jackson never glanced at Howser, and the coach asked the umpires for time so he could speak with Jackson.

Told to forget bunting, Jackson instead squared and missed. He then fouled off another bunt attempt.

On a 1-2 pitch, surely he would swing away, perhaps even put one into the bleachers in the dramatic way Reggie Jackson often did things.

Instead, he once more tried to bunt and fouled out. He meekly walked back to the dugout, head down.

Kansas City won in the 11th inning, and Martin was livid in the locker room.

"I'm the manager and he's the player, and it's pretty simple, isn't it?" Martin fumed. "That was out-and-out defiance of an order from the manager. That will not be tolerated by me or by this club.

"He did it because he expected me to punch him and it took the most control it has ever taken in my life not to do it."

Jackson, for his part, believed he was helping the team. In a weird, convoluted way, that would become true. But, at this moment in July, he'd messed up so badly that even the fractured locker room came together in support of Martin—and the subsequent five-game suspension and $10,000 fine handed to Jackson.

"The manager runs the club on the field," Rosen noted. "He has the full authority to do this and the full backing of the front office on this matter. No player or players are bigger than the team."

Even the usually silent Munson chipped in by emphasizing that "everyone has to be treated the same, and everyone has to treat the manager the same way. You do what you're told to do for the team."

Jackson had contacted Steinbrenner before the bunting incident and expressed, once again, his displeasure with the manager. Indeed, Jackson told the owner there was "no way this team can ever win again with Billy Martin managing it."

Steinbrenner, for his part, had a love-hate relationship with Martin that bordered on obsession. He recognized that without all the extracurriculars, Martin was a brilliant tactician and motivator. That's why Martin eventually would have five stints as Yankees manager.

But The Boss also disliked the way Martin couldn't control himself—drinking was part of Martin's problems, too—or his clubhouse. And he couldn't stand the bricks Martin threw in public, bricks that shattered camaraderie and the image of his ballclub.

Still, this was one instance where Steinbrenner and Martin were in total agreement.

And then Martin pushed his oversized self-destruct button.

The team headed to California to play the Athletics. Jackson was on the flight, but then learned of the suspension and disappeared while the Yankees went about their business. He said he didn't pick up a bat once during his idle five days.

When he rejoined the Yanks in Chicago, Jackson missed the bus to Comiskey Park. When he arrived by taxi after batting practice had begun, Martin couldn't—and wouldn't—hide his anger.

"You'd think he'd be out here a little bit early to hit, you know?" Martin said.

"If Reggie doesn't shut his mouth, he won't play," Martin added, his rage boiling over. "I don't care what George says, he can replace me right now if he doesn't like it. I just want (Jackson) to shut up and play. I don't want to hear any more about Reggie."

Jackson was somewhat contrite, saying he was sorry to cause "grief and uncomfort" on the team. "Knowing what the consequences were, the suspension and the amount of publicity this generated, I probably would have swung."

That further fueled Martin's fire. Jackson didn't play in Chicago as New York won its fifth in a row. Yes, the Yankees were winning again. But no, it didn't bring peace.

Far from it.

That night, in O'Hare Airport, Martin sealed his fate as Yankees manager for 1978. At a time when Steinbrenner firmly was on his side over the "Reggie Row," and the team was playing better, perhaps more united than ever could be imagined thanks to Jackson's mini-mutiny, Martin uttered his famous phrase:

"The two of them deserve each other. One's a born liar, the other's convicted."

The quote hit the Associated Press wire before it made its way to television, radio, or the tabloids. The AP sent it around the sports world in minutes.

"I don't think Billy had any idea of the impact of those words," said AP sports writer Frank Brown, who was covering the Yankees' road trip. Brown noted that Martin's comments seemed premeditated.

Alerted to Martin's diatribe, which also included more venom directed toward Jackson, Steinbrenner immediately called Rosen, general manager Cedric Tallis, and other front office staff. Admitting he was "stunned" by such phrasing, and wondering if Martin had been drunk when he spoke, Steinbrenner sought to discuss this latest headline-grabber before making any headlines of his own.

But The Boss knew there would be reams of copy, hours of discussion, devoted to whatever decision he made. And when he confirmed that Martin had, indeed, violated a clause in his contract specifically prohibiting publicly criticizing the owner, Steinbrenner had no choice.

Martin was out.

The Yankees actually gave him an out, allowing Martin to re-sign for health reasons. He certainly could have cited stress or insomnia or even a nervous breakdown for his resignation.

In truth, though, he was fired.

"Billy needed to resign for health reasons," Rosen claimed, "but I couldn't let any employee of the Yankees say anything like that about the front office."

Martin did issue a statement at the team hotel in Kansas City. He was accompanied by longtime friend Phil Rizzuto, the short-stop when Martin played second base for the Yankees in the 1950s. Rizzuto feared Martin was about to collapse, but the now former manager got through his quasi news conference.

"There will be no questions and no answers after this statement is made. That means now and forever, because I am a Yankee and Yankees do not talk or throw rocks.

"I don't want to hurt this team's chances. It has a shot at the pennant and I hope they win it. I owe it to my health and to my mental well-being to resign. At this time, I'm also sorry about these things that were written about George Steinbrenner. He does not deserve them, nor did I say them. I've had my differences with George, but we've been able to resolve them."

And they would resolve matters again in future years. But, for now, the animals in the zoo would no longer have their cages rattled by Billy Martin.

His replacement was anything but a cage-rattler. Steinbrenner hired Bob Lemon, who earlier that season was fired by the Chicago White Sox.

If Martin was the ferocious tiger in the Yankees' menagerie, Lemon was an owl. A former big-league pitcher with excellent credentials, he did his job quietly, usually with efficiency. And he could stay up all night drinking, like Martin, but without losing his faculties.

"There was an enormous reduction in tension when Bob took over," Shannon recalled. "Lemon was like old shoes, a very comfortable and relaxed guy, and everyone respected his baseball knowledge. His philosophy was: Wind them up and send them out there and play.

"Lemon was a seat-of-the-pants guy who most of the time made the right decision. He knew what his guys could do and let them do it. That is what the players wanted; they were not kids, they were veterans who had been through the wars. The players saw that with the talent in the clubhouse, they should win a pennant. I think they kind of felt Billy was getting in the way."

So, 96 games into what had fast become a lost cause, Lemon was in charge of steering the Good, Bad, and Ugly Ship Yankees into calmer waters.

Among his first chores was meeting with the players privately to discuss their roles, and how they would handle them and the team. He told Jackson he would be the cleanup hitter, mostly as a DH but sometimes in right field, and he would play every day.

He told Gossage that he was the best closer in baseball and not to look over his shoulder out to the bullpen if he was struggling.

He asked Randolph and Dent to simply play the kind of ball

both showed they were capable of when healthy. "Don't push it trying to make up for lost time," Lemon said. "Just play."

Lemon told Rivers he had to be punctual off the field and to always hustle on it. He didn't have to say anything to Guidry, White, Piniella, or Nettles, who'd managed to stay out of the debilitating fray much of the time.

Perhaps most significantly, Lemon made Munson his confidante. He sought out the catcher to explain his approach, and asked Munson to take charge of the locker room.

"Just get them together to do the same thing, win ballgames," Lemon said. "You're my captain, you're in the lineup every day, you're running things out there on the field."

Munson told Lemon a less confrontational approach would be just right.

A few days later, Steinbrenner's devotion to Martin surfaced again—in a stunning way.

At Old Timer's Day at the Stadium, with Joe DiMaggio, Mickey Mantle, Whitey Ford, Yogi Berra, and Rizzuto on hand, The Boss found a way to focus the spotlight on his former and future manager. It was as dramatic as any Broadway director might have conjured.

"Bob Lemon will be managing the Yankees for the rest of 1978 and for 1979," said Bob Sheppard, the legendary announcer at Yankee Stadium. "In 1980, he will become general manager."

Sheppard paused as the stir in the stands built. Why, the fans were asking each other, do we care about that now, especially with Lemon having no true Yankees roots before earlier in the month?

Sheppard went on.

"In 1980 and hopefully for many years to come, the Yankees will be managed by number 1, Billy Martin."

Out of the dugout came the man Lemon succeeded—and who would take Lemon's place.

Even Sheppard admitted the cheers were as loud as he'd ever heard in the Bronx ballpark. On a day celebrating the great history and stars of the franchise, Steinbrenner and Martin one-upped them all.

Amid all the back-slapping and celebrations of the eventual return of Steinbrenner's favorite manager—gee, how did Jackson and Figueroa and Rivers and Randolph feel about that?—was this reality:

The Red Sox had run off and hidden from the Yankees.

That Boston would be such a formidable opponent hardly was a shock. The Red Sox won the 1975 pennant, holding off the Yanks, then lost to Cincinnati in one of the most memorable and entertaining of World Series. They still had most of the heroes of '75, including Jim Rice, Fred Lynn, Carl Yastrzemski, Carlton Fisk, George Scott, and Luis Tiant.

But just as the Yankees began putting things together under Lemon, Boston began to slump. By early August, the Yankees were within six and a half games, more because the Sox were sliding than the Yankees were winning.

Boston's players claimed they were unworried.

"We're the best team in the American League," Fisk said. "We know how to win; we did it three years ago. We'll be fine."

As if to punctuate their confidence, the Sox took two straight games from the Yankees, including a classic 14-inning affair in which they rallied from five runs down.

Those losses spiraled the Yankees to fourth place and it began looking like Baltimore, not New York, would be Boston's most potent challenger.

Had Martin been in charge, the soiled atmosphere in the clubhouse might have made any thoughts of a pennant run foolhardy. Martin was gone, however temporarily, though, and Lemon simply held a team meeting marked by its lack of incendiary proclamations.

"If you can't play for him, you can't play for anybody," Hunter said. "Things are different now. Instead of everybody worrying about what the other guys are doing, they are just going out every day and doing their jobs.

"This is a better team than last year. We're playing as a team, not as individuals. Lemon has been very instrumental, especially with our pitchers. As a former pitcher, he spots little things."

Such as how to handle each player in a different manner. Sure, playing as a team ultimately can lead to overcoming 14-game deficits, but individual care—particularly with so many fragile psyches such as the 1978 Yankees had—is essential, as well.

"He treats me like a man," said Figueroa, who blossomed into a superb starter under Lemon. "He lets me pitch to the hitters my way. I have more confidence with him than with Martin."

Even Sir Reginald himself recognized Lemon's contributions to the turnaround. Yes, Jackson acknowledged that someone else could stir this drink.

"This is a whole ballclub now," said Jackson, who ignored a sore thumb to stay in the lineup for Lemon; would he have done so for Martin? "Bob Lemon has me more relaxed. He has confidence in me and it's wonderful coming to the park knowing you're going to play. He doesn't look for reasons to knock a guy or bench him or show him up. He just wants to win, not knock.

"He isn't trying to make a fool out of you all the time like Billy Martin did."

Yet Jackson balked at being placed eighth in the batting order during a personal slump, instead telling a coach he was too ill to play that day. So Lemon sat him, then put him down for seventh in the order the next game. Reggie played.

And the Yanks began winning again, so much so that with several Red Sox, most notably Fisk, Dwight Evans, and Yastrzemski, all playing hurt or sidelined, the once prodigious lead was whittled to a handful of games.

"There's going to be a pennant race," Piniella promised as the calendar hit September. "It's going to be tough, no question about it. But if we play well, the way we've been playing, we have time. I guess this is our push: now or never."

It was now. Gossage had become the preeminent reliever in baseball and Lyle was functioning well in a secondary role. Guidry was headed for the Cy Young Award and Figueroa was on fire. The supporting cast, such as Dick Tidrow, Jay Johnstone, and Ken Clay, was effective.

Boston lost five of six heading into a four-game series at Fenway Park with New York. This was the chance for Piniella and cohorts to make his prediction come true.

While the Yankees were immeasurably confident—"We can sweep these guys," Rivers said—the Red Sox seemed prepared for something more than a four-game, late-summer baseball series.

"Every time we play the Yankees, we suit up a little differently," Red Sox pitcher Bill Lee said. "It's like we throw on the armor and get ready to fight the Holy Wars."

This war began on a Thursday night with a rout of epic proportions. Sox manager Don Zimmer noticed the winds blowing in at about 25 mph and claimed it would be a pitchers' duel.

Not quite.

The Yankees started the onslaught immediately with two runs in the first inning, three more in the second, another two in the third and five in the fourth on the way to a 15-3 victory. With the exception of Hunter leaving in the fourth inning after some pain in his groin—he joked that "the hardest thing I've done in my career is leave with a 12-0 lead"—it was a celebratory night for the Yankees.

And, they believed, a precedent-setting performance.

"This is just a start," promised Jackson, who emerged from a hospital with a virus to single in a run in the first inning and set the tone for the evening. "We're ready for more of this."

They would deliver it, as well.

Zimmer reasoned before Game 2 that at least the 15-3 defeat "counts only as one game." At least it should have, but there clearly was a hangover for Boston.

The guy who should have had a hangover was Munson, who was beaned the previous night by Dick Drago. Instead, the Sox committed seven errors, the Yankees got off to another blazing start, getting seven runs in the first two innings and winning 13-2, with 17 hits. That was four fewer hits than the previous night, but still plenty effective.

Make that devastating.

"Well, I've seen it twice, but tomorrow's another day," Zimmer said, scratching and shaking his head. "All the pitchers are getting the same dose. I bring them in and they hit 'em. The errors have been here right along, but I don't know if it's ever been as bad. These two losses aren't easy to shrug off. But what are you going to do, shoot them because of errors?"

By now, the Yankees believed they were in control of the series and, by extension, the pennant race. After all, they'd romped two straight nights, even winning easily with rookie pitcher Jim Beattie, who earlier in the season was demoted to the minor leagues after being pounded by Boston in a June game.

Who could blame Lemon for saying he would have settled for a split heading to Fenway Park, but now he wanted nothing less than a sweep? Had he heard the doubt in Fisk's voice, Lemon would have been even more confident of leaving Boston with a share of first place.

Fisk was the heart of the Sox and, thanks to his 1975 World

Series heroics, their most popular player. So when he publicly expressed doubts about his team, all of New England gasped.

"I've never seen the Red Sox get blown out two nights in a row in a pennant race the way we did last night and tonight," Fisk admitted. "It wasn't a case of overconfidence or complacency. It is something that's difficult to put your finger on. We weren't uptight or anything like that. Maybe we were over-relaxed.

"The good thing is that this isn't a golf tournament where they add up the score from all four days."

The best thing for the Yankees was that Guidry was taking the mound in Game 3. They knew they wouldn't need all those runs for the 20-game winner, not even against Boston ace Dennis Eckersley.

And Guidry yielded two hits in the first inning, making it appear the Yanks just might struggle and maybe the Sox would come alive. Then "Louisiana Lightning," in his Fenway Park debut, shut down Boston the rest of the way, while New York came up with seven runs in the fourth inning, helped greatly by a wind-blown bloop double.

Clearly, the game was over at that point, and New York's comeback from 14 games down was almost complete. The Yankees, 7-0 victors, trailed the Sox by one game and had three straight lopsided wins in Fenway.

They also had won 15 of their last 17 contests and 33 of 46 since Lemon replaced Martin. Their march to the top seemed unstoppable.

It had gotten so demoralizing for the Boston faithful that by the seventh-inning stretch, most of the fans were stretching their limbs by walking out of the ballpark.

"It's hard to believe that people would desert them so fast," Yankees first baseman Jim Spencer said. "You look up . . . and there are fewer people in the park than there were during batting practice."

Yankees hitters were taking batting practice on Boston pitchers, and Zimmer was left to turn to a rookie left-hander named Bobby Sprowl to slow down the Bronx Bombers. New York would go for the sweep with Figueroa on the mound.

Sprowl, who had seven innings of major league experience, lasted all of two-thirds of an inning, walking four in the first inning, when the Yankees got three runs. They came through with two more in the second and coasted to a 7-4 victory and a tie for first place.

"We came to town looking for a split and came out of it with a whole handful," the always-relaxed Lemon said.

"I don't think we intimidated them," said Gossage, whose only work in the sweep came in saving Figueroa's victory. "But I'm sure we hurt their morale. We stung the ball from the first night on and it was kind of a steamroller."

And the Red Sox were completely flattened.

"We took a shellacking," Zimmer said after the final beating. "We got the crap kicked out of us."

Yep, they did. The Yankees outhit the Sox 67-21, outscored them 42-9, and Boston made a dozen errors.

"In 37 years, this was the worst performance I've ever seen," Boston coach Johnny Pesky said.

It was so bad that one wag said, midway through the series, that it was the first time a first-place team was chasing a second-place club.

All tied atop the AL East after the Boston Massacre, the Yankees knew they couldn't stop winning. And the reeling Red Sox knew they'd get another shot at New York, in the Bronx, the following weekend.

Not that anyone could expect things to change at this point. The Yanks were soaring; the Sox were choking.

Most disturbing must have been how Boston's fielding had turned shoddy. Through 90 games, the Red Sox led the league in defense and had committed just 90 errors. Now, after the Yankees turned up the heat, the Sox were melting.

They lost 3-2 in Baltimore when they made three errors—on consecutive plays. That gave the Sox 32 errors in their last 13 games, leading to 21 runs. Such charity certainly wouldn't lead to the World Series.

The Yankees, meanwhile, cooled just a bit, losing a game in Detroit when sole possession of the top spot in the East was available. But by midweek, New York culminated its surge from 14 games back with a win in Detroit while the Sox were falling at Cleveland.

The scene was repeated the next night and the Yankees held a one-and-a-half-game lead. Some observers wondered if the Red

Sox were looking back at other AL teams and giving up on catching their nemesis.

But the cast of characters in Boston—Yaz, Lynn, Rice, Fisk, et al.—had too much, well, character to give up. And too much talent.

After all, as Zimmer noted when the Red Sox arrived at Yankee Stadium for a three-game set, "If we sweep, we're back in first place. But we can't afford to lose a game."

Sweeping the Yanks meant, for starters, beating Guidry, who was well rested for the opening game of the series. Indeed, Guidry and Lemon had agreed the lefty would be even more formidable—an almost unimaginable prospect considering how unhittable Guidry had been—with an extra day of rest.

And he was, firing yet another two-hitter at the befuddled Bostonians. He threw his eighth shutout of 1978, beating one-time Yankees killer Tiant 4-0.

Yet another error, this one by Yastrzemski, and back-to-back home runs by Chambliss and Nettles settled matters in the fourth inning.

"Boston is not the same team we saw earlier this season," Guidry said. "When a team is in a batting slump like they are, you can get away with a lot of things. They become defensive and take pitches they shouldn't. Once you get ahead of them, you can pretty much get them to swing at your pitch.

"They're just not comfortable."

Nor could the Sox feel comfy about facing Hunter the next day. With their season spiraling out of control, all they needed was seeing a pitcher almost as torrid as Guidry on the mound.

And that's what they got.

Hunter improved to 7-1 since coming off the disabled list in mid-July. He beat the Red Sox 3-2; at least this one was close, with the Yankees winning in the bottom of the ninth after Rivers tripled and Munson, who barely fouled off a suicide squeeze attempt, then hit a sacrifice fly.

The Red Sox appeared finished. One more win over their archrivals and the Yankees pretty much could begin planning for the playoffs with AL West winner Kansas City. Their remarkable rally would be all but complete, with the Sox trampled and done.

"Three weeks ago, my brother called me from North Carolina," Catfish said, "and he told me I'd be home for harvest time. 'None of that World Series foolishness,' he told me. And I just said, 'Sure looks that way.'"

That, of course, was before the Yankees made the Sox look like rank amateurs.

But then something unexpected occurred. Indeed, something shocking, considering how dominant the Yankees were in six straight wins over Boston.

The Red Sox won the final game at the Stadium, leaving the Bronx down two and a half games, but breathing.

Twelve games remained, with the Yankees seemingly holding all the edges. They were winning steadily, often with ease. They had laid the Red Sox to waste by winning six of seven meetings in an 11-day span. Their pitching had reached peak form. Their lineup was potent; their manager was making all the right decisions.

And history clearly was on their side.

The Sox, however, gained a little spark from finally beating New York, and the next day they won in Detroit, while the Yankees were blanked by Milwaukee. The Yanks then split a doubleheader with Toronto, which routed Guidry, of all people, showing some unexpected vulnerability against a weak opponent.

Heading into the final week, the Yankees led by a game. Playing at home, they beat Toronto three in a row, while the Sox swept the Tigers in Fenway Park. New York then won two in a row over Cleveland, clinching a tie for the division, even though Boston was manhandling the Blue Jays.

"You've got to put out of your mind what's going on in Boston," said Gossage.

"We can't worry about them," added Dent. "As long as we win, they can't beat us."

With the ball in the hands of Catfish Hunter, one of his era's best clutch pitchers, for the season finale, the Yankees' attention might have been turning toward the Royals and the AL playoffs. The lowly Indians weren't going to beat mighty New York and negate this amazing comeback, right? No way.

Oops.

Hunter got shelled by the Indians in a 9-2 defeat. Seizing that one gap Dent said wouldn't open, the Red Sox beat Toronto, their eighth successive victory, to close out the season.

Now Boston had pulled off the big turnaround. The Yankees were ticked at themselves.

"They were unhappy having to use Guidry in another must-win," Shannon said. "They thought they shouldn't have been in a playoff.

"I remember Nettles saying: "It's a pain, we should have won this game and it would be over. Now we have to go through this crap again.""

The bitter rivals would stage a one-game playoff for the division crown. And the game would be at Fenway Park!

Not that being at home was much of an edge for the Sox. The only previous AL playoff game was in 1948, and Boston lost to Cleveland. Besides, the Sox had used Tiant and Eckersley too recently, so Mike Torrez, a loser in six of his last seven outings, would start against Guidry. And all Guidry had done was throw consecutive two-hitters at the Sox in September.

"You want me to throw another one?" Guidry said, repeating a question. "I'll go out there and see what I have. It's the most important game, but I've been taking every game as if it's the most important game."

That this game would even be necessary was a victory for the Red Sox, who were almost giddy at the prospect of getting another shot at the Yankees.

"The way we're playing, we will be tough to beat," Torrez said. "How about my tickets in Kansas City? Pack your bags. That's where we stop next."

Neither Lemon nor Zimmer was thrilled that one game would decide the division between two such distinguished teams.

"That's the way it is," Lemon said. "What do you want us to play, four of seven? How about we play the whole season over. We'll be playing during the Super Bowl."

Well, the playoff certainly had the feel of a Super Bowl. It was front-page news in both cities, and it drew tremendous attention elsewhere—in the days before the Internet and all-sports television and radio. Not only were the most heated rivals in baseball duking it out, but there were stars everywhere. From Yaz to Fisk to Rice to Lynn for the Bosox; from Reggie to Munson to Guidry to Gossage for the Bronx Bombers.

So, of course, one of the guys who almost never grabbed the headlines would be the hero.

The game would later be described as "brilliant theater" and "unbearable drama." Neither description does it justice.

"There is no way any of us right now can appreciate or even understand how it came to this," said Sox shortstop Rick Burleson, who would *not* be the shortstop of note on this autumn afternoon in Fenway. "What we do know is this is the biggest day of our lives."

The day began wonderfully for Boston. The beloved Yastrzemski, the best Red Sox player since Ted Williams, homered off a shaky Guidry to open the second inning. Torrez was stymieing New York's powerful bats, and in the sixth, Rice singled home Burleson for a 2-0 lead.

Could the Yankees conjure up yet another rally? And quickly?

Chambliss and White both singled in the seventh and up to the plate with two outs stepped Dent, a good fielder and decent hitter, but someone who normally wouldn't have gotten this opportunity. Lemon certainly would have used a pinch-hitter, except he had no more middle infielders because Randolph was hurt and his replacement, Brian Doyle, already had been hit for.

For sure, Dent wasn't thinking home run when he walked to the plate. Sure, he (and every right-handed hitter who ever played in Fenway Park) noticed the Green Monster so tantalizingly close in left field. But Dent had managed all of 21 homers in his career.

Dent fouled the second pitch from Torrez off his foot. While the trainer tended to Dent, the pitcher simply watched.

"I should have thrown a couple of pitches because I was standing on the mound waiting to see what was going on," Torrez said. "I should have asked for a delay, just let me throw a couple of pitches, loosen up after I've been out there waiting for five minutes."

Before Dent stepped back in, though, Rivers had the batboy deliver another bat to his teammate.

"Mickey had talked me into using a different bat earlier because my hands had been dragging a little bit," Dent noted. "Actually, I thought I had the new one with me when I went up to the plate. But after I fouled the ball off my foot, Mickey noticed it was not only not the new bat, but a chipped one."

Dent dug in and Torrez fired. The pitch was over the middle of the plate and Dent sent a lazy but long fly ball to left field.

Of course, this was not just any left field. And the ball soared into the netting above the Monster for a three-run homer.

"When I hit the ball, I knew that I had hit it high enough to hit the wall," said Dent, who sensed the game would be tied and he would have a double. "But there were shadows on the net behind the wall and I didn't see the ball land there. I didn't know I had hit a homer until I saw the umpire at first signaling home run with his hand.

"I couldn't believe it."

Nor could Red Sox Nation.

"I was so damn shocked," Torrez said. "I thought maybe it was going to be off the wall. Damn, I did not think it was going to go out."

Soon, the shaken Torrez was going out. He walked Rivers and was replaced by Bob Stanley, who gave up an RBI double to Munson, making it 4-2. Jackson homered in the top of the eighth and the Yanks led 5-2.

But this passion play for the pennant, this epic chapter of Yankees-Red Sox lore couldn't end swiftly. Boston put together four hits in the eighth off Gossage to move within a run.

So it all came to this: Fenway in a frenzy as the Sox came up in the bottom of the ninth, trailing 5-4. Gossage was starting his third inning of relief, and Lemon wasn't looking to anyone else to close out the game.

Burleson walked with one out, and Jerry Remy lined the ball to right field, where Piniella either misjudged it or lost sight of it. (Through the years, he explained it both ways). Regardless, Piniella played it cool, as if he was going to catch the ball, so Burleson couldn't take off for second base.

The ball fell in front of Piniella, who then stabbed it brilliantly with his glove before it skittered by to the wall.

First and second, one out. Fenway Park was shaking to its foundation, the fans' cheers echoing throughout the Back Bay and, perhaps, throughout New England.

Up stepped Rice, who would win the league's Most Valuable Player Award in 1978 as the most feared power hitter in the game. In the on-deck circle was the Boston icon, Yaz.

Gossage, who threw nothing but heat, faced Rice, who regularly crushed fastballs out of ballparks.

"When they had two on in the ninth with Rice and Yaz coming

up," White said, "I was just holding my breath. You want to close your eyes and not see him swing. The wind was blowing out and I could feel that wall creeping closer behind me."

Gossage got Rice to hit the other way, though, and Piniella spotted this one right away and caught it for the second out. Burleson tagged up and went to third, and up stepped Yastrzemski, ready to become the most popular man in Beantown since Paul Revere. Or maybe Ted Williams.

"When it got down to Yaz," Nettles said, "I was thinking, 'Pop him up.' Then Yaz did pop it up and I said, 'Jeez, not to me.'"

Nettles, as sharp a third baseman as anyone this side of Brooks Robinson, caught the lazy popup in foul territory. The Yankees mobbed him and Gossage and anyone else wearing pinstripes. All the Fenway faithful could do was watch in stunned silence.

"In 18 years, you think you have seen everything, and then you come to a season like this and realize you haven't," Yastrzemski said as he pondered the most bitter of defeats. "I've gone through every emotion there is this year, and right now I'm feeling that I'd like one more shot at the Yankees, that I'd like to play them six more games.

"But I also take my hat off to them and I'll be rooting for them to go all the way."

Which the Yankees did. And, yes, they needed yet another comeback in the World Series to beat the Dodgers in six games.

After which Steinbrenner wondered "if my heart can take much more of this."

Oh, c'mon Boss, you would take it every year.

7

STAMPEDING BACK

1992 Buffalo Bills

Buffalo Bills fans are a hardy lot. Even they have their limits, though, and on January 3, 1993, their faith was tested to the very edges.

Not by bitterly cold weather—the faithful at Rich (now Ralph Wilson) Stadium show up no matter what the thermometer says, with some of the crazies wearing nothing more than painted lettering on their chests to spell out B-I-L-L-S.

Not by snow. Bills fans have been known to plow their driveways, neighbors' driveways, and strangers' driveways, then to free up the roads to get to Orchard Park. If you're wearing a Buffalo blue jersey and you need someone to clear a path for your car, no problem.

And certainly not tested by the skill of the opponent, particularly in the glory days of the early 1990s.

Still, coming off two straight losses in the Super Bowl and a disappointing regular season (for them), the Bills hadn't exactly prepped their followers for a big postseason run.

Indeed, in their final regular-season contest, at Houston, the Bills had a chance to wrap up the AFC East for the fifth straight year. Not only did they flop 27-3, but star quarterback Jim Kelly was sacked by defensive tackle Ray Childress and sprained a right knee ligament.

Their opponent the following Sunday in a wild-card playoff game: the same Oilers.

"The scouting report will be easy, just add one week to it and we're done," Oilers coach Jack Pardee said. "It will be the same for them. I'm sure both teams will have some changeups next week."

"It's good we get to try them again next week," Bills linebacker Shane Conlan added. "We'll be all right in the playoffs, especially at home. We get them next week and their plays are very fresh on our minds."

Also fresh, though, was the injury to Kelly, one of the league's most indispensable players. How at home could the Bills feel, even against a team accustomed to the regulated comfort of the Astrodome, with their star quarterback sidelined?

And with several other starters, including dynamic defensive end Bruce Smith, special teams standout Steve Tasker, and linebacker Cornelius Bennett also aching, the Bills looked particularly vulnerable.

"Percentage-wise, some of those questionables ought to be ready," coach Marv Levy said. "If not, (others) will have to step up and be counted.

"Are we a longer shot than someone else? Sure. Long shots win sometimes."

Under other circumstances, the Oilers would have been the longer shot. Unlike the Bills, they had virtually no postseason success on their resume in the previous decade and their last appearance in a conference title game was 1979. They'd never lost a Super Bowl because they'd never been in one.

And they felt their window of opportunity closing.

"For a lot of us, this year or next year, if we don't get it done, we'll probably see ourselves making some major changes around here," said quarterback Warren Moon, an eventual Hall-of-Famer. "The urgency is that we have the chance to do it this year. That should be the only urgency, not looking down the road that we're getting old. It should be that the opportunity is right here in our face and we should take advantage of it."

Why this year?

"This year, we're playing better at the last of the year than we have since I've been here," Moon said. "That's what propels you into the playoffs. Hopefully, that momentum carries you through.

"If you do not do well down the stretch of the season, you're not going to do well in the playoffs."

The Bills hadn't done well down the stretch, losing three of the last five games. And they were banged up.

So the uneasiness was palpable in Western New York when the game kicked off before 75,141 fans—not quite a sellout. A difficult economy, the timing of the game (just after the holidays), and the sense that this was not the Bills' year all contributed to enough empty seats by the NFL's deadline for a sellout that, for the first time in 23 home games, the Bills were blacked out in the area.

What occurred in the first half made it better that the game was not on local TV.

Houston's run-and-shoot offense ran over and around the Bills and shot to a 28-3 halftime lead. The Oilers held the ball for more than 21 of the first 30 minutes, averaged 7.3 yards per play, and kept the Houston attack moving at such a furious clip the Bills, minus the injured Bennett, simply couldn't keep up.

Moon twice found Haywood Jeffires for TD passes, and also connected with Webster Slaughter and Chris Duncan. When Buffalo had the ball, with backup quarterback Frank Reich behind center and star runner Thurman Thomas battling a painful hip, it was no match.

"Warren came out throwing darts," Bills linebacker Darryl Talley said. "He was a surgeon. He could have been a plastic surgeon today and given 9 million facelifts."

The Bills were the ones in need of a major facelift.

Reich was concerned that his mediocre performance and inability to get into the end zone had erased his teammates' confidence in him.

"If Jim has a bad series or two, it's, 'Well, we know he's going to turn it around,' and no one even second-guesses that," Reich said. "Whereas when you're a guy who doesn't play that much, as soon as you make even the littlest mistake, the doubt can creep in a lot faster.

"There's been a point in my career where I hadn't proven myself to my teammates. Hopefully that point is past. You can have a bad series or two and people aren't going to jump ship and say, 'Get him out of there.'"

How about get everybody out of there?

At halftime, all those hardy fans might have been considered foolhardy for sticking around. Instead, they fortified themselves for the second half and what they hoped would be a sensational rally by the Bills.

Buffalo's players, meanwhile, hoped to give a better account of themselves in the second half.

"I think each individual player took it upon himself to say, 'I've got to play better. I have to do the job. I have to make the plays. I have to make the effort,'" wide receiver Andre Reed said.

There were coaching adjustments, as well. The tattered defense dropped its nickel-and-dime alignments and went back to a more basic set, hoping to put some pressure on Moon, who already had completed 19 of 22 passes for 218 yards and four touchdowns. *Four Touchdowns!*

"This is an attitude game," said Bills defensive coordinator Walt Corey. "Sometimes you start playing a game and you're afraid to make things happen or afraid to make a mistake. We didn't do anything the first half. I thought the scheme of the dime was good, but we didn't make anything happen. We felt we had to take big chances in the second (half), even if they blew us away 56-0."

When Bubba McDowell grabbed Reich's first pass of the second half and sped 58 yards to the end zone for a 35-3 lead, the exodus began. The stadium started to empty and even Van Miller, the longtime radio announcer of Bills games, was dismissing his team.

"It really did look bleak," Miller said. "When the Oilers went up by 32, you had to be thinking about it being the end of a great ride and time to look to the next season. You had a lot of injured players, a backup quarterback, and the Oilers were just so hot, doing everything right.

"Who really thought the Bills had a chance?"

Good question. But one man who still believed was Reich, a secret weapon of sorts for Buffalo.

More than eight years before this game, Reich came in for starter Stan Gelbaugh at Maryland, the Terrapins trailing powerful Miami 31-0 at halftime. Talk about lost causes—and miracle comebacks.

"I remember when we played Miami, that game was away, so

we didn't have the advantage like we did today, of the crowd," Reich said.

The rowdy crowd at the Orange Bowl had seen the Hurricanes, led by coach Jimmy Johnson and quarterback Bernie Kosar, out-gain Maryland 328 yards to 57 in one half.

There were other differences. Terps starter Gelbaugh was inefficient, not injured, so when Reich got onto the field, it was not for the opening series, and he'd had no hand in digging such a deep hole for his club.

"He wanted to know why he wasn't going to be the starter against Miami and I told him that we had won five straight and so we stayed with Gelbaugh," said Bobby Ross, the coach at Maryland in 1984. "I said you're one play away and just be ready to play.

"When it was 31-0, I made the decision walking off the field I was going to change quarterbacks. It wasn't that Stan was doing anything wrong, it's just sometimes you do something to try and do something."

One of the things he did was threaten the players that he was going to turn on the lights at the stadium when they returned to Maryland and make them run a 40-yard dash for every point they allowed in the Miami game. Then he would hold a full practice.

"Sometimes a speech like that doesn't come off well, but there was just something about the fire in his eyes that let us know he wasn't going to settle for anything less than a total effort," Reich said of Ross. "We came out and kicked off to them. We intercepted a ball to start the second half, and that started it."

Reich immediately turned the turnover into points with a 39-yard touchdown pass to Greg Hill. After the Canes punted for the first time, the Terps marched 60 yards and Reich scored from the 1.

Although Miami kicked a field goal for a 34-14 lead, Reich threw another TD pass. Maryland got the ball back and a 14-yard TD run by Tommy Neal made it 34-28.

The Canes were reeling and Reich sensed it. His 68-yard touchdown bomb to Hill gave Maryland the lead. Each team scored another touchdown, but when Miami missed a 2-point conversion with 50 seconds on the clock, the biggest comeback win in college football history was secured.

Reich went 12 for 15 for 260 yards—yes, 21.8 yards per completion—and three touchdowns in one half.

"What was ironic about that one was we were losing 31-0 and we threw only 15 passes in the second half," said Reich. "Certainly when you're behind by 31 points, you would think you'd have to throw 30 passes to come back and win.

"It just goes to show that when everyone works together, everything is possible."

Johnson, who went on to coach a national champion at Miami and two Super Bowl winners in Dallas, called the 42-40 defeat "the most disappointing game I've ever been associated with." He did take the time to search for Reich after the final whistle and said: "You did a great job. That's something you'll remember for the rest of your life."

But now it was time to build more memories.

More unlikely memories, because this was the NFL. The NFL playoffs, for that matter.

Behind 35-3, there remained a sense of calm on the Buffalo sideline, although some might have considered it a state of shock.

"I just said this is a humiliating day," Levy said to himself at that point. "Did I think we still had a chance? Well, there was a lot of time left, and there was a glimmer of hope. But it's about the same chance you have of winning the New York lottery."

"I don't think any of us had been in that position before," Conlan added.

Well, one of them had, of course: Reich.

"Frank is a person of high character," Levy said. "He's intelligent. He's a well-rounded family man. I know he's religious. I think sometimes the guy who has other things in his life doesn't clutch up. There's other things that makes him able to retain equilibrium.

"These people who think the only thing in the world is a win, I don't think they retain their poise as well as a person that maybe is as rounded as Frank."

The rounded Reich needed to get right to work. Promptly, the Bills got a break, with a weak Houston kickoff setting them up at midfield.

With the Oilers laying back a bit on defense—a huge miscalculation—the Bills drove in 10 plays for Kenneth Davis's 1-yard TD run. Davis was playing for injured star Thomas.

That might have seemed like a drop of water in the Atlantic, but Steve Christie's onside kick was grabbed by . . . Steve Christie. Perhaps it was an omen, because kickers rarely cover their own kickoffs, let alone recover them.

"Yeah, maybe that was a sign," Christie said with a laugh. "But we were still down 25 points."

Not for long. Reich found Don Beebe down the left sideline for a 38-yard score, and it was 35-17. Game officials never saw Beebe step out of bounds on his route.

Many folks who'd left the stadium but not gotten very far headed back. With no TV coverage available, the rest of the region began perking up just as Miller's play-by-play calls did.

"When the Bills forced a three-and-out and a punt on the next series, you got a feeling if they could score again, anything was possible," Miller said.

They could, indeed, score again. Reich capped a quick 59-yard surge with a 26-yard pass, again down the left sideline, to Reed. Suddenly, it was 35-24 and 4:21 remained in the third quarter.

"That's when I thought it was within reach," said Reich. "If the defense kept playing the way it was playing, and we kept executing on offense, there was plenty of time to come back and win the football game."

On the Houston sideline, the smiles had faded. So had the swagger. Things had gotten out of hand. The offense was sputtering and the defense was invisible.

"It was like, 'Oh, here they come, they're getting back in the game,' which was fine because I was still real confident we would win the game," Houston defensive end Sean Jones said.

His confidence was severely misplaced.

Two plays after the kickoff, Moon's pass deflected off receiver Slaughter and directly to safety Henry Jones. Buffalo set up at the Houston 23, the end zone clearly in sight.

By now, a few hundred fans had filtered back into Rich Stadium. Soon enough, more would return to the stands. By game's end, a million would claim they were there.

It appeared nothing but the clock could stop the Bills—and there was more than a quarter left.

But somehow the Oilers got stingy on defense and Buffalo gained only 5 yards on three plays. Fourth-and-5 on the Houston 18. Levy, sensing that holding the Bills to a field goal might inspire the Oilers, or at least wake them from their lethargy, never called for Christie to kick.

"I told the other coaches if we hit a fourth down, we're going for it if it's anywhere near reasonable distance for the first down," Levy said. "The reasoning was that if we made the field goal, we were still down by eight. That quarter was nearly over and we'd be going into the wind, and you'd have to get very close to try a field goal in the fourth quarter."

Reich was only mildly surprised by the gamble.

"I came over to the sideline and Marv said we were going to go for it," Reich said. "A couple of other coaches were talking, 'Do we want to kick the field goal?'

"I felt real good about the play, so he said, 'OK, go ahead and go for it.'"

First down? How about touchdown?

Reich hit Reed behind coverage for an 18-yard TD pass and it was 35-31. In a span of 6:52, Buffalo had outscored Houston by 28 points.

But the Bills still trailed. There was more work to do.

Again, Houston couldn't move the ball and punted. But the Oilers got some comfort when the defense held and Moon—finally—began finding time to throw and open receivers to throw to. They ate up more than seven minutes with a 76-yard drive helped greatly when a Buffalo interception was negated by a late hit on Moon.

So the Oilers were in position to stem the surge, but stalled at the Buffalo 14. Al Del Greco never got to try a chip-shot field goal, because holder Greg Montgomery bobbled the snap.

"We just kept compounding the problems," Pardee said.

Their exhausted defense was no match for the Bills on the next drive, which covered 74 yards on seven plays into the wind. Reed, not surprisingly, was on the receiving end of Reich's 17-yard TD pass and, unfathomably, the Bills were ahead 38-35 with three minutes to go.

"We knew they'd concentrate on Reed and he hurt us anyway," Pardee said. "We tried to blitz and that put us in some one-on-one coverages."

Confusion seemed to be the calling card of the Houston defense, with players sniping at each other and the coaches. Cornerback Cris Dishman claimed Reed could have been slowed down, but the coaches never adjusted.

"We knew they were going to feature Andre Reed in the second half, but we stayed in the same zones," Dishman said. "When you play the same things all the time, teams are going to beat you. It was the same old coverage.

"You can beat around the bush and say they got plays. It's not really something that they did. I keep saying over and over . . . we just basically choked. As coaches, as players, everyone. We just basically choked."

While the defense was in shambles, Moon wouldn't allow the offense to give up. There still was time to reverse Houston's fortunes.

"It just seems like it kept going and kept going and we couldn't get it stopped," Moon said of Buffalo's momentum. "But we weren't going to stop there, stop trying. We knew with all that had gone wrong, a touchdown still would win it for us."

Maybe on this day of illogical spurts, the final stroke would belong to the Oilers. With Buffalo in a prevent defense, Moon finally got some time to look downfield, to read the flow of plays. Houston relentlessly moved deep into Buffalo territory.

Could such a memorable rally be thwarted? Each Bills defender, on the edge of exhaustion, had to be asking himself that question as Moon ate up the yardage.

Then the Bills' amazing resolve, which carried them back from 35-3 one quarter earlier, emerged yet again. The defense held, and Del Greco kicked a 26-yard field goal with 12 seconds to go.

38-38.

Overtime.

Which side could claim the advantage heading into the extra period?

Certainly the Bills felt good still being alive. And surely the Oilers felt a spark after tying the score in the dying seconds following such an unnerving collapse.

"No, no, no, I don't think any of us felt any edge," Reed said. "We just knew this was one of the strangest, wildest games we'd ever play in. We had no idea how it would end."

Houston's luck seemed to have changed, what with the dramatic drive to tie the game and then when it won the coin toss and received the kickoff to start overtime.

"Sure, we felt we were going right down the field and we were going to win it," Moon said. "We had just moved the ball so well to get the field goal for the tie, and we knew they were tired, maybe even a little down after we came back to tie."

On third down from the Houston 27, Moon was pressured by Jeff Wright. He avoided the sack with a throw that floated directly to cornerback Nate Odomes.

Odomes's interception was compounded by Jeffires drawing a 15-yard facemask penalty for his tackle of the defensive back.

This time, Levy wasn't forgetting about Christie. On third down, he called on the kicker to try a 32-yard field goal.

Christie's kick was good, capping the greatest comeback in NFL history. Final: Buffalo 41, Houston 38.

"You dream about kicking winning field goals in playoff games. Every kicker does," Christie said. "But nobody in his right mind dreams of coming back from 32 (points) down in the second half before you get that field goal to win it."

The wounds were deep for the Oilers, who would never win another playoff game before moving to Tennessee in 1997. Defensive coordinator Jim Eddy immediately was fired. So was defensive back coach Pat Thomas.

Eddy and Thomas worked for Pardee in the USFL and at the University of Houston, too.

"We've been together the last 10 years so this is very difficult, but we felt for the organization it was something that had to be done," Pardee said. "It's no secret we had a few problems in that area and we've got to get them corrected. This is a tough business. At this time of year, you'd rather be selling insurance or doing something on TV."

One TV viewer of the game was Hall-of-Famer Joe Schmidt, who was with the Lions in 1957 when Detroit rallied from a 27-7 hole to beat San Francisco in the playoffs.

"What I think happened with the Oilers was they were so happy to be up 35-3 that they just sat back," he said. "They can't use the clock with that run-and-shoot offense. It doesn't allow that. If they could have worked their way down the field on each possession, then they would have won."

Could the Bills carry the momentum deeper into the playoffs, on the road?

Absolutely. They beat Pittsburgh and Miami to make their

third straight Super Bowl—where they lost to Johnson's Dallas team with Reich on the bench at the outset and Kelly back in the lineup.

"It's motivating, a great feeling to have that experience," Schmidt said of the incredible comeback against Houston. "You think to yourself, 'We have the ability to come back from anything. We did it before. We can do it again.'"

8

THE STREAK STOPS HERE

Notre Dame's Win over UCLA
in Basketball, 1974

If there is anything like a sure thing in sports, it was the UCLA basketball team of the 1960s and '70s. In a 12-year period from 1964 to 1975, the Bruins won 10 national championships and came painfully close to notching another.

The Bruins' record of 38 straight victories in the NCAA playoffs might stand forever. So might their 88-game winning streak, which came to a shocking end one January day in 1974 on the campus of Notre Dame.

To say that the Irish "stole" one from the Bruins was not too far from the actual truth. Notre Dame coach Digger Phelps took a page out of the UCLA book, using John Wooden's famous full-court press to pull out an unlikely victory in the final minutes.

The big, bad UCLA Bruins—No. 1 in the country—were dealt a sample of their own medicine and literally stopped in their tracks.

Wooden had brought the philosophy of the full-court press with him when he headed west from Purdue in the early 1960s. At Purdue, Wooden had played for Piggy Lambert, a Midwestern basketball legend.

At the time Wooden made his move to California, West Coast basketball wasn't considered on a level with the rest of the country, even though San Francisco and California had won national titles in the '60s.

In a short time, Wooden changed that thinking, winning with little men (Gail Goodrich and Walt Hazzard), big men (Lew Alcindor and Bill Walton), and in-between men (Sidney Wicks and Curtis Rowe).

In Alcindor, later known as Kareem Abdul-Jabbar, and Walton, Wooden had two of the greatest centers in college basketball history. Each was devastating in his own way. UCLA's full-court press was equally devastating. It went baseline to baseline, grudgingly giving up ground to frustrated opponents. At UCLA's Pauley Pavilion, the students got into the act, riotously counting off the seconds as opponents attempted to bring the ball upcourt. Very often shaken, they couldn't make the half-court line within the allotted 10 seconds, resulting in a turnover.

Of course, in order to play the demanding style of the press, UCLA's athletes had to be extremely well conditioned. Wooden made sure they would be.

"I told my players that I wanted them to be in better condition than any team we meet," Wooden said. "Not as good, but better."

The UCLA press confounded opponents, prompted steals, and inspired awe. "What do you do with the ball once you have an advantage?" one frustrated coach said about the Bruins' pressure defense.

He had no answer.

Playing for Wooden was not easy. Getting access to the UCLA players was equally as difficult for the media.

"[He] shields his team at all times and often assumes the pompous air of his days as an English teacher at South Bend Central High School," Kenneth Denlinger wrote in the *Washington Post*.

Wooden's practices, where UCLA's games were essentially won, were tough and usually closed to prying eyes. During a game, Wooden very rarely called a timeout; his players had been well schooled in just about every situation possible. Besides, he saw the calling of timeouts, unless absolutely necessary, as a weakness. And he trusted his players implicitly to do the right thing.

Wooden was usually unemotional on the bench, his game program tightly rolled up in his fist as he watched the action. He kept himself in control for the most part, rarely getting into heated attacks on officials during the game. He waited until halftime, out of public view, to do that.

If he was displeased with the officiating, reporters said, Wooden waited at a side door for the referees to walk through. Then he would put on his own full-court press, giving them an earful.

"On the Coast, we call him Saint John," one opposing Pacific-Eight coach said in a sarcastic tone, indicating a darker side to Wooden's squeaky-clean public persona.

While Wooden was making his mark out west, Phelps was just starting to make some noise in the East in the early 1970s. The son of an undertaker—thus the nickname—Dick "Digger" Phelps played his collegiate ball at Rider College.

As a coach, he burst on the scene in 1970 at the age of 29 with a break-out Fordham team that captured the heart of New York.

With a full-court press (like UCLA's) and an undersized band of sharpshooters, the Rams were suddenly the pride of the city. College basketball excitement was back in town after two decades of apathy following the point-shaving scandals of the early 1950s.

"There hadn't been a national championship won by a New York team for 20 years (CCNY in 1951), and we wanted to correct that," said the swaggering Phelps.

Fordham's star was Charlie Yelverton—"King Charles" to his adoring fans. Yelverton was a 6-foot-2 skywalker who played one of the forward positions.

"Yelverton was the spirit of the team," Phelps said. "Everybody looked up to him."

Yelverton not only led the Rams in scoring most of the time, but usually defensively took on the best player on the other team. And it didn't matter how much bigger he was.

A memorable performance early in the season: Yelverton blocked a jumper by Julius Erving, then took the ball away from the Massachusetts superstar, who was 6-7. Yelverton wound up with 30 points and Fordham finished with an 87-79 victory.

The Rams played a far-reaching schedule, from Florida to California, but weren't immediately recognized in the national polls despite winning their first 10 games.

"That was our challenge," Phelps said. "We played a pretty

tough schedule, and my kids kept winning and looking forward to getting ranked week to week."

The Rams were easy to overlook because the tallest starter on the team was only 6-6 sophomore Bart Woytowicz. Finally, after improving to a record of 11-0, Fordham broke into the Top 20.

Fordham continued to move up in the rankings with the help of a 94-88 win over Notre Dame in a raucous, sold-out Madison Square Garden. The crowd of 19,500 chanted, "Number One," a reference to the fact that Notre Dame had beaten top-ranked UCLA.

Maybe they weren't "Number One," but the Rams were certainly one of the nation's most formidable teams at 19-1. When second-ranked Marquette pulled into the Garden, Fordham was ranked No. 10 in the United Press International poll and No. 11 in the Associated Press.

As expected, there was another sellout crowd at the Garden and electricity in the air. The game was everything the fans expected. There were 14 ties, including at 68 at the end of regulation.

Finally, Marquette's muscular front line prevailed in overtime, with star Jim Chones leading the way. Marquette held on for an 85-80 victory over Fordham in one of the most exciting college basketball games seen in the Garden in many years.

By the end of the regular season, Fordham had earned a spot in the NCAA playoffs. The Rams beat Furman in the first round before losing to Villanova, the eventual finalist against UCLA.

The season ended faster than Phelps planned, but it had been an incredible ride. From a 10-15 team the year before, Phelps had built the Rams into a powerhouse that won 26 of its 29 games.

Next stop for Phelps: Notre Dame. Phelps was soon on his way to his dream job. It was a match made in basketball heaven: the ebullient Phelps and the most famous collegiate athletic program in the country. Certainly basketball didn't come close to matching the far-flung fame of the football team. But, after all, it *was* Notre Dame.

Phelps's first year at South Bend was rocky, as the Irish went 6-20 in 1971–1972. Looking back on that disastrous season a couple of years later, the son of a funeral director quipped, "I was thinking then of going to embalming school."

By his second season at Notre Dame, the Irish corpse was blinking. The big win: 66-64 over Kansas in overtime.

"That was the key game for us," Phelps said. "We had a 1-6 record and needed a win badly."

By his third season at South Bend, the Irish corpse was not only blinking but beating everyone in sight. The Notre Dame revival was on, and it was going full steam.

Phelps liked to keep things relaxed around the team, giving reporters total access and basically letting the players regiment themselves—the extreme opposite of Wooden. Not that he couldn't be stern when the situation called for it. Once, when Dwight Clay was slow in raising his arm after a foul call, Digger tore off the bench. The player shot to attention and wasted little time putting up his arm.

In the 1973–1974 season, Phelps had assembled one of Notre Dame's strongest teams, with John Shumate, Adrian Dantley, Gary Brokaw, Clay, and Gary Novak.

Shumate, a physical 6-9 center who was in place when Phelps arrived, was Notre Dame's biggest star. But basketball seemed secondary after he survived a viral infection in 1972 that almost took his life.

"When I woke up one day and overheard the doctors saying I couldn't play basketball again and might die . . . I got very depressed and upset, and I felt like giving up," Shumate told the *Los Angeles Times*.

However, a comforting visit from his father, a minister in New Jersey, made Shumate feel better. Two years later, he was the focal point of a Notre Dame team that was winning and climbing steadily in the national rankings.

Starting with Phelps, just about everyone on the team had a nickname. Shumate was "Big Shu." Novak, a pencil-thin forward, was "Goose." Dantley was "Magic," a reference to his long-range shooting touch and high field-goal percentage. And Clay, a Pittsburgh native, was called "The Iceman" because of a history of making big shots under stressful conditions.

"Not everyone can handle a pressure game," he said, "but I thrive on it."

With a modest winning streak early in the season, the Irish were slowly sneaking up on people. The Bruins couldn't very well do that. They had won seven straight NCAA titles and were favored to win another with a team nicknamed "The Walton Gang."

The "Gang" was led by the imposing Walton, a 6-11 center who ignited UCLA's frightening fast break with his enormous rebounding skills. Walton was surrounded by UCLA's usual wealth of talented players, just about all of them high school All-Americans. Among them: Keith Wilkes, Dave Meyers, Tommy Curtis, Pete Trogvich, and Ralph Drollinger, Walton's backup, who could have started at center for most any team in the country.

The 1973–1974 Bruins would be tested early with tough out-of-conference games against Maryland and North Carolina State of the Atlantic Coast Conference. The Bruins beat Maryland and the basketball world soon turned its eyes toward St. Louis, where UCLA and North Carolina State met in a neutral-site contest.

The Wolfpack had won 29 straight games, second-longest active streak only to UCLA's 78. State's featured player was David Thompson, a do-everything forward with incredible leaping skills. Walton's personal challenge was Tom Burleson, who at 7-foot-4 was five inches taller than the UCLA center. Monty Towe was the Wolfpack's sparkplug point guard.

↬

It was a matchup of No. 1 against No. 2 and was being built up as the "Game of the Decade," comparable in some ways to the great UCLA battles with Houston in the late '60s featuring Alcindor against Elvin Hayes.

But the UCLA–NC State game was no contest. Even with Walton sitting out a large part of the match in foul trouble, the Bruins turned the expected classic into a rout, 84-66, as Wilkes scored 27 points. The headline in the *Los Angeles Times*: "UCLA's Still No. 1 . . . and N.C. State's No. 79."

The Bruins marched into January still unbeaten, looking ahead to a Midwestern swing that included the Notre Dame game. The Irish had moved up to No. 2 in the polls, and there was concern in the UCLA camp that the Bruins would have to play them without Walton. The All-American center had a bruised back muscle that had not responded to treatment.

↬

How important was Walton to the UCLA team? Famed odds-maker Jimmy (The Greek) Snyder made Notre Dame 4-point favorites if UCLA was to play without Walton, the two-time player of the year. With him, the Bruins would be favored by 4.

Turned out, the Bruins would have Walton in uniform, although not for the first game of the trip with Iowa. He was still not at his best and felt that playing in the Iowa game would set him back. The Bruins didn't need him, as they routed the Hawkeyes 68-44.

The UCLA streak was now up to 88, the longest in college basketball history by a wide margin, eclipsing the 60-game streak of the San Francisco Dons in the mid-1950s.

On January 19, 1974, UCLA took the court against Notre Dame at the jam-packed Athletic and Convocation Center with 11,343 in attendance. The last time the Bruins had lost was on January 23, 1971, when a Notre Dame team led by Austin Carr's 46 points pulled off an upset on the very same court.

For most of the day, the Bruins didn't look like they would lose there again. Their front line of Walton, Wilkes, and Meyers took 11 shots together in the first 10 minutes—and made them all. UCLA led by 17 on two occasions and went into the dressing room at halftime leading by 9 points, 43-34.

It wasn't so much the score that was so demoralizing to Notre Dame fans; it was the ease with which the Bruins made their points. They hit an astounding 70 percent of their shots in the first half against a lifeless Notre Dame defense.

The Irish rallied at the start of the second half. The Bruins rallied back.

Notre Dame made another run, but UCLA again answered.

It seemed as if UCLA was just toying with the Irish, letting them get just close enough to smell the lead, but not enough to taste it. When the Irish closed within 5 points at 64-59, UCLA again came back with 6 straight for a 70-59 advantage.

There were just 3 minutes, 30 seconds left, and hope was failing among the Notre Dame fans.

Not on the Notre Dame bench, though.

Phelps called timeout and told his team to go with the man-to-man press. He had used it unsuccessfully early in the game. But now he readjusted the lineup so that faster players would be on the floor.

Suddenly, the momentum changed as:

- Shumate scored after the Bruins threw the ball away against the press.
- The Notre Dame press forced another turnover as Shumate made an interception and scored again.
- Dantley stole the ball and drove for a layup, cutting UCLA's lead to 70-65.
- The press caused yet another turnover, and this time, Brokaw converted to trim UCLA's lead to 70-67.
- Notre Dame rebounded a UCLA miss and Brokaw converted to cut the score to 70-69 with 1:23 remaining.
- Wilkes was called for charging with 43 seconds left, and Notre Dame moved quickly downcourt. "The place was rocking," reported the *Los Angeles Times*. And the Bruins seemed to be panicking.
- Failing to get a pass inside for a close-in shot, the Irish finally whipped the ball to Clay in the corner. It was not the shot they wanted, but the Irish had no choice. Clay had no choice. He fired from long range and stumbled back into the crowd.
- *Bingo! Basket!*

"Now the noise was deafening," the *Los Angeles Times* said after the Irish took the lead at 71-70.

Finally, Wooden called a timeout. He had to set up UCLA's last play.

But the unnerved Bruins missed several shots, including an eight-footer by Walton in the final 29 seconds, before the buzzer sounded to end the game. Shumate grabbed a loose ball and happily heaved it toward the ceiling as hundreds of celebratory fans poured onto the court.

The 88-game streak—the most impressive in the sport's history, if not in the annals of all sports—was shattered. All Wooden could do was congratulate Phelps and wait for their return game in Los Angeles the following week.

"We'll get a better measure about the two teams after next Saturday's game," Wooden said, knowing full well what his team was capable of in the return engagement.

And "The Rematch" became "The Mismatch," with UCLA winning in a blowout at Pauley Pavilion, 94-75.

Beating UCLA two times in a week was too much to ask of Notre Dame—or probably anybody else. But the memory of the miracle finish at South Bend still remains as a highlight of Irish basketball.

9

KINGS OF QUEENS

1986 New York Mets

In 1969, they were the Miracle Mets. Four years later, they were the Amazin's.

And in 1986, the New Yorkers were World Series favorites.

The Mets? That bungling bunch whose first manager, Casey Stengel, once asked of: "Can anybody here play this game?"

By '86, not only weren't the Mets providing comic relief for the baseball world, but they had won one World Series crown, played for another, and were the dominant diamond team in the Big Apple. Yes, they not only were the Kings of Queens, but the Mets owned all of New York in those days because the Yankees were also-rans.

Even more distasteful to George Steinbrenner's bunch in the Bronx, the Mets would play the Boston Red Sox in the Series. It was the kind of postseason matchup that would make Yankees fans barf: can't root for the hated Sox, and can't root for the local rivals.

Not that the Yankees mattered whatsoever to either side—even if there would be an extra tinge of satisfaction for the champions that they were masters over Lord Steinbrenner and his minions.

Oddly, early in September, the Mets visited Fenway Park to

play an exhibition game. It was the first meeting in a two-year, home-and-home deal for charity.

It also was a preview of the World Series.

"Games like these are great for the game and great for both cities," said Mets catcher Gary Carter. "When you have charities like the Jimmy Fund or the sandlot leagues involved, it's something special."

Enough so that many of both teams' regulars not only played in the game, but participated in a home-run derby before the contest. Carter sent five balls over the left-field wall, the Green Monster, as the Mets won the long-ball exhibition 9-5.

And they also won the charity game 7-3.

Had the Mets delivered a message?

"We take all games seriously," manager Dave Johnson said. "We wanted this one, too. But this was more for fun. We still have to win our division and win in the playoffs before we see these guys again."

Added Red Sox manager John McNamara: "Is this a preview of the Series? Well, they are 20 games in front in the NL East, we're 4½ in front in the AL East. We haven't even won our division yet.

"I'd like to trade places with the Mets and take my chances."

Turns out, both sides' chances of getting to the World Series were pretty good. And the seven-game series they would stage wound up a classic featuring one of baseball's greatest comebacks.

But first, each needed to get by formidable opponents to win their league pennants. That was hardly a simple task.

New York won 108 games during the season, the best record in baseball. With superb pitching led by starters Dwight Gooden, Ron Darling, and Bob Ojeda and relievers Roger McDowell and Jesse Orosco, the Mets moved into first place on April 23 and never fell out of the top spot.

But they weren't a slam dunk to get to their third World Series. Indeed, it took a magnificent comeback in Game 6 of the National League championship series to subdue the Houston Astros.

Leading three games to two, the Mets headed back to Houston well aware that their nemesis, Mike Scott, master of the split-fingered fastball before it became a common pitch, would go in Game 7 if the series got that far. They were well advised to avoid

Scott by ending the proceedings in the sixth game, because Scott had yielded one run and eight hits while striking out 19 in winning Games 1 and 4.

So what did they do? How about fall behind 3-0 in the first inning on an RBI double by Phil Garner and run-scoring singles by Glenn Davis and Jose Cruz. The Astrodome was rocking, the Mets were being rocked.

They also were looking helpless against Houston starter Bob Knepper, who was 17-12 during the season, including a 3-1 mark against the Mets. As he mowed down batter after batter, Houstonians began making plans not only for a Game 7, but for their first trip to the World Series.

Knepper allowed two hits through eight innings and carried the 3-0 lead into the ninth.

"For eight innings, that's the best I've ever pitched," the left-hander said.

But he needed nine.

Displaying the heart of champions, the Mets rallied.

Len Dykstra pinch-hit and Knepper made his first mistake, on an 0-2 pitch, no less. Dykstra lined it into center field for a triple.

"It was frustrating that our guys were going up there inning after inning with two out and nobody on base," Dykstra said. "I went up with the idea that I had to get on base."

Mookie Wilson singled off second baseman Bill Doran's glove to score Dykstra.

Keith Hernandez's double knocked in Wilson and knocked out Knepper. His eight innings of stunning work would be forgotten if the Astros couldn't hold on with Dave Smith on the mound.

Smith had 33 saves during the season, and he was facing the slumping Carter, who'd managed a mere two hits in 22 at-bats in the postseason. But Smith walked Carter, bringing up slugger Darryl Strawberry.

Strawberry sent a majestic shot deep into the upper deck as the dome fans held their breath. But it was a foul ball.

Not that the locals got much relief when Strawberry also walked, loading the bases with one out.

Up stepped Ray Knight, who admitted to a "case of nerves" even though he was one of the most experienced Mets. Knight made solid contact, sending a deep drive to right-center field, a sacrifice fly that tied it.

If this game wasn't already a classic, it certainly would become one as the teams battled through four scoreless innings.

"During the 10th, 11th, 12th, and 13th innings, I was thinking that none of this would have been necessary if I'd done my job," the unfortunate Knepper said." We'd be out there tomorrow."

In the 14th, it would be the Astros' turn to make a comeback. They had flailed away against McDowell, who allowed one hit in five innings, a far longer stint than he'd been accustomed to. When Wally Backman singled home Strawberry in the top of the 14th, Houston was on life support.

McDowell, however, was done, and Johnson turned to Orosco, the left-handed portion of his dynamic bullpen duo. But Orosco wasn't nearly as sharp as McDowell.

Billy Hatcher stepped to the plate with the Astros' season on his bat—and rocketed a homer to left field to tie the score.

After another scoreless inning, the Mets struck again in the 16th, with some good fortune.

Strawberry's pop-up fell between Houston's fielders in short center for a double and Knight singled him home against Aurelio Lopez. Knight took second on the throw home, went to third on a wild pitch, and scored on another wild pitch by reliever Jeff Calhoun.

Dykstra eventually singled home another run for a seemingly safe 7-4 lead.

"I'm not sure there was any point we could feel comfortable," Dykstra said, "but we were up by three runs with Jesse on the mound."

Orosco was struggling, though, and Johnson really had no other options. So he stuck with the lefty even after Davey Lopes walked and Doran and Hatcher singled.

How confident was Johnson at that point?

"I was scared to death," he admitted. "I was scared they were going to come back one more time."

Almost. Davis also singled, and it was 7-6.

With two outs, the tying and winning runs on base, Kevin Bass faced the faltering Orosco. The count went to 3-2 amid the bedlam in the Astrodome.

"I've never felt this kind of heat before," Johnson thought.

Orosco had enough heat left to fan Bass, and the Mets stormed from the dugout and the bullpen to mob each other in ecstasy. Who knows where they got the energy from.

It was the longest game in postseason history, and certainly the most exhausting.

"My ballclub never gets down," Johnson said. "My ballclub handled the pressure very well. They said we never played a tough game all year. Well, the pennant is the toughest thing to get. Even if you lose the World Series, you've won the pennant."

But Carter felt little relief.

"If we don't win the World Series, this is all for nothing," Carter yelled amid the celebrations in the locker room. "To come this far and not get to the World Series would be very sad."

The sadness enveloped the Astros, who fought gallantly and understood they would have been strong favorites to beat the Mets in Game 7 with Scott on the mound.

"There's no question in my mind that we should be in the World Series," Knepper said. "We just made too many mistakes. They didn't make the mistakes. We did.

"During the last six or seven innings, I had plenty of time to cry inside about letting the game slip away."

Slip away? Perhaps in Houston's view. New York had another perspective, believing it fully earned the trip to the World Series.

"This is my 16th year in pro baseball and I've never been involved in anything so emotional or been under such a mental strain and under such physical pressure as I have been in this series," Knight noted.

All Knight needed was to wait a few days to match those feelings. And surpass them.

⌒

The Red Sox didn't have a joyride into the World Series, either. They needed seven games to down the California Angels, coming back from a 3-1 deficit in the AL Championship Series, becoming only the seventh team to mount such a rally. Their comeback was as impressive as what the Mets staged in Game 6 at Houston.

But the final two games were romps of 10-4 and 8-1 at Fenway Park behind ace Roger Clemens and the power hitting of veterans Jim Rice and Dwight Evans.

It was extremely noteworthy how the Sox put away the Angels, because Boston's well-documented history of folding in such circumstances hovered over the team and its fans like a plague. The Sox hadn't won baseball's prime prize since 1918, with some monumental chokes leading many to believe the team was cursed.

Perhaps this was the squad to break through, particularly after the way it had arisen to win Game 5 of the ALCS. These Sox were the first in franchise history to capture a win-or-go-home contest with a division, pennant, or World Series title on the line since the team moved into Fenway Park. That was in 1912.

The Angels, who never had been to the World Series, had some of California's finest vintage from Sonoma on ice for their celebration after going up three games to one.

Boston led 2-1 through five innings when Dave Henderson replaced injured center fielder Tony Armas. A few moments later, with a man on base, Henderson leaped up the wall for a long fly ball off the bat of Bobby Grich. The ball hit his glove, bounced off it and over the fence. Home run. Angels lead 3-2.

"I went up, the ball hit the heel of my glove, and when my wrist hit the top of the wall the ball got away," Henderson explained. "It was kind of a fluke thing. I thought I had it all the way."

Henderson threw his arms up and bowed his head. Sox pitcher Bruce Hurst kneeled down near the mound, refusing to watch Grich circle the bases—or look out toward Henderson.

When the Angels added two more runs and took a 5-2 lead into the ninth behind powerful right-hander Mike Witt, the Sox appeared doomed.

"No Knute Rockne speeches," McNamara said. "I just said a few words that I thought were appropriate to a few individuals."

One of those individuals was Don Baylor. The veteran, no stranger to succeeding in difficult situations, delivered a two-run homer off Witt with one out, making it 5-4. But Witt recovered to get Evans, and the Angels stood one out from the pennant.

To get that out, manager Gene Mauch brought in left-hander Gary Lucas to face lefty batter Rich Gedman.

With all the fans on their feet, yelling, clapping, stomping—yes, even in Anaheim they can get that excited—Lucas nailed Gedman with an errant pitch.

In came closer Donnie Moore. Up came Henderson. How juicy: the goat of a few innings earlier with a chance for redemption.

The count reached 2-2.

"We're ballplayers. We fail most of the time," Henderson said. "I had to step out of the batter's box and gather my thoughts."

He gathered them very well. Henderson fouled off the next pitch, then sent a forkball deep to left field, into the seats, and, stunningly, the Sox led 6-5.

"I haven't got that many chances (since he was acquired from Seattle in August), but it's nice to get the big hit. It came at the right time," he said.

No kidding.

"We got down to the last out and we did what we've done all year," Baylor added. "When you get down to your last out, your last pitch, there's a lot of emotion. We did what we had to do. We've been pushed to the wall a lot this year and after this you have to believe in this ballclub."

But the Angels weren't done. In the bottom of the ninth, they tied it on Rob Wilfong's RBI single. They still had a two-game edge in the series, and as they headed to extra innings, Wilfong said, "our confidence was high."

In the 11th inning, though, Boston capped the dramatic comeback, Moore hit Baylor with a pitch—Baylor made a career out of being plunked—and Evans singled. Gedman beat out a bunt before Henderson's fly ball to center was deep enough to plate the go-ahead run.

On came reliever Calvin Schiraldi, who blew Game 4 when he forced in the tying run with two outs in the bottom of the ninth by—oh, the irony!—hitting Brian Downing with a pitch after getting two strikes on him. Schiraldi wept in the locker room after that debacle, but this time, no tears: Schiraldi was untouchable and the Sox stayed alive.

"I was just hoping for a chance to get into the game and make up for last night," Schiraldi admitted. "I'm glad Mac had the confidence in me to put me in there and give me the chance to make it up."

Added McNamara: "This might have been the most exciting, most competitive baseball game I've ever seen. It was very exhilarating for us to win, and very tough for them to lose."

So the Red Sox, a team that destiny had played cruel tricks on for decades, suddenly were charmed.

And their blitz of the Angels at Fenway seemed to certify that this was their year—as well as ensure that Mauch, who won 1,901 games in 26 years as manager of Philadelphia, Minnesota, Montreal, and California, would never manage a World Series game.

"Ever since Sunday's game, we've been saying to each other, over and over, that we shouldn't even be here anymore, we should be dead, the season should be over. So it's all gravy now," said second baseman Marty Barrett, who was the playoffs MVP.

"It got to the Angels, too. The (security) guards were in their dugout on Sunday, the batboys already popped the champagne. They had it dangling right there . . . then it was gone.

"After that, there was more pressure on them than on us. We were going back home and we were playing with house money."

The World Series opened in New York. The city is renowned for its cosmopolitan nature and for its role at the center of the business, media, and artistic worlds. But when it comes to baseball, New Yorkers are as parochial as anyone. "Let's Go Mets" had become the rallying cry throughout Queens, where they play, and the other four boroughs. Plus Long Island, Westchester, Rockland, New Jersey, and Connecticut.

The Big Apple and its environs was swept up in Metsmania.

The floodlights on the Empire State Building displayed blue and orange—the Mets' colors—after sundown. A sign near Shea Stadium advertising a bread company instead repeatedly flashed the word *Champs*.

Banners flew from apartment buildings and private houses. Sales on New York state champagne soared. Experts predicted the direct impact on the city's economy could approach $10 million.

And in Boston? Well, talk of the Red Sox falling apart at every critical juncture was replaced with the optimism inspired by their remarkable rally against the Angels.

"If you ever weren't a believer, that series with California should have made you a believer," Baylor said. "There were so many guys that played a role in getting it back to Boston, and when we got back to Boston, we knew we had a chance."

One of those guys, first baseman Bill Buckner, was hitting just .214 in the playoffs. He began wearing specially made high-top shoes just before the World Series to alleviate pressure on his sore ankles.

"I feel like I'm walking in slippers," Buckner said of the new shoes. "They feel real good.

"It's been 12 years since I've been in a World Series (1974 with the Dodgers). To not be able to play now would be awfully disappointing. All the pressure is in the playoffs. The World Series is the reward for all that hard work."

In an attempt to match New York's efforts to dress up the Series, in Beantown's Prudential building a pattern of lights was set up inside offices to display the number 1.

On both sides, there would be much angst heading into this matchup. As one fan told the *New York Times,* "The Mets are dynamic, like the Red Sox. Both teams have played games that drive your stomach into your throat."

As they would do over the next week or so.

The opener was a pitching classic between Hurst and Darling, neither of them the ace of their staff. On a typically chilly late October night at Shea Stadium, where the wind whips off Flushing Bay even in the dead of summer—yep, football weather—Hurst allowed only four hits and fanned eight in eight innings before former Met Schiraldi finished a 1-0 win.

And the only run came thanks to an error by Mets second baseman Tim Teufel in the seventh inning.

So Boston's first World Series appearance in New York in 70 years was a resounding success. The Sox stymied the best offense in baseball, and while they didn't do much with the bat either, they won.

Mets manager Johnson absolved Teufel of the role of demon.

"When you don't score any runs in nine innings, do you think that's one man's fault?" Johnson said. "We didn't score runs. You get shut out and you lose, that's it."

If the Mets were distressed, they didn't let on too much. After all, Gooden would be on the mound for them in Game 2.

But Clemens would pitch for Boston.

Another scintillating pitching duel seemed likely. So, of course, the Red Sox hammered Gooden and, while Clemens wasn't overpowering, he was good enough to lead a 9-3 victory for a two-game edge as the Series headed back to the Fenway bandbox.

Johnson shook up his lineup hoping to find some potency, and the Mets did manage eight hits. None of them were for extra bases, though.

And the Sox were getting 18 hits off Gooden and three relievers. Both Evans and Henderson homered, driving Gooden from the game after five innings. He surrendered eight hits and six runs, and it was clear that the Sox were feeling no aftereffects from their emotional playoff series. The Mets, meanwhile, seemed lost.

"How do you explain this? I don't know any answers," said Knight, who was benched for Howard Johnson, who then went 0 for 4. "I have no idea why we're not hitting, but we're slumping."

Slumping, but not obsessing about it. As Strawberry understood, "If we sit around and cry like babies, we'll lose the next two in Boston and it will be over."

Indeed, the Mets faced a formidable task. Quirky Fenway is a difficult enough ballpark for visitors from the American League who get there periodically. Other than that summer exhibition game, most of the Mets were total strangers.

Talk about lost.

In turn, the Sox were strutting, and deservedly so. They'd won five in a row, three of the games in romps that featured heavy hitting. When they needed to clamp down the opposition, their pitchers managed it. Boston, the city, was beaming with hope, boasting about its baseball heroes. Boston, the team, couldn't have carried more confidence into Game 3.

"I think it's fair to say we're feeling good about how we're playing: hitting, pitching, defense, running the bases, it's all been good," Gedman said. "You want to hit your stride now, and we've done that for the last few games."

McNamara, embodying the typical New England attitude about positive outlooks, wasn't going overboard with his optimism.

"After what we've been through, we're not going to be overconfident about anything," he said. "I do feel comfortable, though. Now, we get back the DH (which is not used in National League parks). We can use our regular lineup that got us to the World Series. We don't have to mess around with bunting and have the pitchers hit and all that stuff."

Everything pointed Boston's way. The Mets even canceled a Fenway workout to rest.

McNamara sent to the mound the mercurial Dennis "Oil Can" Boyd, best known not for winning 16 games in 1986, but for throwing a tantrum after being bypassed for the midseason All-Star game. His opponent was a former Red Sox pitcher, Ojeda, a left-hander who would not just be dealing with the hot-hitting Sox, but with the Green Monster.

That, Boyd offered, might be in Ojeda's head when he took the field.

But Ojeda had won 18 games and hardly was a slouch. At times, he was as good as any of New York's hurlers. This would be one of those times, setting off the first of three memorable Mets comebacks.

While Ojeda went seven innings, yielding just one run, it was Boyd who was jumpy, unnerved. The Oil Can got crushed, allowing four runs in the first inning. The Mets' bats awakened and so did their championship chances with a 7-1 win. Ojeda was the first left-hander to beat the Sox in a postseason game at Fenway in 68 years.

The victors' reaction to their triumph was filled with relief. Those creeping doubts whether they could hit Boston's hurlers suddenly were erased in a one-inning outburst. The questions about winning in Fenway Park disappeared.

They all immediately credited Dykstra, who hit the third pitch of the night inside the right field foul pole for a homer. That ignited the four-run inning that was decisive.

It also got the Mets believing.

"We wanted to show Oil Can what we can do," Knight said. "And when we got that quick run with one swing of Lenny's bat, it had a snowball effect."

A snowball that turned into an avalanche.

Buoyed in Boston, the Mets won Game 4 by a 6-2 score as Darling, a New England native who once rooted for the Sox, pitched seven shutout innings. He didn't allow a run after escaping a bases-loaded jam in the opening inning. Carter's two homers were more than enough support, and—shades of Henderson against the Angels—Evans saw Dykstra's drive bounce off his glove and over the fence in right.

Boston's bats had now gone silent, particularly third baseman Wade Boggs, a perennial .300 hitter now in the Hall of Fame, and the struggling Buckner, who had stranded 17 runners.

"We've had our backs to the wall all year," Evans noted. "Our backs really aren't to the wall, but we had a two-game lead and they tied it. For them to come in here and get three in a row, sweep us in Fenway, is going to be tough."

It was only the third time the visiting team won the first four games of a World Series, and the Mets' comeback to square matters at two games apiece might not have offered them much advantage with the final two of the best-of-seven scheduled for Shea. At least one of those games was now necessary.

"I don't really understand this," Darling said. "They win two in our park, where we feel really comfortable, and then we win two in their park. It just shows one thing: Baseball makes no sense."

Perhaps. Particularly when one of the home stadiums is as idiosyncratic as Fenway.

"Someone's going to win at home," Hernandez said. "Hopefully us."

Uh, no. At least not right away, because the Red Sox showed their resilience by taking Game 5, the last one in Boston, 4-2.

Hurst beat the Mets for the second time in a week. Even worse for New York, its ace, Gooden, lost—and barring a couple of rainouts, would not be available to start again in the Series. Meanwhile, the Sox had their top pitcher, Clemens, all set for the sixth game in New York, where, remember, Boston was 2-0.

"I guess we got the home-court advantage off our backs," Henderson said.

"We've played five games and we've got two more to play," Knight promised. "Basically, we're all even in my mind. It's all down to one game. We've got to win Game 6, then one more."

Oddly, the team that scored first had won every game, a factoid worth remembering heading into that sixth contest.

Much of the buildup to the game at Shea centered on whether the Red Sox really could win a championship after a drought that lasted since before Babe Ruth became an icon. Since before the Roaring Twenties.

"We're right where we want to be—a game up with Roger on the mound," Henderson said.

And on five days rest. Clemens was 8-0 with a 2.12 earned-run average in such situations in 1986.

But Clemens didn't sound like someone ready to dominate and carry his team to the long-anticipated title.

"I don't like the mound there and I don't like a lot of things with that ballpark," he said. "It's a brutal mound. It's built so high that you don't use your legs. Now I know why Dwight Gooden has that high leg kick and turn. He has to keep balanced."

The Sox needed to keep their balance, not get beyond the task at hand. In the past 40 years, they had been in three Game 7s of World Series and lost all of them. So ending it in the sixth game was paramount.

And the Sox got going exactly as they needed to. They scored once in the first on Evans's double—moments after a parachutist landed in the infield, to raucous cheers from the sellout crowd.

They scored again in the second on three singles, with Barrett knocking in the run for a 2-0 edge. With Clemens mowing down the Mets, Beantown was beginning to believe.

New Yorkers were beginning to wonder about their squad; maybe only the Yankees could continue the Curse of the Bambino.

What happened to "Ya Gotta Believe?"

Hope resurfaced in the fifth when the Mets tied it without benefit of a big hit. Strawberry ignited the two-run inning with a walk and a stolen base. An error helped the cause, and suddenly it was 2-2.

Just as suddenly, Clemens developed a blister and left after seven, with Boston on top 3-2 thanks to some shoddy fielding by the Mets.

On came Schiraldi to preserve the lead. Would it be the Schiraldi who blew one contest against California, or the one who later shut down the Angels in another? Or a little of both?

Lee Mazzilli led off the eighth with a single and Dykstra's weak bunt came back to Schiraldi—the bad Schiraldi. He wheeled and threw wildly to second, with both runners being safe.

Backman sacrificed both runners and Hernandez was walked intentionally.

"We have the bases loaded, one out, and Gary and Straw coming up," Knight said. "We had to be feeling good about this."

Back in Boston, and throughout New England, they had to be feeling miserable about this. Historically, the Sox never escaped such a bind.

They didn't entirely escape this one, but after Carter—on a 3-0 pitch, no less—flied out to left to drive home Mazzilli, Schiraldi the good got Strawberry to fly out.

Neither side scored in the ninth, and it was on to extra innings. Excruciating extra innings.

The 10th would be remembered forever, and not just in these two cities. It would be chronicled by sports writers and announcers, by poets and singers. It would become a part of World Series lore.

With both of New York's top relievers, McDowell and Orosco, already out of the game, Johnson turned to Rick Aguilera. And Aguilera turned arsonist.

Henderson, who went from loser to savior against the Angels, homered to break the tie. Boggs doubled, Barrett singled, and Shea Stadium became a makeshift mausoleum.

"Ya Gotta Believe?" Nope, "Ya Gotta Wonder."

Schiraldi was still on the mound, so the Sox had an edge. He was their closer and, for all of his inconsistencies, Schiraldi was the guy who was supposed to have the ball in his hands needing three outs.

He got the first two, retiring Backman and Hernandez. In fact, Hernandez didn't even remain in the dugout after flying to center. He trudged into the clubhouse, sat in Johnson's office and prepared to watch the Mets' demise on TV, with Carter about to make the final out.

Aguilera sat on the bench, his eyes moist, his soul aching. He had failed and, ultimately, he felt he'd caused the Mets to fail.

"My heart was breaking," he said. "It was just a terrible, terrible feeling."

Some fans got up to leave as they saw the police brigades line the edge of the stands in foul territory.

Inside the visiting locker room, the bubbly was iced, the attendants ready to pop the corks. And was New England ever ready to celebrate!

Carter singled, though. There were mild cheers.

Up stepped rookie Kevin Mitchell, who was hitting for Aguilera. Difficult spot for a rook.

"I'm not experienced with things like that," he acknowledged. "But I feel if I concentrate a lot, I can come through."

Which he did, with another single.

Schiraldi now faced the veteran Knight, the guy who'd never been so emotionally involved as in the epic Game 6 against Houston.

How cool was Knight in the midst of this crucible?

"I've never been so mentally exhausted," he said. "My legs are trembling. You're up there numb. I let my eyes guide me."

Knight guided the ball into center field, Carter scored, Mitchell went to third and the "faithful" who were getting ready to vacate Shea suddenly rediscovered that faith.

Still, there were two outs. The Sox led 5-4. But McNamara knew he had to yank Schiraldi.

His choice was Bob Stanley, who would face Wilson. At third base, the coach, former Mets shortstop Bud Harrelson, offered Mitchell some advice: "Stay alert, he might throw a wild pitch."

Stanley got the count to 2-2. The Sox were one strike away from that elusive championship. If you rooted for them, you were on your feet in anxious, oh so anxious, anticipation—or on your knees in prayer.

Every Sox player was on the dugout steps. So were most of the Mets. Only Hernandez, who wouldn't budge from his manager's chair because "the seat had a lot of hits in it," superstitiously stayed put.

Stanley had thrown just one wild pitch in more than 82 innings during the season. But his fastball sailed too far inside, deflected off Gedman's glove and past him as Mitchell sped home.

5-5.

"I was excited," Stanley said. "I've always dreamed that I wanted to be on the mound to clinch it. I was on the mound, but I couldn't clinch it.

"It was supposed to run back in toward the plate, and it just went the other way."

By now, it seemed inevitable that the Miracle Mets had resurfaced. So had the Bambino's Curse.

Still, if Stanley could retire Wilson, the game would go to the 11th. The Mets weren't getting great work from Aguilera, so maybe Boston could get some more runs.

Wilson, the fastest man on the team, simply wanted to make contact. Knight, one of the slowest players on the Mets, if not in the entire league, was on second in great part because his manager had nobody left to replace him on the base paths and, if the game went to more innings, at third base.

Wilson sent a lazy grounder toward Buckner at first base. After hours standing on the infield dirt with his sore ankles and bad knees, Buckner barely could bend down to make the play.

But, as McNamara noted, "Billy Bucks has good hands."

Not on this night. Not on this play. Not during this comeback.

The ball skidded between his legs and under his glove. As he incredulously turned around and saw where it headed, Buckner knew even Knight would score.

The rest of the Mets stormed from the dugout; Hernandez nearly broke himself in half running out of the clubhouse to join the festivities. They awaited Knight as he leaped on home plate with the winning run.

With the latest miracle.

With the path to Game 7.

"You sit back and say to yourself, 'How in the hell did this happen?'" Knight said. "I was on second base and Mookie hit the ball. Because it's a 3-2 pitch, I am moving anyway and had a good jump. But you don't have time to grasp everything, you just want to make it to the next base.

"I knew if Buckner catches the ball, even if Mookie beats him to the base, I'm not going to score. So I was watching the play as I got to third base. And then I was headed home and I was mobbed."

Mobbed by a delirious bunch.

"This one ranks right up there with Bobby Thomson," said Hernandez of the "Shot Heard Round the World" that lifted the Giants to the 1951 pennant over the Dodgers. "This was sweet. Incredible. I don't care how we did it."

Maybe it was King Kong Karma playing another nasty trick on the Red Sox.

"I don't know anything about history," McNamara insisted. "I don't know anything about choking or any of that crap."

The folks back in Boston and environs knew. They'd been through this so many times before.

To his credit, Buckner emerged after a long spell in the trainers' room. His eyes were moist, but his voice was strong.

"I knew it was going to be close at first because that guy runs so well," he said. "The ball went skip, skip, skip. It didn't come up. It just missed my glove.

"I have to live with it."

His whole team did. All of Red Sox Nation did.

"We got a little bit of our own medicine tonight," Evans said. "We know what that's all about."

© *Sports Illustrated.*

A New York Mets fan says it all at the conclusion of the 1986 World Series.
Photo by Chuck Solomon.

"I thought we were out of the inning," Stanley added. "I made a mistake. Buckner made a mistake.

"I've walked off mounds a lot losing a game. But to be one out, one pitch away, is a desperate feeling. I probably won't sleep tonight."

The Red Sox probably didn't sleep much for a couple of nights. In a cruel twist, as if to deepen Boston's anguish, Mother Nature stepped in and poured down buckets of rain. Game 7 was postponed for 24 hours—another full day for New England to mull just how close it had come to Nirvana. And how close it now stood to another trip to baseball Hell.

McNamara certainly knew he was being blistered back in Boston, but he wasn't about to doubt himself or his players or the staff's strategy at this point. After all, if the Sox won Game 7, they would be champions—although they tested themselves and their fans to the point of exhaustion, panic, even fright.

"This is an outstanding second-guess situation," McNamara

said after the seventh game was postponed. "I don't second-guess myself at all about anything that happened in that baseball game."

Mac also set himself up for more criticism by opting to start Hurst over Boyd in the seventh game. With the rainout, Hurst would have three days of rest and he'd already beaten the Mets twice in the series.

Hardly someone to hold back his thoughts, Boyd was refreshingly candid about the switch.

"It hurts so bad, what can I do?" Boyd said. "Bruce is on a roll and Mac thinks the Mets have a better left-handed lineup.

"It's just that it was my turn, and after all I've been through—I'm sorry, my sensitives are going to show through every time. This one hurts more because I was so psyched to pitch the one game that means everything. Mac said I'd be the first one out of the bullpen, but I don't know if the intensity will be there."

And this from the unfortunate Buckner:

"It's been a lousy World Series for me and it just got worse. I feel lousy about what happened, but you have to live with it. I can't remember the last time I missed a ball like that. But I'll remember that one."

Or this from Henderson:

"Losses like that haunt you. They haunt you for a while."

Uh-oh. Not exactly what anyone rooting for the Sox to break nearly seven decades of championship disappointment wanted to hear.

The Mets were eager to play Game 7 right away, but the elements didn't cooperate. Their sensational comeback win had them stoked; the rain didn't put out that enthusiasm.

"I think it would have been to our advantage to play tonight," Hernandez said. "The kind of win we had last night kind of carries over."

Added Carter: "Coming after last night's loss and going into tonight's game, it had to be depressing for them. This may let them pick up the pieces."

Darling would pick up the ball for the Mets when Game 7 began. With the one-day delay, just about anyone would be available for relief work.

Quickly, it appeared the whole staff might be needed. Darling, so sterling in his earlier performances, yielded three runs in the second inning and would not get through the fourth.

Gedman, seemingly unaffected by the pivotal wild pitch that bounced off his glove, hit a two-run homer in the second, and Boggs's RBI single made it 3-0.

Joy in the Back Bay and in Fenway, in Narragansett and Naugatuck, in Burlington and Bangor. Joy tempered with worry, of course; these were the Red Sox, after all.

The Mets would need to rally once again. Did they have another comeback in them? Or had they depleted their supply of grit and guts?

"Considering what we'd been through, I guarantee none of us thought anything was over," Knight said.

Once again, Knight was right.

The crowd's concern was evident heading into the later innings, well aware that the Sox had a pretty full bullpen to rescue Hurst. But when Hurst tired in the sixth, the Mets tied it.

Mazzilli, pinch-hitting for Sid Fernandez, who was brilliant in relief of Darling, singled. So did Wilson, and Teufel walked. That brought the left-handed Hernandez to the plate to face the lefty Hurst.

"I knew I was swinging the bat very well and I just felt if I got up with guys on base, I'd be a big part of what we did."

What Hernandez did was single in two runs.

With Shea rocking to chants of "Let's Go Mets," Carter looped the ball to right field that Evans, a superb fielder, dived for. Evans couldn't make a clean catch, but he did quickly throw to second base for a force-out.

Still, Teufel trotted home to tie it.

Manager Johnson complimented Fernandez for his key role.

"No doubt about it, he was the hero," Johnson said. "He shut them down and got the crowd back on our side. If he can shut them down, we can come back."

They were all the way back into a tie. They needed more.

One inning later, the Mets got it.

McNamara ignored Boyd and chose to bring in Schiraldi, usually his closer, in the seventh—awfully early. The likelihood of Schiraldi going three innings was slim, even if it was the good Schiraldi.

This was far from that Schiraldi.

His fourth pitch was sent into the left-center-field bleachers by Knight. Delirium in the stands.

And the Mets weren't through.

Dykstra hit a pinch-single, took second on a wild pitch (on a pitchout, no less), and scored on Rafael Santana's single. Hernandez made it 6-3 with a sacrifice fly.

Schiraldi failed to get out of the seventh, retiring one batter, allowing three hits and three runs.

"I had the chance Saturday and didn't do anything," Schiraldi said of Game 6. "I had the chance tonight and didn't do anything, so there's no consolation for me."

And nothing but consternation in Boston.

The Sox, though, weren't through. Given the way this postseason had played out, why should anyone believe another rally wouldn't be in the works?

In the top of the eighth, the gallant Evans doubled in two runs with none out, and the Red Sox were in position to force another tie. Orosco came on for the ineffective McDowell and got Gedman on a lineout, fanned Henderson, and forced Baylor to ground to shortstop.

It was Boston's last gasp.

Strawberry led off the bottom of the eighth with a homer, and Orosco, batting for only the fourth time all season, singled in Knight to make it 8-5.

So Orosco stood on the mound, as he had in Houston, with a chance to finish off the miracle the Mets had built in Game 6. Heck, in two Game 6s.

"I wasn't thinking about baseball, I was looking for a bathroom," Orosco offered. "I was really nervous."

Maybe Orosco needed not to be calm, because he pitched a perfect ninth. Moments after a smoke bomb exploded in left field, he fanned Barrett for the World Series title. The lefty sank to his knees and the players mobbed each other—not nearly weary enough to pass on this hard-earned celebration.

There was a little more passion in this revelry than in most. When you've been to the brink of the most demoralizing kind of defeat and escape, the level of joy (and relief) is unmatched.

"I know what it's like to be in the cellar," said Wilson. "I know what it's like to be home at this time of year watching the World Series with a pizza and a beer. I know I might appreciate this more."

Added Backman: "I remember in the sixth game having an

empty feeling in the 10th inning and knowing I would feel that way all winter. I just would not have been satisfied without winning the World Series.

"But now I can go home with a smile on my face knowing I'll have a ring on my finger."

The Red Sox would trudge home with yet another excruciating defeat. It seemed to be their lot.

"There's no telling how long it will take me to get over this," Gedman said. "It's the type of memory I'll never forget. We came a long way for things to turn out this way."

10

TOPPING TILDEN

*Bill Tilden Loses Shocker to
Henri Cochet, 1927*

Henri Cochet, "dead man" running.

While his crestfallen countrymen slumped on the sidelines in despair, one of France's "Four Musketeers" of tennis was about to be vanquished.

It was the semifinals of the 1927 Wimbledon singles championship and American star "Big Bill" Tilden was putting on one of the greatest displays of tennis ever seen on either side of the Atlantic.

The end was near for Cochet. He had dropped the first two sets of their match. Now the Frenchman was one point away from losing to the American star for the second time in less than a month.

There was so much national pride at stake, so little room for error.

"Tilden is a great master," Cochet said. "He had me cross-eyed."

"Big Bill," after all, was the No. 1 player in the world from 1920 to 1928—the only one to challenge France's dominance in international tennis in the late '20s.

In 1920, Tilden had been the first American to win the singles championship at Wimbledon. He repeated in 1921, and now was looking for his third Wimbledon title in eight years.

Nothing less was expected. Tilden was a golden name in the golden age of American sports in the Roaring Twenties, alongside baseball's Babe Ruth, boxing's Jack Dempsey, and golf's Bobby Jones.

On even terms Tilden was tough enough to beat. Holding a 2-0 lead after two sets and a 5-1 advantage in the third, Tilden had the match all but won. No one in his right mind would have given Cochet a chance at that point.

The situation seemed hopeless for the little Frenchman.

But Cochet wasn't one to give up easily. Could he win the match? He had beaten Tilden before. The 5-foot-6 Cochet squared his shoulders and waited for Tilden's big serve . . .

Like Tilden in America, Cochet was one of the leaders in French tennis—part of the famed "Four Musketeers" along with Jacques Brugnon, Rene LaCoste, and Jacques Borotra.

At the time of the 1927 Wimbledon tournament in London, the "Musketeers" were already on their way to international prominence. Cochet hoped to match his famed countrymen by adding another Wimbledon title to their growing cache that started in 1924.

Cochet already had won the singles title at the French championships in 1926, although the tournament was only open to French nationals.

To say Cochet was born on the tennis court would not be very far from the truth. He practically grew up on one.

His father was the groundskeeper at the Lyon Tennis Club, and Henri started playing tennis at the age of seven. He quickly fell in love with the game. He first gained national recognition when he won a regional tournament in 1921. Five years later, he was the singles winner at the French championship.

By that time, Tilden was already at the peak of his amateur career, ranked No. 1 in the world. He had won two Wimbledon titles and 31 national crowns in singles, doubles, and mixed doubles.

Tilden gained his greatest amateur glory as the ace of the

American Davis Cup team. In 1920, he helped bring the trophy back to America from Australasia, and never lost a singles match in Davis Cup play from 1920 to 1925.

"From 1920 through 1925 he was so invincible that no player in the world stood a chance against him in any competition," noted the Associated Press.

For many years, Tilden was the mainstay of American dominance in Davis Cup play until the "Four Musketeers" of France finally loosened the United States' long hold on the trophy in 1927.

Tilden's tennis career was not without controversy.

In 1928, the United States hoped to regain the Davis Cup after losing it to the French in 1927. Then, suddenly, a scandal broke.

While in France, Tilden was ruled ineligible to play by the United States Lawn Tennis Association (USLTA) because of a furor over his writing activities. Tilden was a journalist and actor, as well as a tennis player.

The USLTA stripped Tilden of his Davis Cup captaincy and sent him to the sidelines because he was being paid to write articles for American newspapers. It was a mystery as to why the USLTA decided to come down on Tilden at that particular time for this activity—he had been writing professionally for quite a while.

The United States didn't need Tilden to beat Italy in Davis Cup play. France was another story.

With its "Four Musketeers," the French eagerly awaited the Americans in the challenge round.

When the Frenchmen found out Tilden was ineligible, they were up in arms. It was the first time the French staged the Davis Cup challenge round and the idea of doing it without Tilden was simply out of the question. They had even built a new stadium at Auteuil, knowing that Tilden's singular drawing power would help fill it.

"It was like putting on Hamlet without the Melancholy Dane," the Associated Press wrote.

The public outcry was so strong that the U.S. ambassador interceded. Tilden was reinstated at the last minute by the USLTA for the Davis Cup match, restoring unity between the two countries.

When Tilden defeated Lacoste, the French might have had second thoughts about wanting the American star to play. However, France went on to capture the championship for the second straight year in a successful run that continued through 1932.

When the Americans returned home, Tilden was again charged with violating the amateur rule involving professional writing. He was banned from the national championships in 1928—one of only two times from 1918 through 1929 that he did not appear in the national championship final.

In his private life, Tilden also made headlines. In 1947 he served jail time for contributing to the delinquency of a minor. He served again two years later for violating his probation.

Tilden, son of a prominent businessman, was born in Germantown, Pennsylvania, a suburb of Philadelphia. He was introduced to tennis by his older brother, Herbert, who had developed a local reputation as a player. It wasn't long before Bill's reputation and achievements exceeded that of his brother.

Bill Tilden entered his first tournament at age 17 and quickly made a name for himself. He won the national mixed doubles championship in 1913-1914 with Mary K. Browne. In 1915, his name appeared in the national rankings for the first time. In 1918 he was ranked No. 2 behind William M. "Little Bill" Johnston, his main rival in the early 1920s. By 1920, Tilden was ranked No. 1 in the country, a position he would hold through 1929.

Tilden managed to mix in schoolwork and army service with his tennis activities. He graduated from Germantown Academy in 1917 and enlisted in the army during World War I. He never got overseas, serving most of his time in Pittsburgh. Tilden later entered the University of Pennsylvania and graduated in 1922.

That same year, a mishap on the court nearly cost Tilden his tennis career and almost cost him his right arm.

He was playing in an exhibition match in Bridgeton, New Jersey, when he cut the middle finger of his right hand and developed blood poisoning. The infection became so bad that surgeons feared they might have to amputate Tilden's right arm. At the last minute, they decided to amputate only the infected finger at the first joint, hoping for the best.

It worked. The procedure saved the arm and allowed Tilden to recover and go on to even greater glories on the court.

Wherever Tilden played, there were crowds—big crowds. In

his time, he was the biggest draw in tennis. A Tilden appearance usually ensured a capacity crowd.

His popularity helped change the way the sport was perceived by the American public. Largely because of Tilden's speed and blistering shots, tennis was no longer a "soft" sport for the country club set and the idle rich. It became as seriously competitive as any of the major sports in the States.

While Tilden was intensely competitive, he also had fun with his game. "Tilden was fond of 'clowning' on the courts, setting the stage for dramatic comebacks when seemingly on the verge of defeat," the *Los Angeles Times* noted. On occasion, it backfired, when too much "clowning" cost him a match he should have otherwise easily won.

Tilden and his American colleagues had crossed the Atlantic in 1927 hoping to avenge their loss to the French in the U.S. championship the year before. They were scheduled to make several stops in France before heading into London for Wimbledon.

"It's about time Tilden showed us something on the courts again instead of in the newspapers with his pen or typewriter," a sarcastic Jacques Brugnon said.

On his way to Wimbledon, Tilden showed the French plenty. In the French Hardcourt Championships at St. Cloud, he swept past Cochet 9-7, 6-3, 6-2.

"Big Bill Tilden proved conclusively today that he has 'come back,'" reported the AP. "The veteran American stormed about the court stroking with all his old power, leaving no spots uncovered and fighting for every point to the bitter end."

Tilden lost to Lacoste in the French Hardcourt finals, but it didn't seem to affect his confidence at Wimbledon. Showing his old form, Tilden "awed the customers with a dazzling assortment of strokes" in doubles play, according to the *Chicago Daily Tribune*. It was the singles competition that entranced everyone, though, and Tilden showed good form there, too. He vaulted into the semifinals against Cochet, who was struggling because of rheumatism in his right arm. The condition had kept him away from the courts since the previous fall.

Cochet did not look his best in a match against Holland's Henrik Timmer, coming within a point of elimination. "Cochet finally won the greatest uphill battle of his career after trailing up to within five minutes of the end," the *Chicago Tribune* reported. It was Cochet's center-court battle against Tilden, however, that truly caught everyone's attention. A buzz ran through the packed stadium as the fierce international rivals looked across the net at each other . . .

Tilden took charge immediately, winning the first two sets, 6-2, 6-4.

"Tilden played amazingly the first two sets, hitting his powerful drives to all parts of the court," reported Dave Darrah in the *Chicago Tribune*. When Tilden wasn't hitting his "cannonball" serves, he was charging to the net for "brilliant volleys."

He forced Cochet to "stick around the baseline until the Frenchman was bewildered, worried and disheartened," Darrah said.

Tilden continued his surge in the third set. He won the first game with powerful returns of Cochet's serves, then went up 2-0 with a love game. The Frenchman seemed dazed.

Tilden was in command, and even after losing the third game came back strong in the fourth for a 3-1 lead. The *Tribune* reported Tilden hit three aces so hard "that one rebound nearly overturned a chair at the end of the court."

The fifth and sixth games were the same. Up 5-1, all Tilden needed was merely one point—a single point—to advance to the Wimbledon finals.

Not so fast. Cochet hadn't given up.

Despite the seemingly impossible task at hand, and the fact he had lost to Tilden so recently at St. Cloud, Cochet still was confident.

"I felt that he was only human and could not keep up that pace and that my chance might come," Cochet said.

Cochet was right. Tilden couldn't keep it up, not even when he required just that one more point. Cochet was the Little Frenchman Who Could.

Suddenly, Tilden started to falter. Cochet broke through to win the 7th game of the third set. He continued his relentless attack through the 12th, winning 6 straight games to take the set, 7-5.

Cochet wasn't quite finished. Now he had his confidence back. From the court, he waved and smiled to a young woman in the stands, his wife.

"My Henri will win," she told the nearby French players, once morose but now thrilled by the sudden turn of events.

And it was the Frenchman who was on the attack, the American in retreat. Tilden's drives were suddenly inaccurate. His pace slackened. He lost speed on his shots, and more importantly, he had lost his fire.

He was described in the *Los Angeles Times* as "pale and haggard" staggering through the last half-hour of the match with "sagging knees."

Tilden was unable to keep up with Cochet's net game. The Frenchman rushed the net time and again, placing tricky shots just out of Tilden's agonized reach.

When Cochet took the fourth set to even the match, "pandemonium reigned in the area," the *Chicago Tribune* said.

In the fifth set, Tilden showed flashes of his greatness with a stunning backhand passing shot that momentarily tied it 2-2. He went ahead 3-2 before Cochet took charge of the match again.

For good.

"Cochet played better and better," a newspaper said, "and after reaching 4 to 3, swept on to the end. Tilden had played himself out."

The tally of Cochet's remarkable victory: 2-6, 4-6, 7-5, 6-4, 6-3.

Cochet tossed his racket in the air, vaulted the net, and embraced Tilden.

One newspaperman reported that Cochet was on the verge of kissing the American great. Both were probably too tired to appreciate the wild ovation they received from the crowd as they walked off the court.

"I used to win that sort of match once," a wistful Tilden later told a reporter.

Did Tilden lose focus at the end because he had such a big lead, or was he just tired? Perhaps it was a little of both, and the *Los Angeles Times* offered yet another possibility.

"Tilden's defeat just illustrates the extent to which the former champion's desire to give the crowds a treat affects his game," Bill Henry said. "He gets Cochet two sets down and 5-1 in the third set and then decides to show everybody a good time by fooling around, with the result that the game youngster took advantage of Tilden's theatricals to stage one of the great exhibitions of super-tennis for which he is justly famed."

Tilden's career was far from finished despite the collapse at

Wimbledon. In 1930, at the age of 37, he brought the Wimbledon singles title back to America. He turned pro at 38 and added to a legacy that in 1950 earned him the honor as the AP's "greatest tennis player of the past 50 years."

Maybe not invincible, as Henri Cochet proved at Wimbledon in 1927, but still the greatest.

11

ONE FOR THE THUMB

2005 Pittsburgh Steelers

Joey Porter likes to talk. And talk and talk.

If you are a fan of the Pittsburgh Steelers, Porter is a funny chatterbox. If you are from Cleveland or Cincinnati or anywhere they hate the Steelers, Porter is a loudmouth.

Whether you wanted to hear everything Porter uttered or wanted to see someone kick in his dentures, there was no denying his accuracy after he took his turn holding up the Vince Lombardi Trophy in Detroit.

"This one will always be remembered," Porter said, a huge smile creasing his face. "It's never been done before what we did. We kept being told we couldn't do this, and that's what we needed."

Actually, it's what every football fan—every sports fan—needed in February 2006. The Steelers' stunning ride from the brink of failing to make the playoffs to winning their fifth Super Bowl crown should turn on everyone who follows any sport. If they could struggle just to get into the postseason, then win four straight times away from Pittsburgh against nothing but division winners, well, there has to be hope for any team chasing a championship.

"We wiped the slate clean," coach Bill Cowher said. "Each week was a unique set of circumstances. We gained some confidence and we started to have a pretty good team."

The Steelers never weren't a good team. The previous season, they went 15-1, not only the best record in the league in 2004, but the best in their history, which dated back to 1933 and included four titles in six seasons from 1974 to 1979.

In 2004, with a rookie quarterback, Ben Roethlisberger, who exceeded every expectation so early in his career, the Steelers won their final 14 regular-season games. They sent nine players to the Pro Bowl, the most since their heyday with Terry Bradshaw, Franco Harris, Mean Joe Greene, and Jack Lambert. They won close games and they won routs.

But come the postseason, they sputtered badly. The Steelers should have lost to the New York Jets in the second round of the playoffs. If not for some ultraconservative coaching and shoddy placekicking, the Jets would have walked out of Heinz Field with a victory.

Pittsburgh survived that day, in overtime, only to be routed by the resident dynasty of the early 2000s, the New England Patriots. On their way to a third Super Bowl crown in four years, the Patriots won 41-27.

It was a difficult loss for the Steelers, particularly Cowher, who was making his fifth trip to the AFC championship game but had only one win thus far. And all of those games had been at home.

"You feel empty when it happens," said Cowher, who didn't even tune in the Super Bowl. "You feel like you didn't do enough. Sometimes, it's hard to remember all the good things your team did because you didn't win that game.

"I never like losing, and the losing can gnaw at you and it is tough to deal with. The longer you're in this, the losses hurt more. The longer you're here, the higher the expectations that are placed upon you and, when you don't succeed, it eats at you."

So the Steelers entered the 2005 season with an extra sense of purpose. They sought to prove the magnificent '04 record was no fluke. With so many proven pros—Porter, running back Jerome Bettis, receiver Hines Ward, offensive linemen Alan Faneca and Jeff Hartings—and rising stars in Roethlisberger, safety Troy Polamalu, and receiver Antwaan Randle El, there was a strong belief this would be their year.

While preferring to avoid comparisons to the Steel Curtain teams of the 1970s, these Steelers believed they could build their own identity. No nickname needed, either.

"This was the greatest football team that was ever put together," team chairman Dan Rooney said of the 1970s Steelers. "No teams should be compared to them."

Ah, but when you wear those distinctive black and gold uniforms—oddly, white would be the color of choice this time—and have such an illustrious résumé, comparisons inevitably will be made.

"We're happy with the way we operate, and if it's successful it will continue," said director of football operations Kevin Colbert, a Pittsburgh native who revered the Steel Curtain teams as a youngster. "They've been doing it this way a lot of years with success. The philosophy was built and they set their standards by winning all those Super Bowls and you understand that when you come to Pittsburgh."

Understanding that another 15-1 record was unlikely, Cowher needed to convince his team that something like 12-4 would be just fine, as long as the players performed to their maximum and the Steelers won the AFC North. If they also got home-field advantage during the playoffs, fine—not that it had helped them much in his tenure.

And that tenure was entering its 14th season, the longest with one team among any NFL coaches still on the job. But Cowher carried an 8-9 postseason record into 2005. While such a mark should not have negated the strong work he'd done through the years, it did overshadow that work.

"I'm driven every year," Cowher said. "But there are no shortcuts. No easy way. You can't take anything for granted, regardless of who you have coming back or their performances. I told the players, just because you played well last year, don't think you're going to get it done by just showing up."

Bettis showed up for his final season, although he playfully never made it official throughout the regular schedule or the playoffs. Expected to be a prime ball carrier, along with similarly built and powerful Duce Staley, Bettis wound up as more of a figurehead. His popularity never waned, though, as unheralded second-year pro Willie Parker took his job.

Parker burst onto the Pittsburgh scene with a sensational

debut, gaining 161 yards on 22 carries, adding one reception for 48 yards and scoring a touchdown in a 34-7 victory to open the season. The Steelers were off and running, thanks to the undrafted free agent who was a backup at North Carolina and was discovered by team owner Dan Rooney's son.

Their regular-season winning streak reached 16 with a 27-7 victory at Houston, but then the Patriots played spoiler again. New England won 23-20 on Adam Vinatieri's 43-yard field goal with one second remaining—a typical victory for the Pats and another painful home loss for the Steelers.

It also was Roethlisberger's first in-season defeat as a starter.

"All this loss means is we can't go undefeated," Roethlisberger said.

Surely, these Steelers had the resolve to handle such a setback, right? Well, they did win the next week in San Diego, but Roethlisberger hurt his knee late in the 24-22 victory.

Sidelined the next week against Jacksonville, Roethlisberger watched backup Tommy Maddox struggle and the Steelers lose 23-17 in overtime.

Pittsburgh would win its next four games, even without Roethlisberger, whose gimpy knee kept him out of wins over Green Bay and Cleveland.

Then things went sour. From 7-2, the Steelers spiraled to 7-5 in the very competitive AFC, losing to Baltimore (without Big Ben), Indianapolis, and Cincinnati (with Roethlisberger).

The 38-31 home loss to the Bengals was the most disconcerting. Not only did the Bengals tear up the vaunted Pittsburgh defense for all those points, but they forced four turnovers. And the victory stamped Cincinnati as the front-runner in the division, giving it a two-game lead over the Steelers.

With a visit from Chicago up next—the Bears had the league's most ferocious defense and, at 9-3, were the surprise contender of the NFC—the Steelers were in the unthinkable position of needing four straight wins to close the season, or else a playoff berth was unlikely.

The team that had dominated pro football throughout the previous regular season was stuck in the morass of mediocrity. One more slip and Cowher could skip watching on television *all* the postseason, not just the Super Bowl.

Cowher certainly wasn't thinking that way. He stood up at a

team meeting and compared the journey ahead to what Christopher Columbus went through in 1492.

"He was convinced we could still do it, and because of that, so were we," Porter said.

But Columbus? The Nina, Pinta, and Santa Maria?

"Guys kind of liked that," Cowher said, his legendary jaw unable to overpower a toothy grin. "There's a lot of people telling you that you can't do it, but that doesn't mean you don't go try. I told our guys that history is not going to determine our fate, but we could determine history."

Cowher was correct. His players did like the approach, even if some of them were looking at each other in wonderment when Cowher went exploring for the proper metaphor.

"He did a really good job of making sure we were focused, making sure we had good weeks of practice, making it tough on us," said Faneca, the All-Pro guard and one of the steadiest of Steelers.

Tough it would be. Roethlisberger hurt his thumb against Indianapolis and it was affecting his throwing. Parker, who never had been a featured back, was in danger of wearing down. The defense, particularly the secondary, had sprung some leaks.

"Where we are right now, we put ourselves in that situation, and it's up to us to get ourselves out of this situation," Porter said. "Winning is the only thing that can make things better, and that's what we're trying to do this week."

And they did. First against Chicago, with Bettis having, by far, his best game of what had been an ordinary season. He rushed through the snow for 101 yards—his team-record 50th 100-yarder in 11 seasons in Pittsburgh—and the defense clamped down for a 21-9 victory.

Next up was a visit to Minnesota, another team on a hot streak. The Vikings had won six in a row and suddenly were a challenger in the NFC. The Steelers had never won in the Metrodome. In veteran Brad Johnson, they would not be facing an untested quarterback, as they had against Chicago and rookie Kyle Orton.

"They're kind of a resurgent team," said Roethlisberger, who was characteristically efficient in beating the Bears. "Probably at the first of the year everybody was counting them out, but they've turned it on of late and won a bunch of games in a row and they're playing like a new team. Brad brings 14 years of experience and more of a throwing mentality, and he's doing a great job of leading that team."

Forget the throwing mentality. The Steelers were in their, pardon the comparison, "Curtain" mode. The defense dominated in an 18-3 win, intercepting Johnson twice, yielding only 54 yards on the ground and 185 in all, and even getting a safety in the fourth quarter.

"They beat our butts," Johnson noted.

Two games into their string of four with no margin for error, the Steelers had allowed a total of 12 points. Back to their trademark manner of winning with defense, a powerhouse rushing attack and clock management, they were halfway to the first goal: climbing out of the hole they'd excavated and into the playoffs.

They would have to get there via the wild card, though, because the Bengals hadn't faltered. They'd already clinched the AFC North with two weeks remaining.

"We ain't supposed to be a wild-card team," Porter opined. "But that's what we've got to be now."

If they kept playing as they had the previous two weeks, the Steelers looked like a good bet to grab the final AFC spot. Jacksonville already owned the other, with San Diego, Kansas City, and hard-charging Miami chasing the final slot.

So the Steelers kept right on at it, with the defense positing its first shutout in more than five years, a 41-0 romp past archrival Cleveland. Pittsburgh had eight sacks, three by Porter, and the Steelers silenced the Dawg Pound by taking an early 14-0 lead.

"We made a statement," said linebacker James Harrison, who blocked a punt, and also tackled a Browns fan who ran onto the field. "We won, that was the statement we wanted. Margin of victory, stuff like that, is nice. But winning and going to the playoffs is our goal. That's what we want."

Making the win even sweeter, Parker displayed the kind of spark he'd seemed to lose in previous games, rushing for 130 yards and a touchdown. He scored on an 80-yard run, foreshadowing the Super Bowl, and surpassed 1,000 yards rushing for the season.

"I never thought I would lead the Steelers in rushing or get 1,000 yards," Parker said. "It's an emotional moment for me."

There would be more such moments.

Having moved to 10-5, the Steelers knew a win over Detroit in the finale would push them into the playoffs. Just as significantly, they sensed things were coming together on both sides of the ball.

There was another theme to Game 16: it figured to be the final game in Pittsburgh for "The Bus."

Bettis, whom Cowher once called "the most respected player in the NFL," originally planned to retire after the 2004 season after 12 years in the NFL. Considering how the Steelers ran away from everyone during that season, he expected his career to end in his first Super Bowl appearance.

But then came the postseason flop—and a promise.

Roethlisberger vowed that if Bettis came back for one more try at the ring, the young quarterback would get him one.

"I was crying my eyes out last year when Ben came over to me," Bettis said. "I was happy that none of my teammates came over and pressed me, because that's when it gets to you.

"He was boohooing, and I was boohooing, and he turned to me and said, 'Come back next year, I will get you to the Super Bowl. Give me one more year.' That meant a lot."

With Terrible Towels waving in tribute, the Bus drove his way to three short touchdowns in a 35-21 win. The Steelers were in the playoffs. Not exactly as they planned to be, as division champions, but in nonetheless, as a wild card.

"It's disappointing for us," Bettis said of going 11-5. "We know we're a better team than that. But everybody is 0-0 now. We did everything we had to do to get in. Now we're in, and let's see what happens."

What usually happens for sixth seeds in the NFL is a quick exit. But the Steelers might have been the most unique No. 6 seed ever.

At 11-5, they matched the record of five other playoff teams and were better than two qualifiers. They also were on a hot streak, with their four successive must-wins to close out the schedule tying Denver for the best finish among AFC playoff clubs.

Their first opponent would be a very familiar one, too: Cincinnati, which was making its first playoff appearance in 15 years. That and the facts that the Steelers were hot, the Bengals had lost two straight to close the season, and Pittsburgh won 27-13 at Paul Brown Stadium during the season made the visitors the betting choice by three points.

The Steelers, aware that no sixth seed ever won the championship, weren't buying it.

"We know we're going to be the underdogs and we probably like that role a little more," Roethlisberger said. "We've had to come back from a lot, and that's going to help us."

"It's obviously a big challenge," added Hartings. "Nobody's ever done it. We're going to try to make history and be the first ones."

The Bengals were in the midst of a sensational turnaround under coach Marvin Lewis. They'd gone from NFL doormat, perhaps the worst franchise in the league for more than a decade, to contender. In Lewis's three seasons at the helm, they'd gone 8-8, 8-8, and 11-5.

All the NFL marveled at the way Lewis eliminated the negative atmosphere in Cincinnati, bringing in a winning attitude.

But nobody seemed surprised to see the Steelers as the oddsmakers' choice.

"We shouldn't be favored. We should be in a position where we have to come out and fight our way and prove ourselves to everyone," said longtime Bengals tackle Willie Anderson. "I'm glad we're not favored. Pittsburgh is an experienced team, coming off a 15-1 season (last year), they've been in playoffs year-in and year-out."

And the Steelers had momentum

"Everybody's saying they're the scariest team in the playoffs and they definitely are," Pro Bowl QB Carson Palmer said. "It's a huge game and more so because it's a big rivalry now."

For all the rhetoric, though, the simple fact was that the Steelers had more to lose than the Bengals. Even if Cincinnati failed to advance, the season had been a success, something special to build on after so many years of disappointment and underachievement.

The Steelers, however, would have seen a first-round elimination as a complete and utter failure considering how they'd dealt with adversity down the stretch just to make the Super Bowl chase. It would have been a huge leap backward after the 15-1 record of '04 and the promise that '05 held back in September.

As if the Steelers weren't despised enough in Cincy (and all of Ohio), the first play from scrimmage for the Bengals would forever (if unfairly) reinforce the hatred. Palmer dropped back to throw a long pass, which connected with Chris Henry for 66 yards. While the fans cheered wildly at such an early success, Palmer was writhing on the ground, grabbing his left knee.

Steelers defensive lineman Kimo von Oelhoffen, who was falling during his pass rush, rolled into Palmer's knee with his shoulder. Replays indicated von Oelhoffen had nowhere else to go on the play and there was no malice or intent to injure.

"I knew right away that it was bad," said Palmer, who tore several ligaments. "I felt my whole knee pop. I didn't feel a lot of pain. It was just a sickening feeling because I knew what it was and that my season was over."

Von Oelhoffen, a former Bengal, was sickened by the incident, too. After making contact and seeing Palmer was hurt, he signaled to the Bengals' sideline and to the officials to get the quarterback some medical help.

"I'm not going to lie, it affected me a little bit," von Oelhoffen said. "That kid deserved a shot to play in this game. It's always horrible when somebody gets hurt. We're all football players—we're together, we compete against each other, but we're together."

But Palmer was done. And although backup Jon Kitna came on to guide Cincinnati to 10-0 and 17-7 leads, the Steelers never sensed they wouldn't rally. After all, they'd already made one stunning comeback just to get this far.

Ward caught a 5-yard touchdown pass late in the second quarter, and the defense took charge from there. Pressuring Kitna with four sacks, not allowing the Bengals' running game to get started, the Steelers relentlessly grabbed control.

Bettis scored on a 5-yard run and third-stringer Cedric Wilson caught a 43-yard TD throw on a fleaflicker in the third quarter. Pittsburgh picked off two passes to secure a 31-17 win.

It was Pittsburgh's first road playoff win since 1989; the Steelers were 0-3 under Cowher in such games.

Getting another road victory would be much more difficult. Next up were the Colts, who'd begun the season 13-0, beaten the Steelers 26-7 during that streak, were coming off a bye, and were the odds-on choice to represent the AFC in the Super Bowl.

The Colts also had become the choice of many fans who'd seen how impressively coach Tony Dungy dealt with the suicide of his son three weeks earlier.

"No one has handled it more inspirationally than Tony and his wife, Lauren," Cowher said. "That's the unfortunate part of our profession, that we live in a fishbowl and we have to experience that with the rest of America. Sometimes those are things you'd just like to share with those you are very close to, but Tony has found out that he's very close to a lot of us."

Dungy's pain, played out so publicly, figured to be a source of inspiration for the Colts. Not that they needed any further edge.

"They're as good as it gets in the NFL," Roethlisberger said. "It's going to take our A-plus game to go out and beat their B-minus game."

For 45 minutes, that's exactly what everyone got.

Pittsburgh moved ahead 14-0 in the first quarter with a pair of lengthy drives capped by TD passes from Roethlisberger to Randle El and to Heath Miller. It was the Steelers who were using a multi-faceted air game to establish control, throwing on 12 of their first 19 plays.

The Colts, meanwhile, seemed nervous and a bit rusty—they hadn't played a truly meaningful game since clinching the AFC South and home-field advantage throughout the playoffs in Game 13.

Often under siege by a relentless pass rush that came from all sorts of angles and areas, Peyton Manning resembled a novice, not an all-time great quarterback.

Manning nearly was sacked for a safety late in the third quarter, Indy punted, and Bettis finished a short drive with a 1-yard TD for a 21-3 lead heading into the fourth period.

Time to celebrate for the Steelers? Not quite.

Taking over at their 28-yard line, desperate to get back into the contest, the Colts finally began looking like the team that won those 13 straight regular-season outings. Manning and Dallas Clark hooked up on a 50-yard TD pass play early in the fourth quarter.

Pittsburgh then ate up a chunk of time with a drive that netted nothing, and then things got wacky.

Polamalu made a diving interception at the Pittsburgh 48 with 5:26 remaining. He got up to run and fumbled the ball, then recovered it.

It was a brilliant play by an All-Pro player, and all Dungy could do was make a last-ditch stand with a challenge of the call. After reporters in the press box of the RCA Dome watched the replay, they began banging out their stories of the Colts' demise and the

Steelers' continued surge. Fans moaned and sat down in their seats, despondent about another imminent playoff loss.

But referee Tony Morelli somehow saw something else. In a call that the NFL would admit the next day was totally wrong—and ultimately could have changed the outcome of the game and the entire playoffs—Morelli ruled that Polamalu never had control and the pass was incomplete.

"I know they wanted Indy to win this game; the whole world loves Peyton Manning," Porter said. "But come on, man, don't take the game away from us like that."

Given another chance, the Colts mounted a vintage drive of 80 yards in six plays. Manning's completions of 20 yards to Marvin Harrison and 24 to Reggie Wayne set up a 3-yard touchdown run by Edgerrin James. Manning connected with Wayne for a 2-point conversion, making the score 21-18 with 4:24 to go.

Sensing a miracle comeback of their own, the Colts instantly held the Steelers, forcing a punt. But Pittsburgh got its fifth sack of the game, downing Manning at his 2 with 1:20 left.

Game over? Steelers' streak continues?

Sure seemed that way as Cowher ordered his offense to ride the Bus into the end zone for the clincher.

"They had three timeouts," Cowher explained. "At that point, the last thing I thought we would do is fumble with Jerome Bettis."

So the Steelers fumbled with Jerome Bettis.

He was hit hard by linebacker Gary Brackett and the ball popped into the air to Colts DB Nick Harper. Harper took off toward the far end zone—and one of the most stunning reversals of fortune in sports history.

"We had all the slow guys out there," Roethlisberger said. "It was our goal-line offense; heck, I probably was the fastest guy on the field, and you know that's not good."

Harper wasn't up to speed because his knee had been cut with a knife the previous day in what was termed a domestic dispute with his wife. As Harper headed downfield, Roethlisberger retreated, trying to position himself to make a stab at a tackle.

The quarterback reached out with his arm and brought down Harper at the Indy 42.

"Once in a blue moon, Jerome fumbles," Roethlisberger said. "Once in a blue moon, I make a tackle. They just happened to be in the same game."

Given yet another chance, Manning completed two passes and the Colts called on Mike Vanderjagt. Only the most accurate kicker, percentage-wise, in NFL annals, Vanderjagt jerked his kick way right, then slammed his helmet to the turf.

"It's extreme disbelief," Vanderjagt said. "From the Polamalu interception reversal to Jerome's fumble, everything seemed to be lined up in our favor. I guess the Lord forgot about the football team."

In truth, Pittsburgh had earned this win. The game plan was nearly flawless, as was the execution. Except for some peculiar plays and calls, the game would have been a Steelers rout.

With six straight victories, four on the road, in the bank, the Steelers were in the AFC championship game. They headed to Denver with the unshakable belief their destiny lay in Detroit on February 5 at the Super Bowl.

And why not? The Steelers had won 15 of their last 18 road games. They'd beaten the best regular-season team in the league. They had no fear as they headed to the Mile High City.

Indeed, they just might have preferred being road warriors.

"It was kind of more of a distraction than anything; more ticket requests, a lot of people want to come and watch," Ward said of the circus atmosphere surrounding home playoff games. "With us going on the road, we really don't have to worry about that too much. We just go out there and just concentrate on football."

Still, Denver was 8-0 at home in 2005, and the Steelers were about to play their seventh straight game with no margin for error. Win or forget about their dreams.

So they won.

Just as at Indy, the Steelers started quickly, taking a 10-0 lead. After Denver made a field goal, the road to the Super Bowl opened wider than Interstate 25 outside Invesco Field.

Roethlisberger engineered a 14-play, 80-yard drive that ate up seven and a half minutes and ended with Bettis's 3-yard run for a 17-3 edge. It was a dagger for Denver—and the defense twisted it deeper.

Under pressure, Jake Plummer unwisely sent a pass into the flat that cornerback Ike Taylor picked off at the Broncos 38 with 1:48 to go in the half. Bettis had a TD nullified by penalty, but Roethlisberger floated a 17-yard pass just over two Broncos and Ward corralled it in the back of the end zone.

It was a backbreaker with just seven seconds remaining in the half.

"I think they were finished after that," Porter said. "We made sure of it in the second half."

The 34-17 win carried Cowher back to the Super Bowl; he guided the Steelers there after the 1995 season, but lost to Dallas.

Far more significantly for this group of Steelers, they were about to take a Bus ride to the Motor City, Bettis's hometown.

"I can't imagine anything better," said Bettis as he wiped himself dry following a Gatorade dunking in the locker room. "I'm going home."

The night before the Denver game, Bettis spoke to the team. And, for once, he was dead serious, and very emotional.

"He asked for something that he knew we would give, and that's 100 percent," Polamalu said. "With that, the game came into our favor and we took him home, which was the second request."

Added Faneca: "He had me choked up a little bit, it means so much to him, to be in the league this long—to give him a shot like this, it definitely means something."

The Steelers' remarkable comeback from the verge of elimination back in early December easily could have been lost in the fanfare accompanying Bettis. How easy it would have been to forget just where the Steelers stood after the loss to Cincinnati, particularly when they were installed as 4-point favorites over Seattle in the Super Bowl.

"It's amazing, especially to have done it all on the road," Randle El said.

But would the Super Bowl really be a road game? Bettis certainly would be comfortable, and he would set the tempo for the rest of the Steelers. Plus, with Detroit an easy drive from Pittsburgh—and 2,000 miles or so from Seattle—Motown would take on a Steel City look by the weekend of the game.

The Steelers also were designated the home team, but chose to continue wearing white for the big game.

As if that would have anything to do with who went home with the trophy.

"You work hard to travel this path, but if you're not able to finish the deal you'll be forgotten," Cowher said. "You have a chance to put your name up there with some of the great teams. That's the opportunity that you're selling to your players."

Obviously, Cowher had done a marvelous selling job thus far. How many coaches could have kept their team together to mount this kind of run?

He didn't want any of the credit he fully deserved, though.

"This is a great group of guys, how we got here, we're a different team," Cowher said. "We're a focused team; no matter what's happened, we've stayed together. We've got a resilient group."

Resilient, happy, on a roll. Would the Seahawks have a chance?

Well, yeah. Seattle had gone 15-3 to get to its first Super Bowl, including a stunning blowout of a strong Carolina team in the NFC title game. While it didn't have the motivational boost the Bus provided for Pittsburgh, it had league MVP Shaun Alexander, who'd set an NFL record with 28 touchdowns and led all rushers with 1,880 yards.

It owned a big-play defense led by a pair of rookie linebackers, Lofa Tatupu and Leroy Hill, who looked more like 10-year vets.

The Seahawks also had a coach, Mike Holmgren, who'd won a Super Bowl in 1997 as boss of the Green Bay Packers.

"What you remember is the elation and the relief of winning one," Holmgren said. "But you also remember the ones you lose. I've been fortunate to win one with the Packers, but then we lost one the next year and you start questioning yourself. What more could I have done? Was there anything we didn't cover properly in our preparation?

"I think it's very important that the sense of fulfillment and the joy you get from winning outweighs the negative aspects of losing, or else it never will be worth it."

Both coaches needed to balance the desire to be fully prepared with the realization that being wound too tight during Super Bowl week is self-defeating. So many teams have gotten to the big game only to have a big letdown because they allowed the atmosphere to overwhelm them.

The Steelers really shouldn't have been concerned about being victimized by any such stress. After what they'd gone through to get there, responding to pressure came naturally at this point.

Besides, Bettis would always keep them loose.

On Wednesday night of Super Bowl week, Bettis's family held an old-fashioned dinner for the Bus and his riders. Turkey, stuffing, roast beef, ham, green beans, candied yams, macaroni and cheese, jasmine rice, rolls. While the players arrived in limos, cars, and even a bus, Bettis stood on the front lawn decked out in a Detroit Tigers jacket and hat, beaming.

"It means a lot, especially to my mom and dad, who want to be as hospitable as they can, being that this is home for me," he said.

His mother, Gladys, predicted Jerome was about to play his final game.

"I think he will retire, and I hope he does. It's time. What else could he do to top this?"

Well, he needed to do one more thing: Win the damn game.

Things didn't begin well for the Steelers, who were out of sync offensively and didn't register a first down in the opening quarter, which Seattle led 3-0. Indeed, it wasn't until close to halftime— and following one of many controversial officiating calls—that Pittsburgh moved ahead.

A nervous Roethlisberger finally made a big play with a scramble and a sudden stop to unload a pass that found Ward for 37 yards.

Cowher hailed the Bus, but he couldn't get into the end zone on two close-range cracks. Then Big Ben followed Bettis's block to the left and scored from the 1.

Or didn't score.

One official raised his hands to signal touchdown, enraging Holmgren. But he couldn't challenge the call because it came with 1:55 left in the half. Instead, Holmgren anxiously awaited a call from the officiating booth upstairs to review the play. A few agonizing moments passed before the review was requested.

As Holmgren told a linesman the play "was not even close" to a touchdown, referee Bill Leavy reviewed it—and upheld the call. Pittsburgh led 7-3.

An infuriated Holmgren assailed the officials as he jogged off the field at halftime.

Now in front, Pittsburgh wasn't about to fade. In fact, on the second play of the third quarter, Parker took a handoff to his right and, behind a crushing block by Faneca, sped 75 yards for the longest TD run in a Super Bowl.

"I just knew it was going to be a great play," said Parker. "They called it at the right time, and Faneca just paved the way."

Seattle came back with a 16-yard reception by Jerramy Stevens

Pittsburgh's Hines Ward scores in Super Bowl XL, February 5, 2005.
Photo by Bob Rosato.

to make it 14-10, just 53 seconds after Kelly Herndon's 76-yard interception return foiled another Pittsburgh threat.

Ahead 14-10 with an entire quarter remaining, the Steelers needed to stay on course. That meant hard running by Bettis and Parker, steady defense, and solid special teams.

That's the Steelers' way, of course. Now, more than ever, they needed to stick to tradition.

Uh, not exactly.

With about nine minutes left in regulation and the ball at the Seattle 43, offensive coordinator Ken Whisenhunt decided a little trickery was in order. And while the Steelers have a bevy of versatile players, including former college QBs Randle El and Ward, something outlandish at this point seemed, well, outlandish.

Wideout Randle El took a handoff on a reverse, pulled up and let fly downfield—a perfect pass to the galloping Ward. Earlier in the game, Ward dropped a ball in the end zone. This time, he grabbed it for the clinching points, earning him MVP honors.

"We ran that play before," Randle El said. "We ran that play against Cleveland and scored a touchdown then. It was called at the right time, and everything was perfect."

Particularly the ending for Bettis. Teary-eyed, he hugged everybody in sight, kissed the Lombardi Trophy, paid homage to his fellow Detroiters and his second home of Pittsburgh.

And announced that yes, this was it.

"This is why I started 13 years ago, on this quest," Bettis said. "Along the way, I amassed a lot of yards and a lot of Pro Bowls, but none of that was significant because it wasn't the team goals. The team goal has always been to win a championship, and now I have a championship."

"I decided to come back to win a championship and mission accomplished," he said. "So with that, I have to bid farewell. We brought the championship back home.

"One for the thumb."

12

DETHRONING THE KING

Billy Casper over Arnold Palmer, 1966

The King was rewarding his subjects with the kind of display that built his fiefdom.

With his fans in rapturous tow, Arnold Palmer was making a mockery of the 1966 U.S. Open. Arnie's Army flooded Olympic Country Club that Father's Day to roar their approval as their hero would win his second Open title and, for the time being, solidify his place as golf's true royalty.

Heading into the fourth round of the tournament, Palmer held a three-stroke lead over Billy Casper, with whom he was paired. Jack Nicklaus, the man threatening to usurp Palmer at the top of the sport, also was in contention, along with other fine tour veterans Tony Lema, Dave Marr, and Phil Rodgers. But there was little doubt if the hard-charging Palmer got off to a quick start, the rest of the field was playing for second place.

Coming off a back injury that temporarily sidelined him in previous weeks, Palmer was primed for this Open. Although he'd won four Masters crowns (1958, 1960, '62, and '64), two British Opens (1961 and '62) and the American championship in 1960, Palmer's reign clearly was under siege by Nicklaus when the golfing world turned its attention to the San Francisco Bay Area.

After all, Palmer failed to make the cut in the previous Open, won by Gary Player, and there was criticism that Palmer's outside business interests were distracting him on the course.

But Palmer had hired a business manager to handle those matters and rededicated himself to the game. He came to San Francisco with one thing on his mind: winning.

"I had gone back to basics, and I was ready," he said.

"Arnie told me he planned to break 280 at Olympic," Marr said. "I told him he was crazy, that the last time the Open was there, 287 won it and the course might be even harder. But he was sure he could break 280."

In the opening round, it looked more like it was Casper who would be in the 270s, as he shot at 69 to Palmer's 71. The leader was an obscure pro named Al Mengert with a 67.

But when Palmer fired a 66—Casper had a 68 in the second round—Arnie's boast to Marr looked more possible. He and Casper, who'd won the Open the year before Palmer earned his U.S. championship, were deadlocked atop the leaderboard through 36 holes.

Palmer had benefited from playing before the winds off the Bay kicked up. His explanation for a 66: "Simple. I missed one fairway off the tee, on No. 14. And I missed only the 17th green. When you play golf like that, you minimize your chance for errors and you can post a good one."

What Palmer failed to mention was he birdied the 14th thanks to a magnificent 5-iron from the rough to within three feet of the hole.

Casper was quite satisfied with his score, saying he "scrambled more than you'd like to" for his share of the lead.

"It was luck to get pars at the 1st and 11 and then I holed out from a bunker on 17," he said.

Casper and Palmer would be paired for the third round, which no longer was accompanied by the fourth round on Saturday. The U.S. Golf Association changed the format, well aware that in mid-June, with temperatures often in the 80s or higher, a 36-hole finale was more a process of attrition than a true test on the links.

Indeed, in 1964, a dehydrated Ken Venturi hung on for the title, but it was not a pretty sight.

Casper's golf was not very pretty on Saturday as he faltered with a 73. His one-putt magic, which had helped so much in that "scramble" round the previous day, had disappeared.

Palmer, meanwhile, shot an even-par 70 that could have been a bit lower, but was strong enough to put him in command by three strokes.

So they entered the final round with Palmer holding a hefty lead, his Army fully expecting a coronation, and even some of the players resigned to a futile chase.

"There was some thought we were chasing second place," Casper said. "At one point, I thought Palmer had come and gone with the tournament."

That point came midway through the round, a round for the ages through nine holes for Palmer. He scorched Olympic's front half with a 32. By the fourth hole Sunday, he was six strokes ahead of Casper. Every time Casper tried to make a move on the front side, Arnie answered.

"I wouldn't say it was frustrating because Arnold was playing some excellent golf," Casper recalled. "He was playing the way a champion plays."

As they made the turn, Palmer's lead was seven strokes. The King could coast from there.

"Don't worry, Bill," Palmer assured Casper. "Continue playing this way and you'll finish second."

But Palmer, ever the adventurous competitor, had something more on his mind than lifting the Open trophy. And it would be his undoing.

Ben Hogan, considered by many the greatest American golfer up to that point, owned the Open record of 276. If Palmer kept burning up the course, he could break that mark, thus making the '66 tournament the most memorable of all conquests for him.

"I never feel I have anything won until we finish," he said, "but I did start thinking about that 274."

One of the cardinal sins in golf is to start thinking about anything but the next shot. It's tantamount to a football team looking down the road on its schedule, or a tennis player focusing on his next opponent before he's done with the current one. Palmer should have known better. After all, he stormed back from a similar deficit to win the Open in '60.

Instead, he added an unnecessary strain to his round, swashbuckling instead of sailing. And the man chasing him wasn't going away.

Casper wouldn't be bothered by the pressure of the final nine at a major championship. He'd won the 1959 Open at Winged Foot, considered a more difficult layout than Olympic. His swing was smooth, his demeanor perfect for the stress of those finishing holes. Casper simply did not get flustered. Perhaps more known for his exotic diet that included buffalo rather than beef, he was the anti-Arnie. Maybe that was a good thing.

"The only thing that gets in the way of a golfer's success is the golfer himself," Casper once wrote. "Whether he can make a good swing at the ball . . . mechanics. Or whether he has the good sense of where the right place is to aim a shot . . . strategy."

Despite his go-for-it strategy—he bogeyed the 10th hole—Palmer certainly seemed safe when he matched Casper's birdie at the 12th hole. He admitted to feeling that way after the birdie because "I was convinced now I could set the record."

Then, he fell apart.

At No. 13, his 4-iron tee shot to the par-3 soared into the left rough. If there is one place you don't want to be in a U.S. Open, it's in the unmanageable rough. Palmer had avoided it so well all week, but not this time.

He pitched out to 10 feet, a fine shot considering the circumstances. But the par putt didn't fall.

At the 15th, another par-3, Palmer's safe lead became tenuous. His 7-iron to the 150-yard hole was hit toward a tough pin placement rather than to the middle of the green. The ball found the sand.

"A calculated risk," Palmer said. "I've always wanted to go for the pin, ever since I began playing. I believe that's the way to play golf."

But when his bunker shot wound up about eight feet from the hole and Palmer missed the putt, the fans packed around the green groaned in unison. Their leader seemed to join them.

And then Casper, faced with a downhill 20-foot putt "with a break of about 2½ feet," planted it right in the middle of the cup.

The lead was now three strokes, the same as when the day started. But the mood on the course—and among the contenders—had changed.

While Casper rarely showed his emotions, his reaction to several shots in this round, particularly the birdies at Nos. 12 and 15, were worthy of the King himself. He waved his putter high and rushed to the hole to pick up his ball, eager to get on to the next tee.

"I believed I had a chance at that point," Casper said. "I was playing very well."

Arnie, meanwhile, wasn't waving clubs. He was wavering.

"When we got through with 15, it was now a case of Billy trying to catch me and I am trying to protect a lead," Palmer said. "It's a different feel, much different."

Unfortunately for Palmer his performances on the last three holes wouldn't be much different from what he'd done on the two par-3s that allowed Casper to slice the lead.

From the 16th tee, the metronomic Casper struck another drive into the fairway of the par-5. As Palmer hitched his pants and strode to address his ball, the anxious Army voiced its support.

"Right down the middle," someone shouted, followed by a plea of "Make a birdie, Arnie."

Or even, perhaps, an eagle to salt away the title. The fans were certain Arnie would attack, and Palmer later admitted he was somewhat annoyed that Casper wasn't taking any chances while pursuing him.

Palmer lost his drive badly into the trees, by far the worst drive of the day for him. Briskly walking to his ball, Palmer could sense his grip on the tournament slipping.

When he saw his lie and the obstacles between his ball and the green, Palmer had little choice but to turn conservative himself and forget about going for the green with his second shot. At least he was thinking clearly, even if he was not executing optimally.

Casper, meanwhile, was doing what he nearly always did, calmly sending his second shot with a 2-iron into perfect position for an approach to the green. That approach landed about 15 feet from the hole.

Palmer, on the other hand, was left with a fairway wood to the green, a dicey proposition in any circumstances, but particularly now.

"When I hit it, I knew it was a good shot," Palmer recalled. "I just knew it."

*Arnold Palmer grimaces as he misses a shot during the 1966 U.S. Open.
Photo by Walter Iooss Jr.*

He was wrong. The ball landed in the bunker to the right of the green. Palmer was headed for a bogey 6.

Casper was headed closer to the lead. For the second straight hole, he nailed a birdie putt. As they headed to the 17th, Casper was a shot down.

By now, it almost seemed as if Palmer was chasing Casper the Friendly Ghost. If Arnie blew this one, he would be haunted by it for, well, maybe forever.

Even worse, 17 was considered the toughest hole on the back nine, a place where U.S. Opens are lost more than won. Lee Janzen, who would win his second U.S. Open crown at Olympic in 1998, was five over par on that hole in his first three rounds that year. But his par at the 17th in the fourth round was, Janzen said, "the key to winning that championship."

For Casper, it was the key to getting a chance to win the championship.

"I know if you don't drive it well on the 17th, you can come up with a big number," he said. "That's a hole you are only thinking about making par."

Casper's chances of making par, though, seemed crushed when his drive headed right and into the rough. Yet the now-shaky Palmer couldn't put his drive in the fairway, either.

Palmer's hook was in worse shape than Casper's, which seemed appropriate the way things were going down the stretch. Casper's 3-iron came up short of the green, still in the deep grass. Palmer, meanwhile, hit a 6-iron that also found more rough.

So it became a chipping game on 17, and Casper always was a master from in close. He put his third shot within three feet, then knocked it home for par.

Palmer's third shot settled 10 feet from the pin, and his par putt looked good as it slowly trickled toward the hole. And slid just past.

They were even.

"I can't imagine there were many people who expected we would be tied coming to the 18th," Casper said.

Well, there were a few. His family, for instance.

Casper's 9-year-old son Billy and his 11-year-old daughter Linda were spending Father's Day with their dad and their mother, Shirley. They walked the entire 18 and, said Linda: "I have faith in my father." She also said she thought Palmer might "bogey, bogey, bogey—and he almost did"—on the final three holes.

Although he hadn't found the fairway on the 18th all week, Casper was confident enough to pull out his driver on the finishing hole. And when he striped one right down the middle, well, even Arnie's Army had to cheer such a clutch shot.

The Army again moaned collectively when Palmer sent yet another tee shot, this time with a 1-iron, into the rough. Even Palmer would admit he thought he'd blown the tournament right there.

He hadn't.

"I had to pull myself together and do what I knew I was capable of and had done for most of the week," he said. "I just had to play good golf shots."

He also knew that Casper was in grand position and would hit the green with his second shot. Casper did just that and had a 25-foot putt for birdie.

So Palmer gathered all the knowledge and experience—and guts—he'd built through his marvelous career and slashed the ball from the deep grass and high into the California sky. It came down on the tiny green, about 30 feet from the hole as the Army roared its approval.

But the putt was downhill on a fast green, and Palmer missed the hole by about six feet. The putt coming back might not mean a thing, either, if Casper knocked in his birdie putt.

Palmer was required by the rules of those days to putt out, though, and his shot "looked like it was a mile long." Not quite, but certainly no "gimme" after all of his travails on the back nine.

He stroked it firmly and directly into the cup, then turned to watch Casper's birdie attempt.

"I thought I could make it, but I also knew if I two-putted, we would be tied," Casper said. "I would say I was in a very comfortable position if I hit a good first putt."

Which, not surprisingly considering how the last 90 minutes had gone, was exactly what Casper did. He missed by perhaps a foot, tapped it in, and shook the shaken Palmer's hand.

"I should have known on this course you must keep your game together," Palmer said. "I tried for shots that are great when they work. If they don't, you're in trouble. I was in trouble."

When the round was over, Casper and Palmer met with the media, which grilled Palmer on his second-nine flop and, in general, overlooked the impressive golf—32 on the back nine—that Casper had played. After all, the most popular player in the sport naturally draws the headlines when his game falls apart with such a cherished prize in sight.

"It was unbelievable that a pressure performer like Palmer could reach a point where his sharpness could disappear so fast," columnist Arthur Daley wrote in the *New York Times*.

But Palmer, while clearly exhausted and disgusted with himself, answered all the queries. Then, stunningly, he exited the media tent and met with Arnie's Army.

It was an impressive display of Palmer's charisma and his grit. After one of the worst debacles of his career, he still was a man of the people.

And there was hope for them, of course. And for Palmer: With the 18-hole playoff ahead to decide a winner, why couldn't the King reassert his reign?

Palmer thought he had a secret weapon, too. He joked afterward that, like Casper, "I will be eating buffalo meat pretty soon. I would do it if I thought it would get me some birdies."

Arnie would, indeed, find some birdies on the front nine of Monday's playoff. He went out in 33, two strokes under par, which Casper matched.

Then came the decisive back nine. Had Palmer learned anything from the previous day? Had Casper?

First, Arnie:

"I'd had a little trouble on the back nine all week. I'd kind of been fighting it. I never seemed to get myself lined up properly."

And Billy:

"I understood that Arnie's charge meant tearing down the flags with his shots. When I charge, I'm getting the ball into position on the greens for a par."

The playoff turned not deep into the back nine, but on No. 11. Casper's putting touch was precise as he holed a 30-footer. Palmer again drove into the rough, didn't get his second shot onto the green and wound up with a bogey.

They were tied but, as Palmer later admitted, "I think the memory of Sunday hurt me on Monday once we were tied. I played some tight shots after that."

And Casper was as loose as he could be. So loose, in fact, that he put home a 40-plus-foot putt on the 13th and excitedly raised his arms above his head. For the first time in the 66th U.S. Open, Billy Casper stood alone in the lead.

Steady pars on the next two holes, combined with Palmer's bogey on 14, gave Casper a two-stroke edge. It was becoming clear that Casper's consistency was overmatching Palmer's risk-taking.

So clear that when Casper parred the 15th and Palmer again botched the par-3, the lead appeared insurmountable. The Army was silent.

And it soon would be in shock.

On Sunday, Palmer lost two shots to Casper on a par-5 that should have been Arnie's power province. On Monday, it was even worse—604 yards of misery that clinched the championship for Casper and plunged Palmer to the lowest depths of his career.

Again betrayed by his driver, Palmer wound up in the heaviest rough on the hole. Trying to gouge it out, his ball barely moved forward, perhaps 75 yards. His 4-wood third shot didn't reach the green.

Flustered by his shortcomings in golf's hottest spotlight for a second straight day, Palmer failed to clear the bunker in front of him on his fourth shot. He managed to get his fifth on the green, but the King was cooked. He two-putted for a 7 and, even though Casper three-putted, Palmer still lost another stroke.

Down four with two holes left, Palmer was done. There would be no more charges to glory, only an ignominious defeat.

Casper three-putted again on 17, but he still had a three-stroke lead as they teed off on the final hole. With his family teary-eyed in the gallery on 18, Casper nearly jogged the length of the hole. His smile was as wide as the San Francisco Bay after his second shot landed close to the pin. He knocked in the short putt for a closing birdie, a 69—and one of the most outlandish rallies in golf annals.

"I was seven down with nine holes to go in regulation play," he said moments after his wife and kids broke through the restraining ropes to hug their hero. "To come from that and win the Open, it's just like a dream. When Palmer slipped, I slipped inside the door he left ajar.

"It's something I've been hoping and praying for so long. It's very rewarding."

A devout Mormon, Casper tithed 10 percent of his $25,000 purse to the church.

But why did it happen?

For one, Casper was deadly on the greens.

"He's the greatest putter on the pro tour," Palmer said. "He putted the ball in the hole at the right time and that made the big difference."

Casper agreed.

"This was one of my best putting tournaments in a long, long time," he said. "Not as good as 1959, but the best in a long time."

Casper also wasn't intimidated by Arnie and his Army. He never lost his composure, never doubted his game plan.

"You don't attack this course, you romance it," he added. "You have to sort of caress the ball on the greens and wait for the birdies to come to you, not go after them.

"Except for a half-dozen holes, Arnie would be No. 1 and I would be No. 2, instead of the other way around. He played very well, but ran into some bad luck."

It was Palmer's third Open loss in a playoff. This, with a 40 on the final nine, was the worst.

"It's getting to be a damned habit," Palmer said. "I can't figure it. I didn't hit bad shots, but I got bad results."

The 11th man to win two Opens, Casper would go on to take the 1970 Masters for his third major championship and would finish his career with 51 PGA Tour victories.

Palmer never won another Grand Slam tournament. There is no question that his failure at Olympic was the low point of a Hall-of-Fame career in which he popularized golf for the masses and became a sporting icon throughout the world.

Palmer would win 61 PGA Tour events in all, then took 12 tournaments, including 5 majors on the Senior Tour. In 1981, he won a Senior Open.

But Casper's Comeback—or The King's Collapse—would remain among the most memorable finishes in golf history. Palmer's close friend and longtime spokesman, Doc Giffin, once said: "Arnold's loss in '66 at Olympic was an open wound that never healed."

Sometimes, even the King doesn't rule.

13

THE FLYING FINN

Lasse Viren, 1972 and 1976 Summer Olympics

The Munich Olympics will be remembered—and often re-viled—for the massacre of 11 Israelis by the terrorist Black September group. Many of the great performances of the 1972 games were overshadowed by that tragedy.

Where the Olympics should be compelling, they had become calamitous.

For 23-year-old Finn Lasse Viren, not one but two remarkable races should have made him the talk of the sports world. Instead, Viren would have to wait another four years before his magnificent achievements would gain the acclaim they deserved worldwide.

And even then, controversy and doubts would plague him.

Decades before Viren came onto the international track and field stage, Finland had dominated long-distance running at the Olympics. From 1912 to 1936, Finns won 24 gold medals in distances from 1,500 meters (the metric mile) up. The great Paavo Nurmi, the original "Flying Finn," led the charge—if anyone can really charge while running for so long—by taking six of those golds.

Viren, a policeman, came to Munich without much fanfare. His nation had been blanked in the distance races since '36, and his fourth-place finish in the qualifying trials didn't cause a stir. But with only nine 10,000-meter races on his resume, he was in the final, to be held three days later.

The favorites were Mohammed Gammoudi of Tunisia, David Bedford of England, and Emiel Puttemans of Belgium. Bedford and Puttemans had broken the Olympic record in the preliminaries. It was the first time since 1920 that heats were needed for the 10,000; 50 runners had entered the race, although only perhaps 10 had a realistic chance of winning.

Viren was one of those contenders, especially after he'd upset Bedford and Puttemans in a 2-mile race earlier that summer in Stockholm, setting a world record in the event.

"My favorite," he would later say, "because it was the first major international victory."

Because he often trained in the forests and along obscure trails outside his hometown of Myrskyla—as well as spending a stint in Kenya—Viren was not as well known as many of the regulars on the circuit. His 2-mile record had been something of a shock to the track and field community because Viren wasn't rated as highly as one of his teammates, Juha Vaatainen, who won the 1971 Euros in the 5,000 and the 10,000.

But another seismic quake on the Munich track was in store for everyone, courtesy of Lasse Viren.

The bearded, shaggy-haired Viren started well and was keeping pace with his competition through the first half of the race. On the 12th lap, with the racers bunched and little room to maneuver, there suddenly was a commotion.

Viren stepped on the curbing in the pack of runners while trying to avoid running up on Puttemans's heels. The only hope for Finland—Vaatainen had withdrawn with injury—stumbled and flopped. Hard.

A large group of runners could have gone down, too, but only one did: Gammoudi, the 1968 5,000 winner.

"I never could determine why I fell, what caused that to happen so early in the race," said Viren, who has hung on a wall at his home a photo of himself and Gammoudi lying on the track. "You really never are sure when it is happening, but your only thought is, 'Get up. Get up and race. Catch up to the leaders.'

"I was probably fortunate that no one ran over me. In those

cases, often the racers who go to the ground get trampled. Fortunately, that didn't happen to me, even though I was near the lead when it occurred."

So Viren began what looked like a long climb back—he was about 50 meters behind the lead pack when he reached full stride, and wasn't even sure he was running in the correct direction after the fall.

"I was disoriented," he admitted. "But not for long."

Gammoudi eventually resumed running, but after a little more than one lap, he withdrew, his will broken.

Viren didn't know that. He was too preoccupied with drawing in the seven leaders.

And, stunningly, he began doing so. Rapidly.

"There was no reason to believe with so much of the race remaining that I could not get to the front group," Viren said. "You don't think about the tactics of it, you just run."

And run he did. Soon, he was in the lead pack. And as the lead changed hands several times, observers expected him to fade away.

Instead, Viren surged to take the lead from Puttemans, and pull away.

As Viren approached the finish, there was little strain on his feet. Not only was it impossible to tell he'd just run more than six miles, but he'd also taken a tumble in the middle of the event—a fall that should have ended Viren's chances.

Not only did Viren win, he set a world record of 27 minutes, 38.4 seconds, breaking the mark set seven years earlier by the great Ron Clarke. He won by 8 yards; his time breakdown on the final two laps was 60 seconds flat and 56.4 seconds.

And not only was Viren unhurt from the fall—though he did have some soreness in his right thigh—but the crash actually helped, serving as a jarring wake-up call.

With Finland flags waving throughout the stadium, Viren had overcome every runner's nightmare to reach every runner's dream. He was an Olympic gold medalist.

"I remember some fans coming down to the track waving some flags and reaching out to hand them to me," he said. "They were as proud as I was. That medal was the most special of all four, because you have won in the Olympics for the first time. It meant so much to my country, and it was what I set out to be so many years before, an Olympic champion."

Incredibly, Viren was determined to add to his medal count. Yes, he could have stepped away after perhaps the greatest individual comeback in any Olympic race. He would be proclaimed a hero in Finland even if he skipped the 5,000 meters on the final day of the politically smeared games. Viren had done his work—magnificently.

"That was not the kind of competitor Lasse was," said his coach Rolf Haikkola. "Lasse was committed to being the best runner, and by winning (the 10,000), with a fall, he was certain he could win the next race, as well."

The 5,000 generally was regarded as the classic distance race by Europeans, just as the mile is considered the top nonsprint by Americans. So Viren made sure he was one of the 14 runners at the starting line.

American Steve Prefontaine, who boldly (and in character) predicted he would run below four minutes on the final mile of the 5,000, led with four laps to go, but a victory by the American would have been a huge upset. With two laps remaining, Viren surged to the front, looking as fresh as Prefontaine looked spent.

Ironically, it was Gammoudi, the fallen victim of the 10,000, who would provide the biggest challenge to Viren.

On the final lap, Gammoudi moved up alongside Viren and appeared ready to grab the gold. It was here that the Finn's unlimited resolve allowed him to retake the lead. As he rounded the final turn into the stretch, Viren was clear of Gammoudi, and the Munich fans rose to applaud this valiant, dominant racer.

Viren won, again by 8 yards, in an Olympic record 13:26.4.

"It was one of the greatest double victories ever," Gammoudi said.

They certainly thought so back in Finland, where Viren's neighbors built him a sauna in honor of his triumphs. But outside his nation, there was little fanfare.

Black September had ruined any chance of that.

So immediately after the Munich double, Viren decided he wanted to come back for more. But injuries slowed him heading toward the Montreal Games.

He had surgery on some knee ligaments. A 1974 hip problem curtailed some of that season, and he numbed the hip with ice

Lasse Viren celebrates his victory at the 1972 Summer Olympics.
Photo by Jerry Cooke.

before finishing third at the European Championships in the 5,000.

Viren needed hip surgery the next year, making the '76 Olympics a long shot. Then again, what could really be unreachable for Viren after his accomplishments in Munich?

If he felt healthy enough, Viren would have spots reserved for him on the Finland squad in Montreal. The Finnish track federation couldn't deny him; that would have been like the United States excluding a willing Tiger Woods from the Ryder Cup squad.

Viren, who had gone back to his police job, decided to run the 5,000 and 10,000 again in Canada. And—get this—he also entered his first marathon.

His reasoning: "If I am free of injury, I believe there are only the people chasing me, that I am No. 1."

In the Montreal 10,000, there were no mishaps. No flops. Viren was close to the lead much of the way and moved swiftly from second place to first on the bell lap, taking the lead from Carlos Lopes of Portugal and sprinting away.

But even this victory had some sideshow elements to it.

After the race, Viren took off his shoes because of blisters and held them above his head as he ran a victory lap. The IOC summoned him to explain the "commercialism" of his act. Innocently, Viren showed the committee members his blisters, and after initially being suspended, he was cleared to run the 5,000.

Considering how the Olympics has become a commercialism festival since the 1996 Atlanta Games, the IOC's questioning of Viren—or any other athlete—was absurd.

"It was very strange," Viren said. "I had only done something very innocently. There were no motives."

There was a motive in the 5,000: set history with another double-double.

That 5,000 was Viren's most difficult Olympic race. He had to hold off several others in the final laps, and twice looked like he would lose. He had five challengers only one or two strides behind him as the final lap began, and they all took shots at Viren.

"There were many racers who could have gotten past me on that bell lap," he recalled. "I glanced behind me for a second to see what it looked like and I was stunned. It was a big surprise because we had been running some fast laps, some very fast laps. Very fast, yet here were these others staying right with me.

"So the question was whether I could run even faster on the bell lap, and whether they could, also."

One of them, New Zealand's Dick Quax, certainly could. He flashed up to Viren's side, his stride strong and straight, as it must be in the final meters of any race.

Viren now understood his final 5,000 as an Olympian might be his first defeat in the games.

"I needed to summon every last drop of energy and power I had, or else I would not be first to the line," he said. "Fortunately, I found that energy and I was able to pass Quax."

And run the last 1,500 meters so quickly that he would have finished fourth in that event at Montreal.

Breaking the tape, he thrust both hands in the air in a more animated display than what followed his other Olympic wins.

"All of the victories were very sweet," he said. "But I think I knew that might be the last one in the Olympics, and I had done something no one else had, so I was more emotional."

Possibly the most amazing feat for this Flying Finn was his fifth-place finish in the 1976 marathon a few days after the 5,000.

"If you love to run, then you run when you can," he said. "If you love to compete, then you compete when you can."

Added Haikkola: "Lasse knew his limits, or that he had no limits. When he was in form, he was the best runner and the most fit runner. He was almost unbeatable, so why not race in those big (races)."

Unfortunately, much of the rest of the sporting community preferred to believe something other than hard work, smart training, and a passion for his craft were behind Viren's success. Whether it was jealous competitors, envious coaches, or backroom politicians, Viren's name was connected with the unethical, if not illegal, practice of blood doping—now referred to as blood boosting because blood doping has taken on other connotations.

Athletes often would train at high altitudes to increase the number of oxygen-carrying red blood cells in their system. Units of that "prime blood" are removed, frozen and preserved for when the athlete races again. The blood then is injected into the system and it maximizes endurance.

Why target Viren? Mostly because blood boosting had originated through experiments in Scandinavia. And because Viren

rarely won big races between his magnificent Olympic performances, he seemed a likely candidate for the process.

Nothing was ever proven, and Viren always denied he was involved in blood doping. He insisted that his training was a four-
year cycle geared toward only one thing: the Olympics.

A magazine once offered Viren $1 million—a far more lucra-
tive sum in the 1970s than now, when some track athletes get that
amount in appearance money during a season—to reveal "the true
story" behind his victories. The offer was withdrawn when Viren
told the publication the "true story" was exactly what he'd been
saying all along: no blood boosting.

No cheating.

Once, he even offered his secret as a diet of "reindeer milk."

Yeah, and he also kept up with Santa's sleigh on Christmas Eve.

Viren was beyond his prime by the 1980 Moscow Olympics,
even though the field was watered-down by the boycott of Western nations. He finished fifth in the 10,000 there and withdrew
from the marathon with an intestinal infection.

But Viren stands alone as a two-time double winner of the
5,000 and 10,000 in the Olympics, a feat that might never be
equaled.

And if he had not leapt up and continued in the Munich
10,000 after the unfortunate fall?

"That was never in question," he said. "A racer finishes the race
when he can."

In Viren's case, that racer comes back from such troubles to
win . . . and win . . . and win.

14

THE MIRACLE BRAVES

1914 Boston Braves

Before the U.S. hockey team pulled off the "Miracle on Ice" at the 1980 Olympics, there was a miracle on grass in the 1914 National League baseball season.

Miracle. Magical. Mystical. Whatever, the Boston Braves made history in the summer of 1914.

On July 4, the Braves were dead last, dead being the operative word. They were buried 15 games off the pace of the first-place New York Giants with no hope of competing for the pennant.

That's where the "miracle" part comes in. The schizophrenic Braves, who were having trouble winning in the first half of the season, could hardly lose in the second. It was as if someone had waved a magic wand.

Welcome, surprising NL pennant winners.

And welcome "Miracle Braves." The tag stuck with the Boston club after making the greatest comeback in major league baseball history.

In a sizzling finish, the Braves had caught and surpassed by a wide margin John McGraw's heavily favored Giants—the same Giants that had finished a whopping 31½ games ahead of Boston in 1913.

It hardly seemed possible to McGraw and the rest of the base-ball world. The Braves were an imperfect patchwork of castoffs, journeymen, and youngsters with little experience.

The year before, the Braves continued their tradition of finishing in the second division. True, it was fifth place and an improvement over previous seasons, but the Braves were still considered a lower-echelon club. A dark horse when compared to McGraw's thoroughbreds who had won three straight pennants.

In George Stallings, the Braves had a manager with a spotty record in the majors. After some success managing in the minors, he received an offer to come back to "The Show" with the Braves. It was 1912 when Stallings was invited to sit in owner Jim Gaffney's box at the Polo Grounds. As they talked, the Giants rolled up a big score and crushed the last-place Braves. "Well, that's the team you'll be managing next year, George," Gaffney said. "What do you think of them?" Stallings was honest—almost too honest.

"Mr. Gaffney, I've been stuck with some terrible teams in my day," he said. "But this one beats 'em all."

Stallings didn't need the money. A wealthy plantation owner in Georgia, Stallings could have retired to the gentleman farmer's life. But baseball was in his blood. Stallings wanted to show he belonged, and the Braves were probably his last chance in the majors to prove it. He took the job.

Stallings, son of a Confederate war hero, had the opportunity to be a doctor, but baseball was his passion. He quickly found out he wasn't good enough to be a major league player and turned to managing. With the Braves, he hoped to last longer than he did with the teams in Philadelphia, Detroit, and New York's American League club. As the Phillies' manager, Stallings brought the team in 10th in the 12-team National League in 1897. He was fired during the 1898 season as the Phillies finished sixth. He lasted just one year in Detroit, despite a third-place finish in 1901, and less than two with the old New York Highlanders.

He was back in the minors until a call came from the Braves. He brought with him to Boston a wildly superstitious nature. His son, George Jr., remembered that his father carried a rabbit's foot around all the time. "All the hair had been rubbed off from wishing, and the hide had the brilliance of a bald head," George Jr. recalled in a 1964 interview with *Baseball Digest*. At any given time, George Stallings would be wearing a "lucky cap" or a "lucky suit." Or sitting in a "lucky seat" at the top of the grandstand in Boston before they opened the gates to let the fans in.

"All ballplayers are superstitious, but I still think my father was the champ," George Stallings Jr. said.

Consider the time Stallings was managing in the minors. A player came up to him and said, "George, we're going to win today."

"How do you know?" the manager replied.

"I saw a load of barrels go by," the player said.

The team won, and Stallings immediately hired a man to drive barrels around the ballpark in future games.

When he went on road trips, Stallings preferred to arrive at the train station extra early and board as soon as the gates opened. He wanted to avoid friends and acquaintances that wanted to wish him good luck. He believed that any good luck wish would somehow result in bad luck.

Stallings, usually attired in the dugout with a straw hat and bow tie, was an extremely vocal man on the bench. His players were used to hearing colorful language from their boss when they made a mistake. His favorite word: "Bonehead."

Once he turned to his bench looking for a pinch-hitter and hollered, "All right, Bonehead, get a bat and let's see if you're good for anything." A half-dozen players headed for the bat rack.

Stallings could be kind as well as cruel. During the Braves' spring training in Macon, Georgia, he invited his players to the 6,000-acre family plantation in nearby Haddock at least once a week. There, the players would feast on turkey, ham, and a large assortment of fruits and vegetables.

Stallings was known for his generosity and his neatness. The man dubbed "Big Daddy" couldn't stand to see a piece of paper—or a pigeon—on the field. Oscar Dugey, who played behind the great Johnny Evers at second base, helped Stallings keep things in order.

"Dugey would stuff his uniform pockets with pebbles before entering the dugout," Braves pitcher Bill James said. "If a bird landed where it might displease or distract Stallings, dutiful Dugey would toss pebbles at it and send it flying. If paper landed on the field, he would dash out and pick it up."

Dugey was one of five players on the Braves' 26-man roster in

1914 with no major league experience. None of them had played higher than Class B ball.

But what gave Stallings hope for the season was the acquisition of Evers from the Chicago Cubs in the off-season. Evers had both managed and starred for the Cubs. He played on pennant winners in 1906, 1907, and 1908 and was a natural team leader. He brought a chip-on-the shoulder attitude to Boston that Stallings thought would lend a spark to his club. Famed writer Grantland Rice called the skinny, 140-pound Evers a "bundle of nerves, a human splinter forever on the alert."

He fit right into Stalling's tough-minded philosophy that winning was the only thing important in baseball. As captain, he became Stallings's manager on the field.

"He was good for our club," James said. "We needed him and he gave the club spunk."

Not that everyone liked Evers—or he them. A feud developed between Evers and James early in the season.

"I got off to a bad start with him at the beginning of the season—and he never forgave me," James said.

The Braves were playing in Chicago and James was throwing so hard that batters were late getting around on his pitches and hitting the ball to the opposite field. James motioned Evers to move to his left, but the Braves' second baseman refused. The next batter hit the ball exactly through the spot where James had asked Evers to play.

Even though he was now in a Boston uniform, Evers was still king in Chicago. Evers felt humiliated that a "greenhorn" player would show him up before his adoring fans.

James, only 22 and in his second year in the major leagues, never could make Evers like him thereafter.

Stories of Evers's combative relationship with teammates are plentiful. For years, Evers played alongside shortstop Joe Tinker as one of the great double-play combinations in baseball history, along with first baseman Frank Chance. That didn't mean they had to talk. For some imagined slight, Evers and Tinker went years without speaking. They had numerous punch-outs in the clubhouse.

Evers, by the way, was known as the "Crab," not for his personality but for the way he sidled up to grounders. Evers wasn't the only player Stallings acquired in his continuing attempt to build the Braves into a winner. In Stallings's first year as manager in 1913, the Braves purchased James from a minor league team in Seattle. Then along came outfielder Joe Connolly, who was waived by Washington; outfielder Les Mann in a trade with Buffalo; and pitcher Dick Rudolph in a deal with the Giants. Rudolph joined a pitching staff that featured George "Lefty" Tyler. Along with the promising James, they would be counted on for most of the mound work in 1914. The Braves' other featured players of 1914 included colorful Rabbit Maranville at shortstop and catcher Hank Gowdy.

They were serious players—well, maybe not totally serious in Maranville's case. The team clown and main source of entertainment, Maranville was a crowd-pleaser. He loved to perform for the fans. They adored watching Maranville take throws from the catcher while sitting on second base in pregame practice, or making his patented "basket catch" of high infield pop flies at his stomach. They also loved watching the little "Rabbit" jump into a bigger teammate's arms with his cap askew, posing for the cameramen.

He was a hot dog long before the term ever existed in baseball, an after-hours hell-raiser renowned for jumping into hotel fish ponds and walking on hotel ledges. Stallings didn't care, as long as Maranville, one of the league's crack shortstops, showed up ready to work each day.

"Do what you want, but don't wind up in jail, and come to play every day," Stallings said.

Consistency was Maranville's trademark.

In his first of two long stints with the Braves, Maranville led National League shortstops in putouts each year from 1914 to 1919, with the exception of 1918 when he served in the navy during World War I. In that period, he also led the NL in double plays three times and in assists twice.

Maranville was a daredevil player who could scoot around the bases on strong, piston-like legs—always ready to sacrifice life and limb for his team.

Once in Pittsburgh, Maranville was at bat with the bases loaded and the Braves and Pirates locked in a scoreless tie. He took two pitches for strikes before leaning over the plate to deliberately take a fastball on the forehead.

The umpire had mixed feelings as he eyed the fallen, obviously dazed player sprawled on the ground.

"If you can walk to first base, I'll let you get away with it," he said.

Maranville slowly and carefully pulled himself up and stumbled to first base as the winning run crossed the plate for the Braves.

Maranville had many such humorous exchanges with umpires. As a rookie playing in a game in Brooklyn, Maranville came to the plate and stopped to take a pair of eyeglasses out of his hip pocket. He thoughtfully polished them, then handed them to umpire Bill Finneran.

It was said he gained his nickname while playing for New Bedford of the New England League. A little girl, watching him play a game of pepper, remarked, "You jump around just like a rabbit."

Gowdy came up to the majors in 1910 with the New York Giants as a first baseman. Manager John McGraw traded Gowdy to the Braves the next season.

"I kicked around between Boston and Buffalo for two seasons and it was only in 1913 that I turned to catching."

Gowdy's first season as a regular was 1914, the miracle year of the Braves. He was one of those rare ballplayers who didn't curse. His strongest expletives were "Criminy sakes" and "Holy Cow"—no doubt disgusting many of his teammates such as Evers, known for much stronger language.

Beefy Butch Schmidt was acquired from the minors toward the end of the 1913 season and soon became the Braves' regular at first base. Chuck Deal, purchased from Detroit, handled third base before an injury late in the season. When the Brooklyn Superbas released James "Red" Smith, the Braves signed him to replace Deal.

The outfield and the pitching were the big problem areas. No less than 11 players were used by Stallings in the outfield during the 1914 season. Left fielder Joe Connolly was the closest to being a regular.

"I believe he was the first big league manager to platoon outfielders," James said. "He had a right-handed-hitting outfield play the day a left-handed pitcher was going, and a left-handed-hitting outfield when a right-hander was opposing us."

As for the pitching, Tyler was the most experienced on the Braves' staff, although hardly a grizzled veteran.

The year before, he won 16 games, but in three big-league seasons he had put together an undistinguished record of 35-49. In 1912, he picked up 12 of the Braves' 52 victories, but also lost a league-leading 22 games.

Hub Perdue was returning from a 16-victory season and Dick Rudolph from 14 wins in 1913.

One of the young hopefuls on the squad was James, who was 6-10 in his first big-league season in 1913. James's primary pitch was a fastball—he was one of the hardest throwers in baseball—and he had added a spitball, then legal, to his arsenal.

These four were among the top pitchers on the Braves' staff, which included two rookies and a group of veterans with losing records. It was hardly enough to inspire wholehearted confidence from their manager. Stallings told reporters in all candor before the season that he did expect improvement, but certainly not enough to win the pennant.

The Giants, led by the peerless Christy Mathewson, appeared to have the inside track on that, with expected challenges from the St. Louis Cardinals and the Cubs.

In the American League, Connie Mack's Philadelphia Athletics, with their famed "$100,000 infield" and future Hall-of-Famers, were the class of the league.

While Stallings was trying to figure out his pitching rotation and which players to use in the outfield, the world was having bigger issues.

The guns of war were rumbling in Europe, a fight that would soon engulf the rest of the world. At home, America was having problems with Mexican bandit hero Pancho Villa.

There was positive news, too: the opening of the Panama Canal and the establishment of an eight-hour workday at $5 per by the Ford company.

In Boston, sports fans eagerly awaited the beginning of the 1914 baseball season.

The town was divided between fans for the Braves and Red Sox.

The Braves traced their history to 1871 as charter members of the old National Association, and were one of the original teams when the National League opened in 1876. In 1901, Boston welcomed another team in the Red Sox, who were part of the new American League.

The Red Sox quickly rose in popularity, gaining fans with the opening of fashionable Fenway Park that held more than 30,000. The Braves had no such quality ballpark to call their own, only a measly, cramped space called the South End Grounds. They could squeeze 7,500 into their ramshackle little bandbox if they were lucky.

That's about the number of fans that came to witness their home opener on April 23 against the Brooklyn Superbas. By then, the Braves had lost four of their first five games on the road to open the season.

Tyler was in good form on this day. He pitched a complete-game 9-1 victory over the Superbas, avenging an opening-day 8-2 loss in Brooklyn.

Still, it was one of the few bright moments at the start of the season for the Braves. They dropped their next five games and continued to slip to the bottom of the standings. A 4-1 loss at Pittsburgh on May 20 put the last-place Braves' record at an embarrassing 4-18.

"This bunch of mine is the worst-looking club I've ever seen," Stallings said. "They can't do anything right."

He hadn't seen anything yet. The Braves continued to flounder in May and June, playing before dwindling crowds. Boston's pitching and hitting both struggled. No one on the Braves' staff, particularly Tyler, James, or Rudolph, had come forth to set the tone.

Along with Tyler, Rudolph, Perdue, and James, Stallings sprinkled a mixture of other pitchers into his starting rotation, among them Dick Crutcher, Gene Cocreham, and Dolf Luque, with usually the same results.

On July 4, the Braves dropped a doubleheader to Brooklyn and fell 15 games behind the league-leading Giants. With a 40-24 record, New York held a 4½-game lead over Chicago.

It is baseball folklore that a team in first place on the Fourth of July usually wins the pennant. That would have counted the Braves out by a large margin.

The Braves had a day off to think about their predicament. It was July 5 and their 26-40 record stood five games behind Pittsburgh and Philadelphia, who were tied for sixth.

James had done the best work for the Braves in the first half of the season with a 7-6 record through July 4. Rudolph followed with 6-8 and Tyler with 5-8. Together, they compiled 18 of the

Braves' 26 victories. But they also were responsible for 22 of their 40 losses.

Stallings was bouncing off the wall, and his pitching staff was giving him nightmares.

"I have 16 pitchers and they're all rotten," he moaned.

He hadn't hit rock bottom yet. That came when the Braves lost an exhibition game 10-2 to a minor league farm club in Buffalo that Evers had termed a "soap company team."

Waiting on a train platform with his players after the game, Stallings was livid.

"Big-league ballplayers you call yourselves?" he shouted. "Hah . . . you're not even Grade A sandlotters! I'm ashamed of you."

The Braves continued to make trades. Stallings sent away Perdue, a solid pitcher in 1913 but now was just 2-5. Including other deals, coming to Boston were outfielders Possum Whitted, Ted Cather, Josh Devore, and Herb Moran, and third baseman Red Smith.

Stallings loosened the reins, too. He had been riding his team hard all year. Now he decided to try something different.

Deal said the Braves were in the Metropole Hotel in Cincinnati for a series with the Reds when Stallings called his team together for a meeting.

"He told us he didn't want to see one of us in the hotel that night," Deal recalled. "He figured if we went out and tied one on, it would loosen us up. Well, you don't have to tell us twice. Most of us did.

"Many have called that the turning point in our season, and I guess that was."

Whether it was or whether Stallings had struck a deep chord with his acid remarks following the Braves loss to a "soap company team," it was hard to tell. But suddenly the Braves started winning.

"We'd win six and lose one, win seven and lose one," Deal recalled.

For the Braves, good things started to happen in Brooklyn, where they swept a doubleheader from the Superbas on July 6.

Less than two weeks later, the Braves moved out of the cellar when they took a doubleheader from Cincinnati. In the nightcap, the Braves trailed the Reds 2-0 going into the ninth inning before rallying for a dramatic 3-2 victory. The players were so excited about getting out of the basement that they tossed their hats and gloves in the air at the end of the game and mobbed Stallings in a giant love-in.

Stallings was feeling better about things, too.

"Now we'll catch New York," Stallings told his club, now perched in the dizzying heights of seventh place. "We're playing 30 percent better ball than anyone in the league."

Thanks to a tightly knit second division, the Braves moved into sixth place when they beat the Pirates 1-0 on July 20 behind Tyler. Rudolph pitched another shutout the next day, 6-0, as the Braves leaped into fourth.

Braves pitching was starting to assert itself. In a five-game series with Pittsburgh, Boston hurlers pitched four shutouts. Tyler was involved in two of them and Rudolph and James one each.

Hitting was supposed to be the weak part of the club, but you couldn't tell by some of the heroics supplied by Maranville. His home run carried the Braves to a 5-4, 10-inning win over Pittsburgh on August 6, extending their winning streak to nine. On August 8, Rabbit's single drove home the winning run in a 4-3, 10-inning thriller over Cincinnati. On August 10, Maranville had a double and two singles to back the six-hit pitching of James in a 3-1 victory over the Reds.

By the time the torrid Braves stormed into New York in mid-August for a three-game series with McGraw's Giants, they were in third place, six and a half games behind the league leaders.

The Braves had won 11 of their previous 12 decisions. No one expected them to keep up that sizzling pace.

But the Braves were relentless, sweeping three games from New York to climb into second place, three and a half games behind the Giants.

In the final game of the series, Tyler beat Mathewson in a pitching classic. The teams were scoreless until the 10th inning, when Red Smith singled and Gowdy hit his second triple of the game, then came home on a wild pitch for a 2-0 lead. Tyler preserved it by pitching out of a no-out, bases-loaded jam in the bottom of the 10th.

It was a great pleasure for Stallings to sweep a team managed by McGraw, who always seemed to have some devious trick or other up his sleeve.

One day the Braves were at the Polo Grounds when they noticed that the skinned area around the shortstop's spot was soaked and muddy. Stallings complained to McGraw. The Giants manager explained it away by saying that the groundskeeper left the lawn sprinkler on too long.

"There was no doubt it was a move on McGraw's part to slow down Rabbit Maranville, our shortstop, who scampered around like a bantam rooster," James said in a 1964 interview with *Baseball Digest*. "New York's shortstop was Arthur Fletcher. He played deep on the grass anyway, so it didn't hurt him any."

The Braves' late surge had caught the imagination of baseball fans across the country. Most every park they played in was almost like a home game. They were greeted with cheers everywhere, and James said, "That was largely responsible for our success."

Now they had the attention of the Giants, who couldn't help scoreboard watching. By August 23, the Braves had achieved the improbable—they tied the Giants for first place with a record of 59-48. It had taken them only five weeks to leap from last to first place, wiping out the 15-game deficit.

August ended with the Braves involved in a three-way dogfight with the Giants and Cardinals for first place. The Braves were in the battle of their lives, and Evers personified their fighting spirit.

During the Braves' drive, Evers displayed some of his notorious temper when he traded punches with former Cubs teammate Heinie Zimmerman in Chicago. Before umpires could stop the fight, just about every player from both sides was caught up in it.

The Braves lost the game 1-0, but the fight appeared to inspire them to greater heights. They won seven of their next nine to set the stage for a crucial three-game series with the Giants in Boston, starting with a morning-afternoon doubleheader on Labor Day.

By this time, the Braves were playing their home games in Fenway Park. The owner of the Red Sox, Joseph Lannin, allowed the Braves to use his stadium for the remainder of their season and the World Series, if necessary. It was a perfect opportunity for Lannin to showcase his new park and bring in extra revenue.

It was a box office bonanza for Lannin, who joyfully saw a combined total of 76,000 patrons move through the gates into Fenway for the two games. Until much later in the century, when major league teams started to split doubleheaders as a matter of economic efficiency, it was the biggest one-day crowd ever seen at Fenway.

The crowds began gathering several hours early for the first game. Ticket scalpers were on Lansdowne Street charging $5 for $1 grandstand seats and $2.50 for 75-cent general admission seats.

It was a typical Boston crowd, according to the *Boston Post*: "They yelled, they brought various noisemaking implements along with them to show their allegiance to the Braves and they used them with unabated fury."

The crowd had plenty to cheer about, but had to wait until the ninth inning to really celebrate. With the Braves trailing 4-3 going into the bottom of the ninth, ex-Giant John Devore beat out an infield hit. He raced to third when Herb Moran slammed a double into the overflow crowd in right field.

Evers slapped a drive to left that was sinking fast. Giants outfielder George Burns raced in to try a shoestring catch, but missed the ball by inches. It rolled past him and both runners came in to score as Evers pulled up at second with a double, giving the Braves a 5-4 win.

Boston took over first place, but only for the time it took to play the second game. The Giants came back to win the afternoon contest, 10-1, and once more the teams were tied at the top.

The most memorable part of the game was not the Giants' victory, but a near riot involving New York's Fred Snodgrass. It started when Tyler hit Snodgrass with a pitch, and the Giants' outfielder made threatening gestures at the Braves' pitcher. When he was booed by the fans, Snodgrass made an obscene gesture to the crowd. The fans started throwing bottles and garbage at the Giant. The angry fans were ready to storm the field and tear Snodgrass to pieces until order was restored by police.

By the time the inning ended, the Giants had scored four runs and were well on their way to a win.

The next day, Boston came back for an 8-3 victory as James outpitched the great Rube Marquard with a three-hitter.

The Braves were back in first. This time, they were back to stay.

With James, Rudolph, and Tyler showing the way, the Braves continued their tremendous surge. The top three pitchers on the staff weren't the only ones to make a dramatic reversal. The Braves got a boost from Paul Strand, a relief pitcher who was 5-0 in the second half after a 1-2 record before July 4.

Everything was going right for the Braves. They even got some pitching help from a Harvard law student. Hoping to give his starters some rest, Stallings signed George "Iron" Davis from Harvard to make a couple of starts. All Davis did on September 9 was throw a no-hitter against the Philadelphia Phillies, taking the Braves another step toward the NL pennant.

The youthful Davis showed professional poise in completing his classic. After walking the first three batters in the fifth inning, Davis pitched out of trouble with a strikeout and double-play ball.

The victory expanded the Braves' first-place lead to one and a half games. That lead grew to five on September 22 after the Braves finished taking four of five from the Phillies, two of three from Brooklyn, two from St. Louis (along with a 12-inning tie), and three in a row from Pittsburgh.

The remaining possibility for a Braves' collapse lay in the days ahead. Boston had a brutal schedule of four successive doubleheaders, three against Cincinnati and one against Chicago—eight games in four days!

No problem. The Braves simply won six of those, lost one, and tied one.

They clinched the pennant three days later with a 3-2 victory over the Cubs at Fenway Park on September 29.

By the end of the season, the Braves were on top by an amazing 10½ games over the Giants. Just as remarkable, the Braves finished 34½ games ahead of the Reds, who were 6 games ahead of them on July 4 in fourth place.

All the Braves had done was win 68 of 87 games since their low point on July 4, a torrid .782 pace.

The key was the second-half pitching of Boston's "big three." After July 4, James went 19-1, Rudolph 20-2, and Tyler 11-5 for a combined record of 50-8.

"Tyler gave the Braves that third pitcher in the rotation, which helped to make them almost unbeatable from July 6 on to the end of the season," said historian Frank J. Williams of the Society of American Baseball Research (SABR).

Stallings had been wrong about his "rotten" pitchers. The Braves' staff recorded 18 of its 19 shutouts in an incredible second-half burst, including six by Rudolph, five by Tyler, and four by James.

Stallings had also been wrong in underestimating his team at the start of the season, when he told reporters he didn't expect the Braves to win the pennant. They did more than that, winning the World Series with a shocking four-game sweep of the mighty Athletics as James and Rudolph each won two games.

Miracle men, indeed.

15

TROJAN HORSES
Southern Cal over Notre Dame, 1974

As Southern Cal running back Anthony Davis walked out of the locker room after a victory over Notre Dame in 1974, he was approached by a woman with a crucifix on a chain. She started swinging the crucifix in Davis's face.

"Nobody's ever done that to Notre Dame," the woman said. "A.D., you've got to be the devil!"

The woman, and many other Notre Dame fans, had good reason to think they needed a higher power to bring Davis to his knees. During his football career at Southern Cal from 1972 to 1974, his performances against the Irish were downright ungodly as far as Notre Dame was concerned.

In three games against the Irish, Davis personally accounted for 11 touchdowns and 68 points.

One of those TDs sparked a momentum swing that would be hard to top. That it happened in a Southern Cal–Notre Dame game when the archrivals were in the running for the national championship made it even more spectacular.

Notre Dame, of course, wasn't the only team Davis victimized, as he set a career rushing record at USC. No small feat, considering that the Trojans had been turning out great running backs for years, including Heisman Trophy winners O. J. Simpson and Mike Garrett and, before them, Frank Gifford and Jon Arnett.

From the Thundering Herd of Howard Jones's day, the tailback position had always been the glamour position at USC.

Davis, a quarterback in high school, came to Southern Cal out of a tough neighborhood in San Fernando, California. Before running for touchdowns, he was running with hoodlums and bore the scar of a knife wound on his right elbow as a reminder of his youthful misadventures.

As a sophomore at Southern Cal, Davis didn't become a starter until after midseason, yet still managed to score 19 touchdowns—including an unfathomable 6 against Notre Dame.

"A lot of USC people were upset I didn't get much chance early in the year," Davis said. "I just waited and when I got the shot, I produced, but I had no idea I'd do that well against Notre Dame. That one game made me famous."

Davis played with a great deal of expression, doing a "knee dance" in the end zone after every TD. J. K. McKay, the coach's son, called him a "Hot Dog," and Davis agreed wholeheartedly.

"Yes," Davis said with a wink and a smile, "but I'm a damn good hot dog."

From the moment he started playing football at Southern Cal in 1972, Davis was never short of confidence. In the Notre Dame game that year, Trojans coach John McKay looked concerned at one point when the Irish drew close.

Davis told McKay not to worry, then went out and returned a kickoff for a touchdown—one of two that day against the Irish. It was a remarkable performance for the 5-foot-9, 185-pound Davis, even more so when you consider that an Ara Parseghian team had never given up a touchdown on a kickoff return in 11 seasons.

Southern Cal won, 45-23, as Davis scored those six TDs. It was the first time in the Fighting Irish's legendary history that a player had scored more than four TDs against them.

With the victory, the Trojans continued on the road to the national championship.

Davis kept his feet on the ground despite a fine sophomore season in which he totaled 1,191 yards rushing. He drove a used car around campus, proudly pointing out he bought it with money earned from a summer job working in a museum.

He also was a cadet and recruiter for the Air Force ROTC.

As a player, it was apparent Davis's gang associations as a youth influenced his irrepressible manner. "My style is to scratch and claw for every yard," he said. "I get like a psycho on the field. I think of something that may have happened to me on the street somewhere and I make up my mind it's going to be me handing out the punishment."

Davis did just that in the Rose Bowl, rushing for 157 yards as the Trojans whipped Ohio State 42-17 to finish 12-0.

It was only a couple of weeks after that game that Davis faced a challenge tougher than anything he ever met on a football field. Davis was driving home one early January morning after a party when he smashed his 1969 Triumph sports car into a light pole. The California Highway Patrol said Davis had fallen asleep at the wheel.

Davis's car was totaled, but he got out alive. There wasn't much he remembered about the accident until he woke up a hospital bed, both legs in a cast. Doctors told him he severed part of his left Achilles tendon, among other things, but they expected him to make a full recovery. At the time Davis wasn't so sure.

"All I could think was, 'God, look at those legs. They've brought me this far and made all these things happen, and now it's over. I'm never going to come back.' I thought that all the work I had done would be wasted."

It wasn't. Just a month later, Davis was starting to run with his old flair. By then he was rehabilitating and working hard toward a successful recovery. Now he was thinking more positively.

"The soreness is OK as long as I can run," he said. "There's no way they're going to get me out of first-string tailback."

Or off the baseball team, another sport that Davis loved and played well. A couple of months after taking off a big cast, Davis was playing the outfield for the Southern Cal baseball team.

Davis returned to football for the 1973 season, gaining 96 yards in a 17-0 victory over Arkansas in the opener. Not spectacular, but not bad. He then had 71 yards in a 23-6 triumph over Georgia Tech. Again, not exactly superstar performances. Critics thought perhaps the auto accident had slowed him.

"The accident hasn't cost me any of my speed," he insisted.

His low yardage totals persisted, however. One national magazine called him a "comparative bust" compared to his sophomore year.

What A.D. needed was a TD explosion.

So he scored five touchdowns against California. Then he helped Southern Cal win the rest of its regular-season games, including a beating of crosstown rival UCLA to earn a Rose Bowl bid.

Despite his slow start, Davis did manage to rush for more than 1,000 yards and score 13 touchdowns. Not bad for a "comparative bust."

In 1974, Southern Cal was one of the preseason favorites to win the national championship. The Trojans had a largely veteran team returning and a pair of great running backs in Davis and Ricky Bell. Quarterback Pat Haden knew the Trojans' offense would revolve around the running game.

"I'm just a handoff artist and (receiver J. K.) McKay is a blocker now," Haden said, referring to the coach's son.

But the offense failed in a 22-7 loss to Arkansas on opening day; the only Southern Cal score came on a 106-yard kickoff runback by Davis.

"Life is too short to kick to Anthony Davis," said Arkansas coach Frank Broyles.

Things picked up after that for the Trojans, with Davis and Bell gouging out great chunks of yardage. The Trojans won five straight games before a tie with California, then three more prior to the game with Notre Dame.

With its rich history, the Notre Dame–Southern Cal game has always been a compelling event. Since it began in 1926 with a 13-12 Notre Dame victory, the games have usually been tightly contested and meaningful on the national stage.

One of the early classics came in 1931, when Southern Cal rallied from a 14-0 deficit in the final quarter to win 16-14 on Johnny Baker's field goal with a minute left. The loss spoiled a 26-game unbeaten streak for Notre Dame and cost the Irish the national championship.

When the Trojans stepped off the train in Los Angeles, wearing bowler hats courtesy of a Chicago haberdashery, they were greeted by a crowd estimated by officials at 300,000. The players then rode through the city in one of the biggest parades ever seen in Los Angeles.

"People had torn up telephone books, and they were throwing all this paper out of windows," Ernie Smith, one of the Southern

Cal players, once recalled. "It was a real thrill. It was unbeliev-able."

With Notre Dame's Knute Rockne and Southern Cal's Howard Jones, the game featured two of football's early coaching giants, starting a trend of big-name coaching rivals in the series.

Such was the case when Notre Dame, coached by Parseghian, and Southern Cal, led by McKay, met in the 1974 game.

After replacing Don Clark in 1960, McKay struggled for two seasons before turning Southern Cal into one of the nation's most potent teams. Before the '74 game with Notre Dame, the Trojans had won three national championships, played in seven Rose Bowls, and perennially finished in the top 10.

Players have called McKay cool and aloof, but they couldn't fault his sense of humor. King of the one-liners, McKay always had a ready quip, win or lose.

Once when a Southern Cal player slipped and fell on wet grass at Notre Dame Stadium while returning a kickoff, McKay responded in mock alarm: "Oh, my God, they've shot him!"

McKay in top form:

"If you have everyone back from a team that lost 10 games, experience isn't too important."

"The American youth loves competition, but not at his position."

And, noting that opening games made him nervous, McKay quipped: "I'd rather open with a second game."

McKay played at Purdue and Oregon in the 1940s before joining the Oregon coaching staff in charge of offensive and defensive backs. His coaching role model was Rockne. When asked about Southern Cal's innovative backfield shift, McKay said, "I picked it up from a book written by Rockne in 1927."

Early in his career at Southern Cal, McKay never failed to reference the Old Master when he could, even in a lighthearted manner. Following a 14-3 victory over UCLA in 1962, he said, "I thought about giving the boys a halftime pep talk, but I couldn't find any old Rockne records."

Parseghian seemed to have the magic Rockne touch as well, with his passionate locker room talks and mind games.

Coaching at Miami of Ohio in 1954, Parseghian was preparing his team to play Big Ten foe Indiana. The day before the game, Parseghian brought along a set of ragged hand-me-down practice jerseys that appeared to be rejects from Rockne's era. The Miami players, looking much the worse for wear, went through their final practice looking like ragamuffins on Indiana's field under the haughty stares of the Hoosiers players.

On game day, Miami turned up full of polish and purpose wearing bright-looking, sharp uniforms. Miami looked like a different team. The Hoosiers had been lulled into overconfidence by Parseghian's trick. The result: a 6-0 upset victory by Miami. It was something right out of Rockne's book.

Parseghian was a hard-nosed halfback who played for the University of Akron and then Miami of Ohio after returning from two years of navy war service. He had a short stint with the Cleveland Browns, where he developed a reputation for his toughness.

His pro career was cut short by an injury, and Parseghian signed on as an assistant to Woody Hayes at Miami. When Hayes left for Ohio State one year later, Parseghian became Miami's head coach at the remarkably young age of 27. He had great success there and later turned around Northwestern's program before coming to Notre Dame and doing the same at South Bend.

In 1963, Notre Dame had a 2-7 record under Hugh Devore. In Parseghian's first year with the Irish, the team went 9-1 with essentially the same players.

Parseghian made his intentions known right away that he came to Notre Dame to win a national championship. He fulfilled the promise in two years, sharing the title with Michigan State following a controversial 10-10 tie with the Spartans in 1966.

In 1973, he was all alone at the top with his second national championship in eight years.

Part of his success was built on a wide-open passing game modeled after the professionals, a creative offense that never looked the same from one year to the next.

Notre Dame's defense improved as well, with Parseghian continually challenging his players. He put up a chart in the locker room showing the points scored by the Irish's opponents year by year since 1946, when Notre Dame was coached by Frank Leahy. The 1946 total of 24 was circled in red, with a note next to it that said, "Can you match this?"

Going into the 1974 game with Southern Cal, the proud Irish defense was ranked No. 1 in the country. It had allowed only nine touchdowns in 10 previous games.

For a while that day in the L.A. Coliseum, it didn't look like it was going to be any different for Notre Dame.

Linebacker Drew Mahalic intercepted a pass by Haden, leading to Notre Dame's first touchdown, a 2-yard run by Wayne Bullock. Then Mahalic stopped a quarterback sneak by Haden to give the Irish good field position on the Trojans' 30, leading to a TD pass from Tom Clements to Pete Demmerle.

"That was my fault," McKay said after the Trojans failed to move the ball less than a yard on fourth down. "After the play was called, they went into their goal-line defense. We tried to get Haden's attention to call a timeout so we could change the play, but we didn't."

The Irish added a field goal and touchdown on two long drives in the second quarter to take a 24-0 lead with less than a minute left in the half.

"During the first half, Notre Dame appeared to be invincible," wrote A. S. Doc Young in the *Chicago Defender*. "USC seemed to be a prize patsy."

Davis gave the Trojans, and the crowd of 83,577, some life with a touchdown catch on a 7-yard swing pass from Haden with 10 seconds left in the half. The Trojans missed the extra point and went into the dressing room trailing 24-6, still a long way from catching up with the Irish.

But Davis made up ground in a hurry at the start of the second half.

Davis, who had returned a kickoff for a touchdown twice in one game against Notre Dame in 1972, did it again. He took the ball in the end zone and raced 102 yards in 14 seconds to give Southern Cal a dynamic boost to start the second half.

"Kicking the football to Anthony Davis is a little like going over Niagara Falls in a barrel," Roy Damer wrote in the *Chicago Tribune*. "It may be exciting. It certainly is dangerous."

Even before the kickoff return for a touchdown, the sixth of his career to break an NCAA record, Davis was confident of his team's chances.

"I told my teammates in the huddle just before the second-half kickoff that if we all do our part, each guy does what he's supposed to do, we can win this game," Davis said.

He certainly did his part. After his long kickoff return brought the roaring Coliseum crowd to its feet, he scored on a 6-yard pitchout only 3:25 into the third period. The Trojans only had to go 38 yards for the TD after pinning Notre Dame deep in its territory.

Following a Notre Dame fumble, Davis scored again on a short run with only 6:23 gone in the third quarter to give Southern Cal its first lead of the game, 25-24. Davis then raced around right end on a 2-point conversion to boost the lead to 27-24.

The Coliseum crowd was hopping. But there was still more to come for Southern Cal. Much more.

Haden threw a pair of touchdown passes to J. K. McKay to complete a 35-point third quarter for Southern Cal.

"They were playing man-to-man pass defense and covering our motion very well," coach McKay said, "but we thought Johnny could beat his man one-on-one."

In the fourth quarter, Haden completed his fourth touchdown pass of the day, a 16-yarder to Shelton Diggs. Defensive back Charles Phillips completed the scoring with a 58-yard interception return.

Final: Southern Cal 55, Notre Dame 24.

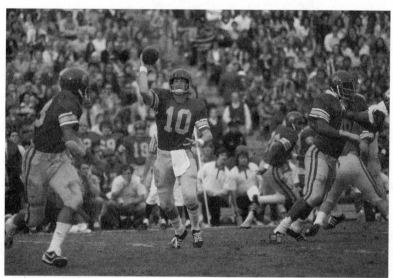

© *Sports Illustrated.*

Quarterback Pat Haden led USC to its improbable comeback against Notre Dame in 1974. Photo by George Long.

The Trojans had scored 55 points in less than 17 minutes! Talk about a Southern California tidal wave.

"They had good field position almost all the second half and they didn't have to drive very far for their touchdowns," Parseghian said. "We had a lot of errors, a lot of fumbles, a lot of interceptions—but the kickoff was the main turning point."

Parseghian, of course, was referring to Davis's kickoff return for a TD to start the second half. Everyone agreed it changed the momentum in the biggest turnaround of the rivalry's history.

The way Davis tormented the Irish, it was easy to see why Notre Dame fans might consider A.D. the very devil himself.

16

MANUELITO'S MAGIC

Manuel Orantes, 1975

In an era dominated by the stoic (Björn Borg) and the stubborn (Jimmy Connors), one man carried himself, on and off the tennis court, with a majestic grace.

Manuel Orantes didn't throw tantrums or belittle volunteers. He rarely questioned a line judge's call or took umbrage with the decision from the match umpire's chair. He didn't collect huge appearance fees and then tank the exhibition match—or worse, not show up at all.

Orantes was known to applaud good shots by opponents and purposely hit balls into the net or wide when he felt a call wrongfully went in his favor.

In fact, in a U.S. Open quarterfinal against Romanian bad boy Ilie Nastase, Orantes forfeited set point in the third set because he believed a shot by Nastase was incorrectly called out.

"My business is to play tennis," Orantes said. "It is not to argue points. I dislike having arguments."

The Spaniard smiled on the court. A lot. He was so classy that his opponents rarely found anything they could seize as a motivator. Orantes was that rare non-American tennis player in the 1970s who actually was popular in the United States.

"He was just a pleasant guy," said Australian star John New-combe.

Orantes was a clay-court specialist who did his most damage on the slow red surfaces of Europe. A native of Barcelona, he won his local tournament three times and made the final there on four other occasions.

The son of an optician, Orantes grew up in the midst of a tennis boom in Spain. Manolo Santana, considered the greatest Spanish player ever, won the 1965 U.S. Open and followed with a Wimbledon championship the next year. He was the first from his country to capture majors, and tennis quickly went from a game of the privileged to a mainstream sport in Spain.

It remains so today, and while Santana is the godfather of the game in Spain, "Manuelito" Orantes holds a cherished place, too.

He also holds a meaningful spot in the lore of the sport because, in the semifinals of the 1975 U.S. Open at Forest Hills, New York, Orantes staged the greatest comeback in tennis history.

The U.S. Tennis Association had switched the event from grass to a synthetic clay (Har-Tru) for the '75 tournament. Not only had the grass become too hard to manage and keep in prime condition for the late August/early September Open, but the tourney was outgrowing the West Side Tennis Club.

Besides, few Americans got the opportunity to play on grass, with hardcourts becoming the fashion throughout the United States. But until the U.S. Tennis Center could be built a few miles away in Flushing Meadows, the Open remained at WSTC—on clay.

Orantes came to the '75 Open hopeful but hardly confident of winning his first Grand Slam title. Indeed, the previous year he made his debut in a major tournament final and fell in five sets at the French Open—on his beloved clay—to the great Borg, who was just 18 years old. Orantes admitted he "choked" in that match after building a two-set lead. Borg, who rarely showed emotion in a match, raised his level of play significantly and blitzed the Spaniard 6-0, 6-1, 6-1 in the final three sets.

Not a bad comeback for the Swede. But nothing like what Orantes would pull off in late summer of '75.

Orantes was an unlikely candidate to do something, anything, on grass. And even when the U.S. Open switched to clay, he seemed an outsider because he was having back woes. In fact, Orantes had stopped playing the tour several months earlier to treat an ailing back.

"I went to the doctors for Barca," he explained, citing the Barcelona soccer powerhouse, "and they helped me with treatments and exercises. I don't know if I could have continued (playing) at such a level without that.

"When I no longer had to worry about my back, it made my game so much stronger."

Orantes also came to Forest Hills off some impressive showings on the summer circuit, including a victory in the U.S. Clay Courts Championships in Indianapolis in mid-August. He beat the popular Arthur Ashe in that match, and the crowd's favor was split between the two, a testament to Orantes's demeanor.

Then he won the Canadian Open in Toronto, although it was an unfulfilling victory because Nastase tanked the final two sets after getting what he perceived a bad call in the first-set tiebreaker.

"I feel badly for the crowd, very sad," Orantes said. "They paid a lot of money to watch a final between two world-class players and to be entertained. They were not entertained by the last two (sets). They were robbed."

Still, to consider him a favorite at the Open was ludicrous. Not with Borg, Connors, Vilas, Tom Okker, and Nastase around. Not with American stars Ashe and Stan Smith in contention.

Sure, he was seeded third, but the two men ahead of him, No. 1 Connors and Vilas, often had proved too formidable for Orantes.

Vilas, in particular, would be problematical for the 26-year-old Orantes. The Argentine also was a clay-court master, and he could run all day to rescue shots.

Certainly Vilas, a loser to Borg in the '75 French Open final, and Orantes were among the players who liked the temporary switch from grass to clay. Neither stood a chance of winning on the green stuff. On Har-Tru, who knew?

These clay surfaces were not like those in Europe or South America, however. And that was intentional, as tournament chairman Bill Talbert explained.

"We think we've come up with a combination of court and ball that favors the all-around player who can both attack and defend, who has all the shots," he said. "Defense will play more of a role than on grass because the ball won't hit and take off as it does on a fast court. But you can still put shots away on this court."

Orantes beat Bernie Mitton of South Africa in straight sets to open his schedule. A win over Frenchman Francois Jauffret got him a spot in the quarterfinals against Nastase.

When asked about facing the man who ruined their recent match in Toronto, Orantes shrugged.

"I think he will be a tougher opponent this time, he will play harder," Orantes said.

Most opponents were careful not to rile up Nastase with bulletin-board material. For "Nasty," however, Orantes was the worst kind of opponent because the Spaniard not only would say nothing inflammatory, he would do nothing inflammatory. No matter how hard Nastase tried to unnerve Orantes, it didn't work.

And that, in turn, helped destroy Nastase's performance against the cool, calm left-hander who eschewed a power game for finesse shots and court management.

Nastase, like Orantes, had all the shots, especially on clay. But he didn't have the temperament it took to win an Open on Har-Tru.

Orantes won the first two sets, then received more applause for surrendering that set point in the third than Nastase could dream of getting for winning it outright. And in the fourth set, Orantes was serving for the match when a shot by Nastase was ruled out by the line judge. He was overruled by the chair umpire, but Orantes then questioned that decision.

And any time the Spaniard wondered about a ruling, it was pretty certain he was correct.

Tournament referee Mike Blanchard was summoned and, after asking several linesmen if they were certain the ball was out, he ruled for Orantes.

"I thought the ball was out. I am sure it was out," Orantes said.

When he finished off the 6-2, 6-4, 3-6, 6-3 victory, Orantes, like the fans in Toronto when he last met Nastase, was the one being robbed. The crowd lustily booed as Nastase menacingly gestured toward a linesman with his racket. What should have been a triumphant exit from the court for the Spaniard was ruined by the tempestuous Nastase.

Regardless, Orantes was among the Big Four with defending champ Connors, Borg, and Vilas in the semifinals. His opponent would be Vilas, his former doubles partner, after Connors and Borg renewed their rivalry on center court.

With so much attention centered on Jimbo and the "Iceman," it seemed impossible that anything Orantes and Vilas did could steal the headlines. Even after Connors dismantled Borg's patient baseline game and dynamic serve in a 7-5, 7-5, 7-5 win—not exactly a classic—the second semifinal seemed an afterthought.

Except, perhaps, to the boisterous Latin contingent on hand.

The Hispanic fans had flocked to the tennis club to watch Orantes and other Latin players such as Juan Gisbert of Spain and, of course, Vilas. When Orantes would win a key point or game, those fans would shout, "*Olé, olé, olé, Orantes, olé.*"

Orantes would just smile some more.

Of course, in Vilas, he was up against a matinee idol who also appealed to the same fans.

Neither player was overconfident heading into the match, perhaps because both knew how formidable Connors, the 1974 champion, figured to be in the final.

"I think anyone can beat me and I can beat anybody," Vilas said. "It's just a question of how I'm playing that day."

Vilas was playing sensationally that evening; the match didn't begin until almost 7 p.m. His court coverage was impeccable, his groundstrokes firm and filled with spin, his volleys well-placed for the kill.

Orantes wasn't doing badly, either, in the first set, but Vilas often had him off-balance in taking the set 6-4.

"I did not feel I was playing badly, but he won the key points," Orantes said. "I was still much in the match, though."

Not so much in the match after the next set, however. Vilas blitzed Orantes 6-1 with an assortment of powerful passing shots, deft touch volleys and slices, and lots of athleticism.

Indeed, Vilas won the last three games of that set and the first two in the third set.

By then, most of the crowd of 15,720 that had paid its way into the stadium to see Connors-Borg was headed home, confident that the final the next day would match a pair of star left-handers in Jimbo and Guillermo.

"I had two sets, I had a 2-0 lead in the third, and I was perhaps thinking ahead a bit," admitted Vilas, who'd won 33 of his previous 35 matches heading into the Open semifinal. "It is a dangerous thing to do against any opponent."

Then again, Orantes's reputation of falling apart in his biggest matches was being fortified by his performance. Had he gone away quietly, no one in the tennis world would have been shocked.

Instead, Orantes put together a shocking run. He won six consecutive games to take the third set. Helped by unforced errors and impatience by Vilas, the Spaniard was back in the match.

"It felt very good to pull it together," Orantes admitted. "But I also knew I trailed two sets to one."

And, very soon, he trailed 0-5 in the fourth. Vilas had awakened with a vengeance, again hitting the lines with regularity, serving precisely, and seizing the momentum. It surely was over for Orantes.

Three times at 0-5 on his serve, Orantes saved match points, twice with dangerous overheads and the third with a brilliant forehand volley. At this juncture, he was going for winners on nearly every shot because Vilas had taken such command of play.

After finally holding serve, Orantes fell down 40-15 in the next game. Vilas now had two serves to move into the Open final.

"The only thing to do is keep going, keep trying," Orantes said. "I wasn't going to give him the last point; he would have to win it."

Vilas couldn't. Orantes saved both match points, and when he passed Vilas with a stinging backhander, the Argentine just stared at the ball as it flew past.

Orantes broke serve, then held. Suddenly, Vilas was making mistakes and looking tired. Orantes seemed refreshed, and he kept running off points. And games.

And then the fourth set belonged to the Spaniard, and the 2,000 or so fans still on hand were standing, cheering and clapping and serenading Orantes ("*Olé, olé, olé,*" of course).

By now, both players should have been exhausted, not exhilarated. But the adrenaline was pumping and each found the extra reserves to seize whatever strength remained.

Orantes broke, Vilas broke back. They reached 4-4 in the fifth—a place Orantes could only have dreamed about one hour earlier.

Vilas served the ninth game and was victimized by what had become Orantes's best weapon in the late stages of his epic comeback: the lob. A series of successful lobs throughout the last two sets allowed Orantes to create some uncertainty in Vilas's mind and strategy. If, indeed, there was any strategy left for the young South American.

On break point, Orantes uncurled yet another lob that Vilas chased and reached. He had no shot, though, and his return didn't reach the net.

Up 5-4, Orantes sat during the break and pondered what had happened.

"You don't give up, but you don't imagine you will be in this position, either," he said. "You are tired, but you also are excited. And you know one more game could be enough to win the match."

It was. Orantes even threw in an ace before Vilas hit a weak return into the net on match point.

If Orantes wanted to jump up and celebrate, he didn't. Worn out? Perhaps. And, after all, this was just the semifinals.

He and Vilas embraced at the net as the crowd roared its approval of a wonderful match and a wondrous comeback.

The 3-hour, 45-minute match ended so late that many East Coast newspapers didn't have a story about it. Who knows how many fans woke up Sunday morning expecting to read previews of Connors-Vilas for the Open crown?

Connors himself figured the Argentine would be on the other side of the net that afternoon.

But at 11 a.m., a mere 12 hours after leaving the court following his heroic rally, Orantes was back at the WSTC, warming up and compiling a game plan to deal with the No. 1 player.

"I went for dinner after the match with Guillermo and I don't think it was before 2 (a.m.) that I was back at the hotel," Orantes said. "I tried to have a bath, but there was a problem with the water. It wouldn't stop running and we needed to call the plumber.

"So it was 3 or later when I got to bed."

And when he arrived at Forest Hills, with about six hours of sleep?

"When I got on the court, I felt fine," he said, shrugging. "I was very excited to be playing in the U.S. Open final."

Connors was fired up, as well. Perhaps too much so.

One problem for the 23-year-old American was his tendency to stick with the power game. He would cure that habit soon, in great part because of the Open final against Orantes.

From the outset, the crowd was as much in Orantes's corner

as in Connors's. What it got was a lesson of tennis subtlety and mastery from Manuelito.

Connors was the student.

"Jimmy likes to hit the ball hard," Orantes told the Associated Press. "If I give him topspin, he will kill me. So I give him soft shots.

"I gave him spins, drop shots, and lobs. I mixed it up. He likes pace, so I don't give him any pace. I know he is not consistent that way."

After Connors blitzed Orantes early, winning the first two games, it appeared the rout was on. But as Vilas learned hours before, this Spaniard wasn't going to be pushed aside by anyone.

Orantes held and broke, held and broke again for a 4-2 lead. Connors took the next two games and Orantes admitted "the next game was very crucial." So Orantes once more held serve, then broke through on Connors for the set, 6-4.

Set point was won on a perfect passing shot down the line as Connors rushed the net. It was a scenario that would be repeated for two more sets.

"I didn't think any man alive could beat me that way," Connors said. "I didn't think I'd ever wave at passing shots so often. He played unbelievable. He hit passing shots throughout the match, from beginning to end, unfortunately for me."

Orantes kept at it with changes of speed, never allowing Jimbo to get into a rhythm. Connors's knack for taking the ball early and blasting returns wherever he wanted was stymied by Orantes's "junk." The lob that helped dismiss Vilas also destroyed Connors.

But not without a fight. The gritty Connors rallied from 0-2 in the third set by taking three straight games. Was he about to assume control of the match? Was Orantes running out of gas? Would Forest Hills witness a second incredible comeback in two days?

"I hoped so," Connors said. "Unfortunately, it was temporary. He got right back into it."

So much so that Orantes won the next four games for his first—and only—major championship.

Appropriately, he passed Connors for the clinching point. Then Manuelito fell to his knees, looking skyward, as the crowd saluted the man who never gave up.

"Now," he said with that ever-present smile, "no one can say I always lose the big ones."

17

CAN'T KEEP THE BLUE DEVILS DOWN

2000–2001 Duke Blue Devils

Super Saturday, the day before the Super Bowl. A perfect time to schedule the renewal of a college basketball classic rivalry: Duke at Maryland.

For more than a decade heading into the 2000–2001 schedule, Duke was the power of the Atlantic Coast Conference. It had won national titles in 1991 and '92 and been to the final game three other times since 1990. Under coach Mike Krzyzewski, the Blue Devils had replaced UCLA as the most prominent program in the sport.

Maryland, for its part, was a perennial contender for the ACC crown and a consistent presence in the NCAA tournament known as March Madness. It simply didn't go very far once it got into the tourney.

In 2001, Maryland would provide Duke with its greatest challenges—and force the Dookies to make two of the most remarkable comebacks in the program's history. Indeed, in college basketball history.

"When we played Maryland, it was always a battle, always a real emotional game," said Duke star Shane Battier. "The records didn't matter a whole lot; neither team wanted to give an inch."

Duke entered the first of three meetings with Maryland in a span of two months with an 18-1 record, 6-0 in the conference, and a No. 2 ranking behind undefeated Stanford, which had beaten the Blue Devils by a point earlier in the season. Maryland was ranked 8th and was 14-4.

The game at Cole Field House, one of the most venerable college sports arenas in America, was something of a grudge match for the Terrapins, who were tired of being the Blue Devils' whipping boys. Duke had won 52 of its previous 54 ACC regular-season games, including 3 straight at Maryland and 22 in a row on the road. It was 92-52 all-time vs. Maryland, 33-13 under Krzyzewski.

With the best 3-point shooting team in the land, Duke had all five starters scoring in double figures.

"It's an accomplishment, but we're not your average team," point guard Jason Williams said. "We have exceptionally great players. We're all able to knock down the 3 if you leave us open. We just take our shots and that's why we always knock them down."

So Duke was averaging 93.7 points per game, second in the nation.

"We have the ability on this team to hit a lot of killer shots," Battier noted.

The Terrapins weren't slouches, though, with victories in 13 of their last 14 games and, at 5-1 in the ACC, off to their best start in conference play under coach Gary Williams. The winner would own sole possession of the ACC lead.

Plus, to beat Duke on a weekend when the rest of the nation was gearing up for the Super Bowl meant plenty to the Terrapins. Not only would this game draw more attention nationally than most ACC regular-season contests, it could establish Maryland as a true conference title challenger to the Blue Devils, and perhaps a Final Four contender.

"If you can beat a team like Duke, it sort of puts you on the map in college basketball," said Maryland star guard Juan Dixon.

Dixon and his teammates were looking like anything but a dot on the map at halftime. The game was tied at 26 before Maryland scored 11 straight points, with Dixon's 3-pointer capping the run. The Terps soon got the lead up to 15, the most Duke trailed by all season, by holding the Blue Devils without a basket for more than seven minutes.

In the final 1.4 seconds of the first half, Williams took a long pass from Mike Dunleavy and scored for Duke, making it 46-37 at halftime. It was an ominous sign of what would happen in just a little while.

Still, the Terrapins were solidly in charge at the break. Their fans, many wearing shirts with obscene Duke references, were chanting "*overrated, overrated*," and a lot less printable stuff at the Dookies.

While it was only the second time this experienced Duke squad trailed at halftime, the players knew the deficit could have been much bigger.

"We were pretty sure that if we played our game, we could win. We sure weren't feeling out of it at that point," Williams said.

Perhaps they got more of a sinking feeling when the chasm grew to 13 points with only five minutes remaining. The building was shaking as the home team's confidence—and shotmaking—surged.

Maryland coach Williams, his suit soaked with sweat as he worked the sideline and the refs nonstop, was within grasp of, perhaps, a program-defining victory that could catapult the Terps into the national basketball consciousness. And, maybe, create some doubt in the minds of Blue Devils players and the coaching staff about which was the better squad.

"Sometimes you think a game like that is over because of the way the teams are playing," said Jim O'Connell, a Basketball Hall of Fame member who covered all three Maryland-Duke encounters that year. "Then you think: 'Nah, this is Duke.'"

And Duke doesn't die easily. Or, many times, at all.

At 90-80 with one minute left, Coach K could have sent in the reserves. Instead, his team sent a message.

"We had a team huddle with 54 seconds left and we could hear the Maryland fans chanting that '*overrated*,'" Jason Williams said. "We said we are not overrated, we are the Duke team we think we are and we made one of those runs."

Williams, a sophomore guard who would lose out to Battier for national player of the year honors that season—he won it the following season—had been averaging nearly 24 points per game over the past two months. He found some of that magic touch to score 8 points in 13 seconds. Yes, 8 in 13!

Included were a pair of long bombs that got Duke within 90-88.

"You could sense there was some panic in the crowd, and I think maybe with (the Maryland players) too," Duke's Williams said. "They were pretty nervous."

But the Terps still had the lead with 41 seconds remaining. And they had the ball.

Coach Williams implored them to protect the ball, work for a good shot, make the Blue Devils work hard defensively, and steal back the momentum. Instead, Maryland turned over the ball just six seconds later.

While Dunleavy failed on a 3-pointer that would have given Duke a 1-point lead, teammate Nate James took in the offensive rebound and was fouled.

"Everyone in that building knew Nate was going to knock down those two (free throws)," Battier said. "We were already planning our defense for their last possession."

James did, indeed, can the two foul shots to tie it. The crowd had gone from hysterical to hushed.

But the Terrapins did have that last possession, one more chance to win in regulation. Duke might have staged an incredible rally, but the scoreboard read: 90-90.

Maryland set up a shot for Drew Nicholas, but his 3-pointer from the corner failed, and the buzzer—sounding more like a death knell to the Terrapins—sounded.

Overtime.

"I'm not sure anyone in Cole really thought Maryland could win after that," O'Connell recalled.

Certainly the Dookies did not think the Terps had a chance. Battier's 3-pointer put them ahead for good with 3:52 remaining in overtime. Up by a point with 1:44 to go, Duke held possession with offensive rebounds for the next 1:18 despite missing five straight shots.

Battier finished the scoring with a foul shot with 16 seconds left, then blocked Dixon's shot to clinch the stunning comeback 98-96 win.

"I knew he was going to take the last shot and I knew he was going to try and get fouled," Battier said. "I didn't even really have to move and then swatted it away."

Simple as that. Although hardly a simple win.

"I'm speechless right now," Battier said. "The fortitude of this team is unbelievable."

"I'm still in awe and will be all night," Jason Williams added. "It was one of those games where everything was going Maryland's way."

Then again, this is Duke-Maryland, where things tend to go the Blue Devils' way when it counts. While Duke plays with a cool demeanor and steps up the defensive intensity, the Terrapins tend to get tight, uncertain.

"We got tentative out there," Gary Williams said. "It's very disappointing, but as I said before the game, I've been here before. You can't let this take away from your next nine ACC games."

Something did take away from the aura of this classic: outrageous behavior by the fans.

The mothers of Carlos Boozer, Jason Williams, and Chris Duhon were hit by debris, including coins, water bottles, ice and plastic cups, thrown at the Duke bench.

"The worst thing you can do is throw objects," said Krzyzewski, who stopped taking his family to games at Cole Field House years earlier because of the treatment from fans.

Maryland athletic director Debbie Yow saw videotape evidence of nearly 100 students throwing debris toward Duke players for about a minute.

"It was an embarrassment to all who value civility and love this great institution. This behavior cannot and will not be tolerated," she said, noting that ice and batteries had been wrapped in some tossed newspapers.

"I don't understand why our fans think they can throw anything on the court, when it's not done anywhere else in the country," Gary Williams added. "We've worked too hard to bring this basketball program up from an embarrassing situation. I don't need idiots throwing stuff on the court, to take something away from what we've tried to do here."

Instead of "idiots," the Terps faced the Cameron Crazies in their next matchup with Duke a month later at Durham, North Carolina. It was Senior Day at the Blue Devils' home—and the Terps ruined it with a 91-80 victory.

No blowing any big leads this time; that would have to wait until March, and a double dose of humble pie.

The win at Duke, still ranked second in the nation, was built on Dixon's superb end-to-end play, something he would refine throughout his stellar career in College Park. It was, perhaps, Dixon's finest moment of the 2000–2001 season as he scored 28 points and had five steals for his 16th-ranked team.

"Dixon was literally sensational," Krzyzewski said, noting that the star guard had 31 points the previous year in Maryland's win at Cameron. "He kept us off-balance all game, and he made the big plays for them."

Many of those big plays came in a second half when both Jason Williams (calf injury) and Boozer (broken foot) were sidelined. Maybe that was a factor in the Terps closing out a victory over Duke so soon after such a painful choke at home on Super Saturday led to Maryland losing four of five games before making a turnaround.

"I can't say enough about our character," coach Williams said after silencing the Crazies in the Terps' fourth successive win. "To go through what we did in College Park, to lose a game like we did and then come down here and get the win, that's really big.

"We've worked a lot on our confidence as a team. We never quit, which this stretch shows. We could have quit with what happened last time against Duke, but we didn't. I have good seniors."

Duke actually was the team falling apart in this matchup, missing 25 of its first 31 second-half shots and blowing a 9-point lead. But Dixon preferred to look at what his squad had done to cause all of that.

"I said we were back on track a couple of games ago," said Dixon, who hit 11 of 20 shots. "We just needed one win, and after that I said we were back, and we're showing it now. Hopefully a lot of people will believe us; if not, we're just going to keep playing our type of basketball."

Maryland extended that string of success to six games when it reached the semifinals of the ACC tournament in Atlanta—and another shot at the Blue Devils. In the buildup, it sounded like Duke considered itself an underdog to the 11th-ranked Terps, particularly with Boozer not available.

"In order to beat Maryland we really have to be on top of our game because they are on the top of their game right now," Krzy-zewski said. "Especially Dixon."

A series of dizzying runs highlighted the third game of the year between these rivals. Dixon helped Maryland score the first 10 points before the Dookies went on a 12-2 spurt. From there, it was close until Maryland outscored Duke 10-2 to end the first half.

Of course, the Blue Devils responded with a 19-2 run that seemed to clinch matters. Well, maybe with two other rivals it might have.

Down 14, the Terps reminded each other that Duke rallied from similar deficits—and that they had beaten Duke at Cameron a fortnight ago—so the game hardly was over.

And it wasn't.

Thanks to the shooting and leadership of Dixon, Steve Blake, and Lonny Baxter, the Terps climbed back.

"Duke came out on fire to start the second half," Gary Williams said, "but we did what we had to do to get back in the game."

Blake's 3-pointer with 8.1 seconds remaining tied it 82-82. So, would Duke finish with a flourish as it had in Cole, or a thud, like it did at Cameron?

"We're a program of championships and every time we're in a championship situation we get up," was Battier's answer.

Yet it was the most unsung of the Dookies who would apply the final touch.

James, in a horrendous shooting slump heading to the ACC tourney, even had lost his starting spot to the freshman Duhon. The senior would seem to have been the least of Maryland's worries.

Surprisingly, Coach K didn't use his final timeout after Blake's bucket. Then again, with the leadership he had on the floor, Krzy-zewski probably figured the players knew what to do.

Not surprisingly, Jason Williams was the first option and scooted downcourt for a runner that hit the rim and didn't fall—except into James' hands.

James was one of the most popular Blue Devils because of his workmanlike attitude and his acceptance of the demotion without causing a stir. He was what coaches often call a "character player," a guy whose guise was more important than his game.

"I run my own race," James said. "People say I'm overshadowed, but I just enjoy every game, every season."

And, in particular, the end of this ACC semifinal. James put back Williams's miss, sending the Dookies into delirium—and ahead to the conference tourney final against North Carolina.

"You don't make the play that he did at the end of the game without being through some wars and having experience in tough games. That was Nate right there," Battier said.

"You just don't fall into those types of plays, you make those plays happen. That's the result of a five-year player making a big play in a big game."

There would be bigger games. And the Terrapins would be on the floor with the Blue Devils once again.

"I told our guys after the game I don't think there's anybody out there who is better than us on a given night," Gary Williams said.

That given night, or day, would be in Minneapolis in the Final Four.

After the ACC tournament loss, the Terrapins regrouped so spectacularly that they marched into the national semifinals for the first time. Along the way, Maryland beat George Mason, Georgia State (coached by former Terps leader Lefty Driesell), Georgetown, and Stanford to win the Western Regional.

So, to many, the 2000–2001 campaign was an overwhelming success for a program Williams had resurrected from the darkest and most tragic of times.

In June 1986, one day after being drafted in the first round by the Boston Celtics, Maryland star Len Bias died of a cocaine overdose. Bias's death led to the firing of Driesell, a coaching icon in College Park whose megatalented teams always fell just short of their goals, often at the hands of that private school from Durham.

Driesell's replacement, Bob Wade, not only couldn't put together a winner, but he violated so many NCAA rules—or at least got caught doing what many claimed Driesell had done for years—that the school was hit with massive sanctions and probations.

Into that mess walked Williams, who left a good job with Ohio State to return to his alma mater.

"The program was ridiculed from the mid-'80s to the 1990s," Williams explained. "People pointed to Maryland as what was wrong with college basketball. Even the faculty felt that basketball embarrassed the university. We had to change that thinking."

It took a while, given the shackles Williams operated with. But by this trip to the Twin Cities for the Final Four, Maryland was making its eighth successive NCAA Tournament appearance.

Krzyzewski pretty much expected to run into the Terps again. Duke had marched through Monmouth, Missouri, and the L.A. duo of UCLA and USC to reach yet another Final Four. All along that path, Coach K had a suspicion Duke would not be the only ACC school to reach the Metrodome.

"The game we had in Atlanta was truly one of the remarkable games played this year," Krzyzewski said. "I thought the brotherhood and camaraderie that was displayed between the coaches and teams after that game was amazing. I think some of the kids even said to each other 'We'll see you at the Final Four,' because I think they know we're good and we know they're good."

Coach Williams had a similar viewpoint. And, perhaps, an advantage because of the adversity Maryland already had overcome.

"I didn't know what to expect when we went through the tough times," he said. "Watching these players react to that situation impressed me because they could have gone in a different direction, but they actually got closer when things got tough."

Close and tough. The perfect description of Maryland vs. Duke.

And Chapter IV of the '00–01 season would be written on the sport's biggest stage.

Nobody outside the two locker rooms could have imagined an even heftier and historic comeback would be needed in the most important matchup of the season between the ACC universities.

Clearly buoyed by their four previous NCAA Tournament wins and by being a newcomer to college hoops' grandest event, the Terrapins weren't a bit overwhelmed. No, they were overpowering out of the gate.

A blitz of sharp shooting, quick transitions, sturdy defense, and unbridled emotion carried the Terps to a 22-point lead, 39-17, in the opening 13 minutes. No intimidation factor here against the top-ranked Dookies.

"We were riding high," Blake said. "But we also knew who we were playing."

Even if it didn't resemble the Duke dynasty one bit in those first dozen or so minutes.

"You're losing by so much, you can't play any worse," Coach K told his players during a timeout. "So what are you worried about, losing by 40?"

That sure appeared a possibility.

"It's a 40-minute game and they beat us for 12 minutes," the freshman Duhon reasoned. "If you're going to beat us, you've got to do it for 40."

Something Gary Williams and his squad surely recognized given the recent history of the series.

And the Blue Devils began chipping away.

"Well, nobody's 22 points better than Duke," Coach Williams said. "I knew they'd make a run. I thought we had enough to sustain it."

The Terrapins didn't have enough. Not even close.

By halftime, the deficit was cut in half, 49-38. Instead of reeling from the Maryland onslaught, the Blue Devils headed to the locker room brimming with confidence, well aware that comebacks were a staple of this rivalry, particularly in 2000–2001.

Besides, Duke's players reasoned they couldn't possibly shoot so poorly all game; they went 2 for 12 on 3-pointers, their strength, in the first half. And they believed by ratcheting up their defensive intensity, they could slow the Terps, who hit 55 percent of their field goals in the opening 20 minutes.

"We felt 11 points down wasn't so bad after being more than 20 down," said Jason Williams, who was only 3 for 14 before heating up. "We knew by playing good basketball—Duke basketball—we could do it."

So Duke began chipping away, and Maryland started getting careless. Three times, the Blue Devils closed within 1 point. Maryland kept responding.

Then Williams finally nailed a 3 to give Duke its first lead. Each team was in front for a few minutes, but it would have been difficult to find anyone in the Metrodome who thought Maryland would seize control again.

Down 77-76, the now-healthy Boozer made two free throws, and Duke led for good. As a measure of just how strong this team was, it then began to pull away.

Duke wasn't slowed much by a collision near midcourt be-

© *Sports Illustrated.*

Duke's Shane Battier finds the hoop at the 2001 NCAA finals.
Photo by Rich Clarkson.

tween Duhon and Blake on which the Blue Devil banged his head hard against the court and, dazed, struggled to reach the locker room. Blake went to the Maryland bench after the contact.

By then, Duke's Williams had drastically turned around his performance, winding up with 23 points, including several baskets down the stretch as Duke pulled away to a 95-84 win. Yes, the Blue Devils outscored the Terps by 33 points in their biggest comeback in the Final Four.

"This team has a lot of heart," Krzyzewski said. "It's the youngest team, so we're prone to getting nervous. But one of the biggest hearts I've coached is Jason Williams, and he carried us on his back."

Williams, like Battier an All-American, sensed what the team had done was something special.

"I just thought we needed a sense of urgency. I thought that was the main thing for us," Williams said. "Take it in steps. We weren't going to get it back in one shot. We did a good job doing that and I think it will help us in the final."

While the Blue Devils headed to Coach K's seventh title game, where they beat Arizona 82-72 for his third national crown, the Terrapins wondered if they'd ever find that winning formula.

They would—the next year. It would take that long to erase the bitter sting of Duke's memorable comebacks.

"We've taken some great steps," Gary Williams said. "We've got a few more big steps ahead. I can't wait to see us do it."

18

AUSTRIA'S DOWNHILL WONDER

Franz Klammer, 1976 Winter Olympics

If it were possible for the glare of a spotlight to melt an entire mountain of snow, it would have occurred in 1976 in Innsbruck, Austria. And the man who would have been caught dead center in the avalanche would have been Franz Klammer.

Klammer was more than a sports hero in Austria. In the midst of a career that would include five World Cup championships and 25 race victories in his specialty, Klammer was coming off the best season of his remarkable career. He won eight of the nine downhills in 1975, an achievement comparable to Tiger Woods capturing 90 percent of the PGA Tour events in one year.

But that incredible run, which made Klammer an icon throughout a land where skiing is more popular than even soccer, also placed expectations higher than the Austrian Alps on the 22-year-old star.

When Klammer arrived for the Innsbruck Games, he was, in many ways, the home team.

"I didn't read any newspaper or watch TV the week before," Klammer said. "I tried to avoid everything that could make me nervous."

Not that nerves ever seemed a part of his makeup. Klammer

was a daredevil on the mountains, a man willing to ski to the very edge of wiping out if it meant finding a faster line down the course. While his main rivals, particularly Swiss Bernhard Russi, tended to be technically strong and analytical, Klammer was all feel.

That didn't make the sporting public feel any less confident that in the biggest race of the Olympics—at least in Austrian eyes—Klammer would find a way to be the quickest down the mountain.

"The pressure was there, anyway," he said. "It came from within me, so I didn't pay too much attention to the fans."

That Innsbruck would host the Games for the second time in eight years was a fluke. Denver had been awarded the '76 Olympics, but after legislation in Colorado rejected the plan for building Olympic sites because they could damage the environment, the International Olympic Committee was forced to move the events. Innsbruck was the host in 1964—Klammer was a 10-year-old schoolboy skiing to classes back then—and had all the necessary facilities to stage another Olympics.

So in 1973, the IOC made the switch.

About then, Klammer had made his World Cup debut and established himself as a threat in the downhill, Alpine skiing's version of a banzai run or a high-speed chase.

"They called the downhill courses 'Autobahns.' You know, just get in a tuck and go fast," recalled noted ski writer Mike Clark, who covered much of Klammer's career. "Klammer was actually a very good giant slalom skier, which was part of the reason he was such a good downhiller. He knew how to carve a ski the way you do in giant slalom and was able to carry that over to downhill. That may have been the thing that helped him most in that downhill at Innsbruck: Klammer was one of the few who could rock and roll through a turn."

Rockin' and rollin' is an apt way to describe Klammer's style. The soundtrack to his races was pure Aerosmith: loud, innovative, funky, and with more than a touch of danger.

Was that how Klammer saw it?

"No," he said. "I was just trying to go fast and get to the finish faster than anyone."

Klammer's skiing roots were set on a farm in Mooswald, Austria. He often joked that his English was weak because he skied to school and it took so long that he missed early portions of his first course, which was English.

Must not have been many downhill runs on his way to school.

Those roots made Klammer even more popular in his land. His work ethic was lauded as much as his surpassing talent.

So it was hardly a surprise when he played a central role at the 1976 opening ceremonies.

"I carried the flag, and it was really relaxing and fun," he said. "At least I had something to do and didn't have to think about racing."

Always, the host country received the loudest and longest ovation at the Olympics' opening festivities. But everyone in attendance knew the cheers and screams and songs would be far more deafening while Klammer was descending the mountain in the downhill.

The course for the Games was not the usual Innsbruck run used for World Cup races. This time, organizers laid out the downhill on Mount Patscherkofel, a course where Klammer won a test race the previous year.

So the different venue wouldn't throw off Klammer; he would have numerous practice sessions on Patscherkofel. But his standing as the world's best downhiller would, oddly, have a negative impact for the Austrian come race day.

During each of those practice runs, Klammer would take the course first because he was the top-ranked skier in the race. Each time, he would descend on fresh snow, tinged with ice, making for an easier run-through in which Klammer could lay out the line he wished to ski. He had gotten quite precise with it, even if that approach lacked his usual panache.

But when the starting spots were drawn, Klammer got very unlucky.

There were 15 skiers in the top flight, the only real contenders to win the downhill, and Klammer drew the last berth. The worst berth.

"My lucky number is three and I was hoping to get three," Klammer said. "But Russi got 3."

While hitting the course third didn't guarantee Russi success, beginning in the 15 slot made Klammer's hopes for gold more precarious.

"Then comes race day and he is starting No. 15, last of the top group, and for the first time when he comes out of the chute instead of hitting clean ice and snow, he is hitting people's grooves," Clark explained. "Imagine coming out, then taking a sharp left and then a sharp right while ascending.

"As he takes the sharp right, he runs into somebody else's marks where they made the turn—something he has never experienced on this course."

There would also be some mind games being played out in Klammer's head because he knew that Russi and the other early starters would go fast on a smoother mountain.

"It was very much a disadvantage," Klammer said, "but someone was going to go first and someone was going to go 15th. I understood I might have to change some things during the race, and maybe that made me think more about what I should do than I would in the past.

"Still, the main thing was to go fast. That did not change."

Klammer had to come back not only from his bad fortune in the draw, but from having new skis, because the ones he had been using, which had perforated tips to lessen the impact of wind resistance, were declared illegal by ski officials.

And then Russi, one of the best big-event performers in Alpine skiing history, made Klammer's chore almost impossible by speeding down Patscherkofel in 1 minute, 46.06 seconds.

Russi had won the 1972 Olympic downhill and was in peak form at Innsbruck. A brilliant technician who later would become a renowned course designer, Russi understood every element of ski racing—including just how intense the pressure was on Klammer even before the downhill began.

"I think he had many things to handle during those Olympics," Russi said. "I knew if I could do a fast time, it would add to those things for Franz."

Add to them? How about quadruple the pressure? Now, not only were 60,000 or so fans lining the course, but Klammer would ski down rough snow with the golden expectations of his countrymen hanging on every millisecond.

And he'd have to beat a superb time posted by Russi, who reached a speed estimated by Klammer himself as 85 mph. As Russi said, "Go for maximum speed, but never force it."

As Klammer's opportunity approached, none of the other competitors came close to Russi. If Klammer was going to surge to the top of the podium, at least he knew whom he had to defeat.

"It was Russi or me," he said.

Klammer readied himself, and the noise on the hill crescendoed. Perhaps it echoed all the way back to Russi's home in Switzerland.

To grasp how brightly Klammer's star shone in his country, consider this story his wife, Eva, told Clark a decade later when the writer sat with Klammer and his bride to review the *Wide World of Sports* tape of the race—the first time Klammer heard Frank Gifford's and Bob Beattie's memorable call. And the first time Klammer was able to dissect the nuances of his performance.

Eva, a non-skiing fan, was working in Vienna and went on a summer vacation. When she returned, the other girls in her office asked about it and she mentioned that she'd met a boy and they were "going to see about staying together."

She called him Franz.

"Then Eva said something about Klammer," Clark recalled, "and the other girls asked, 'His name is Franz Klammer? Franz Klammer? Don't you know who he is?'

"And Eva answered: 'He's my boyfriend.'

"They had to explain who Klammer was to her. And he didn't tell her who he was or what he did. Eva might have been the only woman in Austria who didn't know."

Everyone in Innsbruck knew who Klammer was—and what he was supposed to do as he leaned forward, ready to chase Russi's time. And a gold medal.

Seconds into his run, everything went awry for Klammer.

He made the first sharp right turn and skied right into an earlier competitor's marks where he made the turn. Suddenly, Klammer's left ski shot way up in the air, he was totally off-balance and he barely made it through that gate.

"I almost went into the air there," he said of encountering the rut.

Most of the fans weren't seeing this mishap, but the TV audience must have gasped as one as Austria's great hope nearly went down. Gifford, who had built up Klammer's Superman status, breathlessly warned viewers (who would see the race on tape) to hold on for a wild ride.

That is, if Klammer could hold on.

Somehow, Klammer recovered from his early stumble, but by then he was far off his prescribed course. From here on out, he'd be improvising.

"From that gate to the finish line he was skiing in territory he never had skied before, kind of riding his instincts," said Clark.

"I didn't think about crashing," Klammer noted. "I was going for the gold. My feelings were to give the race everything I had, without fear. I couldn't do anything else but try my hardest."

The icy, choppy course wasn't going to yield anything, either. If Klammer was to come back from this awful start, it would be the most memorable win of his career, and his greatest comeback.

Klammer had fallen .2 seconds behind Russi's pace, a nearly insurmountable margin for someone skiing so late to overcome. But this was Klammer, and he would do his damndest.

"In my mind I knew I had to go for it," Klammer said. "If it was necessary to change the line, to risk more, I would. I knew after the intermediate I was behind Russi. I skied a little different. I decided to go as high as possible and straight and take so much speed with me."

That would require split-second improvisation to go with strength, stamina, a hawk's sight—and a magician's touch.

That, thought Austrian coach Toni Sailer, who won three gold medals in 1956, was too much of a challenge.

"I closed my eyes and thought this was the end of the gold medal," said Sailer, who radioed to several colleagues that he thought Klammer had fallen because Sailer couldn't see the skier in his usual spot on the course. "I only dared reopen them when I didn't hear the sound of a crash."

Crashing was highly probable with Klammer so far from where he and the other Olympians planned to ski. Klammer seemed to spend almost as much time and cover almost as much territory while airborne as he did on his skis.

This onrushing runaway train was a wreck waiting to happen.

But Klammer also had gathered incredible speed, and he was cutting into the time deficit.

He also felt somewhat disoriented, because instead of being perhaps 40 meters away from the mountainside crowd, he was nearly on top of it. He could clearly hear their chants of "*Klammer, Klam-mer*."

He passed the final checkpoint still behind Russi, and made a gliding right turn, then a sharp left toward the finish. As Klammer made a big turn so far from where he expected to be, he heard a woman screaming and thought he'd hit her with his pole.

"That's how close I believed I was to the fans," he said. "But it also was the best turn I ever made in my career."

Klammer probably made up close to a half-second during this part of his wild journey down Patscherkofel. All that time in the air had been beneficial.

"I was in the tuck much longer than in training; that is why I made such a big jump," he said. "Here I thought I have to do something because I am a little behind. I watched the crowd before reaching the intermediate and thought I was far behind Russi and I have to do something."

Entering the dash to the finish line, Klammer had gathered unimaginable speed. If he stood up to the end, he had a shot at the gold.

But he also was skiing so far over the edge that it would have taken a construction crane to straighten him out. Wiping out was a real possibility.

Yet he skied an even tighter line to the finish—Klammer at his gambling, instinctive best.

"I wasn't aware of the actual times," he said, "but I knew I had to do something, and in one split second I made a clear decision to try a different line. It gained me time and was the best decision I made."

As Klammer rushed across the finish to an uproar that seemed to shake the very mountain he'd just conquered, the scoreboard flashed his time: 1:45.73.

Not only had Klammer rallied from that horrendous start, he'd beaten Russi's superb time by .33 seconds, an eternity in downhill skiing.

Even Russi was impressed.

"To be second behind Klammer is no disgrace," he said. "He really is the greatest downhill skier of recent years."

That meant something extra to Klammer.

"The best moment was when Bernhard came running up to me and gave me a big hug," Klammer said. "It was the most sincere congratulations of all."

All of the skiers had been caught up in the drama. This was

considered in many ways the golden age of the men's version of the sport, and Klammer's golden run was the topper.

Immediately after winning—and while slower skiers were coming down the mountain in far less spectacular fashion—Klammer was inundated by media, many of them still unnerved by what they'd just witnessed.

"How in the world did you do that?" he was asked.

"Well, I'm a pretty good skier, you know," he joked.

Asked how he came back from the near fall—falls—and a "terrible start," he added:

"What do you mean terrible? I think gold's a pretty good color."

Klammer later joked that his biggest challenge came after the race, at doping control.

"I was sitting there for two hours and I couldn't go," he said. "Three beers and I was almost drunk and still couldn't go."

There might never have been a more pressurized performance in the Olympics than what Klammer delivered on Patscherkofel. Three decades later, Austrians barely recall that their countrymen won only two golds in 1976. But they still celebrate one of those wins: Klammer's.

19

THE CHOKE AT DOAK

1994 Florida State Seminoles

Thanksgiving weekend, 1994. And the Florida Gators were tearing apart Florida State, making the Seminoles look like the remnants of their holiday turkey.

The score had reached 31-3, and the possibilities for Steve Spurrier's Gators were almost limitless.

Never one to call off his troops, Spurrier was reveling in the rout of Florida's archrival and its Hall of Fame coach, Bobby Bowden, who'd won three of the previous four meetings. And there was still a quarter to go.

"It was typical Steve Spurrier," FSU cornerback James Colzie later would say. "He did some things we didn't work on all week. He came out in five wide receivers, and they hadn't really done that all season.

"If Spurrier would have stuck to his guns, they probably would have scored 60. We were on our heels."

And looking like a punch-drunk boxer about to be knocked out.

"We wanted to embarrass them as badly as we could," Gators center David Swain admitted. "We all talked about scoring as many times as possible. Everything was clicking."

Everything tended to click on offense for Spurrier's teams no matter who they were playing. In '94, the Gators scored at least 31 points in their first nine games, then beat Vanderbilt 24-7 the week before their trip to Tallahassee—clearly a matter of looking ahead while playing a weak opponent. They were ranked No. 4 in the nation and had a 9-1 record before meeting the 'Noles.

FSU was ranked 7th and also was 9-1. Its previous games included a perfect 8-0 mark in the Atlantic Coast Conference, and its only loss was to another in-state rival, the Miami Hurricanes.

"When you play a team like the University of Florida," Bowden said, "you not only have a chance to get beat, you have a chance to get killed. If you play an Alabama, you might get beat. But it's going to be close."

The winner of the Gators-Seminoles matchup would emerge as a solid contender for the national title.

"We feel as if this may be the best team we've taken up there in our three trips. Hopefully that'll give us the best chance to be successful," Spurrier said before the game. He'd lost 45-30 and 45-24 at Doak Campbell Stadium his previous journeys there.

"I think our team has learned that it really doesn't matter what we say, or they say, or anybody says. It doesn't matter sometimes how much we want to beat the other team if we don't play well, if we're not prepared to execute our assignments. The emotional factor is important, but sometimes you can overdo it and not play well."

But Florida played very well—spectacularly—in the first three quarters on FSU's turf. It looked like the Gators would chomp all over the Seminoles for 60 minutes, further embarrassing a school coming off its first national title (12-1 in 1993), but marred by a scandal in which several 'Noles were given free merchandise by a Foot Locker store.

Florida coach Steve Spurrier, never one to resist a good punchline against his hated rival, joked that FSU stood for "Free Shoes University." It wasn't the last time that he would try to disparage Bowden in one of the most heated coaching rivalries in the country.

The 'Noles were hurting as they fell into a deeper and deeper hole.

Florida quarterback Danny Wuerffel threw three first-half touchdown passes, two to Jack Jackson. The Seminoles turned over the ball three times, and when Wuerffel hit Jackson for a 28-yard score with only eight seconds left in the half, it was 24-3. Florida scored 17 points in the second half of the second quarter.

Soon, it was 31-3, after Wuerffel went in from the 1 to finish off an 80-yard drive that probably should have signaled to the Seminoles that this wasn't their day. The FSU players weren't thinking about catching the "Ol' Ball Coach's" ballplayers.

"We just wanted to score some points to make this thing respectable so we could go to class on Monday," said wide receiver Omar Ellison.

"They were running us out of our own stadium," added another Florida State wideout, Kez McCorvey. "My first thought was, 'Hey, let's at least make this respectable. Let's not give up 50. Let's not get totally embarrassed here.'"

"It can always happen if somebody makes a lot of big plays," noted Bowden.

So it was time for the Seminoles to make some big plays.

But could they do so with Danny Kanell in the game? The quarterback was struggling mightily, so much so that many fans—the ones who were still in the stands when the final period began—were eager to see him benched for Thad Busby or Jon Stark. After all, the Seminoles won the national championship the previous year with Heisman Trophy winner Charlie Ward running the offense. To them, Kanell just wasn't measuring up.

But Bowden had made the mistake of sitting down Kanell once before, in the loss to the Hurricanes. Neither Busby nor Stark could handle the quarterbacking chores then, and why should Bowden or offensive coordinator Mark Richt think much had changed in one month?

Indeed, Richt lobbied Bowden to stick with Kanell.

"I don't want to get beat when I've got a guy on the bench who might come in and win it," Bowden said. "I'm just impatient."

This time, though, he was smart. He sent out Kanell for the first series of the fourth quarter.

"It was pretty brutal, but we hadn't given up," Kanell said. "When we were down 31-3, defeat was in my mind. I just wanted to put points on the board to save face."

Florida State got a boost from a nine-play drive that included a fourth-and-10 conversion on an 11-yard pass to McCorvey. Zach Crockett's 5-yard run made the score 31-10. Still not within hailing distance of the Gators, but at least the 'Noles had some momentum.

They also sensed something else. Florida had gone conservative—yes, Spurrier, "Coach Innovation," had pulled back his *players*, trying to eat up the clock on offense. Defensively, coordinator Bobby Pruett had ordered his unit to lay back. The old prevent defense was about to prevent Florida from winning.

FSU had gone to the shotgun on most plays, and Kanell was picking apart the laid-back D.

Ahead by 21 points, the Gators went three-and-out, and FSU quickly made it 31-17. Kanell hit Andre Cooper for a 6-yard touchdown.

The Doak was rocking. The Gators were reeling.

More than 10 minutes remained.

"Every time we scored, I came back to the bench and said the same thing, 'It's not over yet,'" said Kanell.

It could have been. But Florida was stuck in a rut by now. Wuerffel had lost his touch, the offensive line was getting blown off the ball by the resurgent Seminoles, and Kanell was in that zone top-level athletes enter now and again.

"Kanell can do anything Charlie could do, except run," teammate Rock Preston said. "Charlie could come back and so can Danny."

When the Gators couldn't get beyond their 28-yard line on their next series and punted, Florida State broadcaster Gene Deckerhoff told his audience "something special is happening here."

The Florida players probably perceived that, too.

"Our defensive line began shadowing instead of attacking, and the defensive backs were playing 15 yards off the ball," Gators cornerback Larry Kennedy told the *Tampa Tribune*. "Pruett wanted everything to be kept in front of us. But with guys like (Warrick) Dunn, they get the ball in space, they zig and zag, and the offense starts to move.

"We were begging to get back in our base defense. Begging! We tried, but by then we were playing on skates. It was over."

The Seminoles got the ball at their 27 and used brilliant tailback Dunn as a runner and receiver on another quick march toward the end zone. Kanell capped it with a perfect bootleg and a 3-yard touchdown run, bringing Florida State within seven points.

Even better for the 'Noles, 5:25 remained.

By then, Deckerhoff was telling his listeners who had left the stadium that he "felt sorry for them. You don't know what you're missing."

Still, Florida could have stemmed the comeback by making just a couple of plays on offense or defense. Wuerffel did connect with Reidel Anthony for 15 yards on the Gators' next series, a play he called "a breath of fresh air."

Then the air got stale again for Florida: Colzie made a diving interception at the State 40.

"When I got to the sideline, everybody was jumping and slapping fives and we knew the offense was going to put it right in there," Colzie said. "Didn't matter how much time we had, we were going to do it."

Dunn went 37 yards on a swing pass down the sideline, avoiding several tacklers and tiptoeing to stay in bounds. Preston's 4-yard run on third down, sweeping right into the end zone, made it 31-30 with 1:45 to go.

Now, Bowden was faced with a mind-numbing decision. Does he go for a 2-point conversion and the victory, or kick the extra point to tie it, then hope the Gators keep self-destructing and give his team a chance to win it with yet another possession?

Bowden reasoned that by going for an almost-certain one point, the Seminoles would have a tie that felt like a win. And that the spiraling Gators might opt to simply run out the clock.

If the 'Noles went for 2 and got it, Florida finally would go back into attack mode—and that had not been a good thing for FSU in the first three quarters.

And if the Seminoles missed the conversion and still trailed, it would be the first negative play of a fourth quarter they'd totally dominated. It might awaken the Gators, and it would mean relying on the unreliable: recovering an onside kick.

So, Bobby, what do you say?

"I wish we could've won it, but gee, that would've really been asking too much," Bowden said. "With 10 minutes to go, I'd said, 'Lord let us tie.'

"To make a miraculous comeback and then miss it, they (Florida) would have been in a glorious celebration and we would have been in a stupor."

So Bowden opted for the kick and the deadlock.

Final: 31-31.

"I've never had a tie feel as much like a win," Bowden said.

Several Gators were relieved that Bowden ordered the place kick.

"That tie game, as miserable as it was from our standpoint, will probably live in the state's legend forever," Florida star receiver Chris Doering said. "I'm just glad FSU didn't go for two at the end. Without a doubt, they would've gotten it. We couldn't do anything right."

Spurrier and his staff went into spin control after the loss, uh, the tie.

"If some of their fans want to think they won, that's just their opinion," Spurrier said. "It was a tie. It just so happened they got a bunch of points at the end and we got ours early.

"Certainly our play in the fourth quarter was not very good. Basically, we were playing with a lot of coverages we had played the whole season. We just didn't execute well enough. Obviously, if we had to do it over again, we'd try something else."

Pruett didn't back away from the blame for the collapse.

"There's criticism even when you win. That's just part of the job," said the first-year coordinator. "My skin is tough. I've been wearing it a long time."

The Seminoles' regular season was done, and they certainly needed to catch their breath after such a heroic rally. Particularly Kanell, who wouldn't win any Heismans in his career—or even go on to many more star turns like this one.

Kanell had gone 18 for 22 for 232 yards in the final quarter. For 15 minutes, he made Seminoles fans forget Ward.

"Every great quarterback has a defining moment, and this was it for Danny," Richt said.

"What an amazing experience," Kanell explained. "You've got to understand the emotions of the FSU-Florida rivalry. I mean, my 80-year-old grandma was in the stadium in Gainesville (in 1993), wearing a pin with my picture on it and the fans abused her the whole game.

"So to have the emotions turn around so abruptly in a game like that was almost too much to believe. It was like the perfect storm. One less play, one incompletion, and that comeback doesn't get done."

To their everlasting credit, the Gators didn't allow the Choke at Doak to ruin them. The next week, they edged third-ranked

Alabama 24-23 in Atlanta for the Southeastern Conference championship. Their reward: a rematch with the Seminoles in the Sugar Bowl.

"We actually got over that game a lot quicker than a lot of people wanted us to," Spurrier said of the 31-31 epic. "Some people wanted to make us feel like we choked or folded at the end, which is fine. That's just part of the game."

Miraculous comebacks would not be part of the Sugar Bowl. While many Seminoles backers were upset about facing the Gators for a second straight game, FSU had the upper hand. The confidence boost it got from the comeback provided more than enough juice for a 23-17 win on New Year's Day and a No. 4 overall ranking.

That bowl game was a minor postscript on both sides, though. The Thanksgiving weekend classic defined 1994 for both schools.

"Say what you want about what happened, but nobody won the game," Florida's Jackson insisted. "I'm sure they're talking about we were up 28 points and they came back. We're talking about how well we played to get up 31-3. When you get finished, though, you always go back to the same thing. It was a tie."

Not to most everyone else in the nation. And especially not to the FSU faithful.

20

YA GOTTA BELIEVE

1973 New York Mets

When the New York Mets won the National League pennant in 1973, a fan at Shea Stadium held up a sign, "You Gotta Beeleeve!"

The sign could have also said, "The Amazin's, Part II." Similar to the original "Amazin's" team of 1969, the Mets had performed somewhat of a baseball miracle in 1973.

With just a month to go in the season, the Mets were in last place in the National League East. By season's end, league champions.

Before making this gigantic U-Turn, the Mets had to get healthy first. They'd suffered an incredible amount of long-term injuries to top players.

And they needed a return to form of Tug McGraw, the top relief pitcher in the game who had suddenly gone into a season-long swoon. After winning the World Series in 1969 with McGraw's help, the Mets were no longer the lovable, laughable losers of baseball. But in the summer of 1973, they had certainly taken a step backward.

"We've had everything happen," said manager Yogi Berra, noting that the Mets had lost key players with serious injuries for months at a time. Berra's job was at risk. And he was hardly given a vote of confidence by Mets board chairman M. Donald Grant, who told quizzing reporters: "We have not thought of replacing Yogi. We will not do so . . . unless forced to do so by public opinion."

Funny he should say that. Just about that time, the *New York Post* took an informal poll of its readers: Should the Mets fire Berra, general manager Bob Sheffing, or Grant, or all three?

It resulted in a backhanded compliment to Berra, who was third in the poll, trailing Sheffing and Grant by large margins.

Berra shrugged off the poll by the tabloid.

"I don't get the *Post* where I live," he said. "I read the *Times*."

Berra had personal experience with the perilous, high-wire act known as baseball manager. He had been fired by the New York Yankees despite winning a pennant. No manager's job was safe, especially on the tough streets of New York.

In Berra's defense, many of his key players on the '73 Mets were missing in action. Among them: catcher Jerry Grote, short-stop Bud Harrelson, first baseman John Milner, and outfielder Cleon Jones. And many others stayed in the lineup playing through injuries because there was simply no one else of major league quality to fill a position.

Milner was the least troubled by injuries, although he still missed 23 games with a severely strained leg muscle.

"All of the strain fell on Milner when the other guys were hurt," said Jones, who was out most of two months with a variety of injuries.

Jones's comment came late in the season when the Mets had been shut out 15 times and produced a sickly lineup devoid of power.

The Mets could have used a hitter like Berra in his prime. He had been an all-star catcher with the Yankees, winning 3 MVP awards and 10 world championships—the most by any player in baseball history. Berra, a left-handed hitter, was known for his ability to make contact with a pitch as long as it was somewhere in the zip code of home plate. As a celebrated "bad ball hitter," Berra very often could hammer a pitch far out of the strike zone into the seats. He hit 358 homers in a marvelous playing career with the Yankees.

But good as he was during the regular season, he was even

better in the World Series. The clutch-hitting Berra batted .452 in 75 World Series games.

As Yankees manager, he led New York to a pennant in 1964, winning 99 games. But Berra was dismissed because he lost the World Series to St. Louis. He was replaced by Johnny Keane, the man who had beaten him in the Series. Keane didn't last long in New York. He was fired early in the 1966 season with the Yankees in last place with a 4-16 record, and replaced by Ralph Houk.

Berra signed on as a player-coach with the Mets under Casey Stengel, his former Yankees manager. In 1969, Gil Hodges replaced Stengel and led the Amazin' Mets to the world title in the same year a man walked on the moon. Some said the events were related, because few believed either could happen.

Following Hodges's premature death in 1971, Berra was selected the Mets' manager in 1972.

A man of few words, Berra was nevertheless credited with a slew of legendary one-liners that may or may not be apocryphal.

As the story goes, a sportswriter woke Berra out of a sound sleep one morning and apologized for calling him so early.

"That's all right," Berra supposedly said, "I had to get up to answer the phone anyway."

Talking about a restaurant that was very popular, Berra said, "Nobody goes there anymore—it's too crowded."

And, of course, Berra's classic and most everyone's favorite:

"It's déjà vu all over again."

Berra really made sense during the 1973 season with this comment about his injury-plagued team:

"We'd be all right if only we could get all our men playing."

Except for a head injury to Jon Matlack that kept him out of action for 10 days, the Mets at least had their pitching staff in pretty good shape, led by Tom Seaver and Jerry Koosman.

Then there was the strange case of McGraw. The best-paid relief pitcher in the game with a $75,000 salary, McGraw was mostly ineffective for the first four months of the season.

McGraw was injury free and said he felt fine physically. But his screwball just wasn't producing results as it had in the past. At one point, McGraw's earned run average ballooned to 5.27.

For most of the season, McGraw was going through tough times, trying to regain the form that made him the top reliever in baseball. The onetime star of the bullpen admittedly had lost faith.

"When you lose your confidence, you lose everything," said McGraw, the most prominent face of the franchise, along with Seaver.

McGraw also was the most popular player on the team. He was a media darling with a lively personality always good for a quote or a laugh. Fans loved his emotional persona and the way he slapped his glove on his thigh as he walked off the mound. It was his way of saying hello to his wife, who was either watching the game in person or on TV.

But now baseball was not much fun for Tug as he tried to figure out what was wrong with his pitching mechanics.

For practically a month, from early July to early August, Mc-Graw and the Mets continued to tread water. By August 6, following a doubleheader loss to East Division-leading St. Louis, the Mets were still in last place, 11½ games back.

The Mets still needed binoculars to see first place. But they were encouraged by McGraw's sudden return to form. He couldn't explain it, other than to say he had been working hard and had regained his confidence.

On such turnarounds are memorable comebacks built.

With McGraw looking like his old self, something else was happening on the team: The Mets' walking wounded started to heal and hit.

In one of his best performances of the season, McGraw pitched three scoreless innings to save a 6–5 victory over the front-running Cardinals. The left-hander allowed only three infield singles in his third straight strong relief stint. In an era when relievers worked more innings than now, and more often had the chance to pick up a victory, McGraw had yet to win a game. But his solid performance against the Cardinals gave him his 13th save.

On their final West Coast road trip, the Mets finally started to make headway behind superb pitching by Matlack and Seaver, who improved his league-leading strikeout total to 175 and earned run average to 1.85 with a 7–1 victory over the San Francisco Giants.

The Mets realized that even a modest winning streak could shake up the tightly bunched NL East, considered a weak sister to the West.

"I told you in the spring that 85 games would win it," Berra reminded reporters.

Seaver, who had lost 10 of his first 27 decisions despite such stingy pitching, started to get more assistance from the Mets' offense. The Mets also found surprising help from two pitchers acquired in trades, Harry Parker and George Stone.

And McGraw was suddenly in the middle of New York's resurgence with his born-again relief pitching.

Ya gotta believe.

The expression was fast catching on in New York, and now McGraw finally felt comfortable using it. Although continuing to occupy last place in early September, the Mets were, oddly, still very much in the East race.

While the Cardinals and Pittsburgh Pirates were battling for first place, the last-place Mets were starting to sneak into the pennant picture. In early September, they had moved within five and a half games of the top of the division.

Ya gotta believe.

"We always had a chance once we got healthy," Berra said.

The Mets kept gaining ground. By September 5, following a 4–0 victory over Philadelphia behind the pitching of Ray Sadecki and McGraw, they had moved into fourth place. It was the first time they had been that high since June 24.

"What do you want us to do, quit and go home?" Bud Harrelson said in response to a reporter's question about the Mets' chances. "We're still in the running."

Ya gotta believe.

Things were falling into place for the Mets. While they were winning, teams ahead of them kept losing.

After taking three out of four in Montreal, the Mets remained in fourth place. But they had moved within a half-game of the third-place Expos, two and a half games behind the second-place Pirates, and three in back of the first-place Cardinals.

"We're not backing into this race," Berra said, "we're climbing right over it."

Not so fast, Yogi.

Next up for the Mets were the suddenly hot Pirates, who had taken over the top spot in the East. The Mets had five games scheduled with the Pirates, two in Pittsburgh and three in New York.

It was make or break time for the Mets, who started Seaver in the opening game. The Mets' ace had owned the Pirates, winning

14 of 15 decisions in the past five years. He had already beaten them four times in the 1973 season.

Not this time. Willie Stargell and his teammates erupted for five runs in three innings against Seaver and went on to a 10–3 romp. It was as much a blow to the Mets' psyche as their pennant chances; the Pirates had manhandled the Mets' best pitcher with a long-ball attack.

On September 18, the Mets sent Matlack to the mound, but he was tagged for four runs in three innings as the Pirates built a 4–1 lead. Another Pirates binge against another of the Mets' top pitchers.

The Pirates carried the three-run advantage into the ninth, the Mets' last chance before a loss would drop them four and a half games back and virtually out of the race.

Pittsburgh reliever Ramon Hernandez got leadoff hitter Harrelson on a fly ball, but pinch-hitter Jim Beauchamp singled. Wayne Garrett doubled Beauchamp to third and both scored on a triple to right-center by Felix Millan.

After Hernandez walked Rusty Staub, Dave Giusti came in from the bullpen. Ron Hodges lashed a game-tying single. Don Hahn then delivered a two-run single for a 6–4 Mets lead.

It was enough to secure a 6–5 victory that moved the Mets back within two and a half games of the Pirates. It also made their spirits soar; it was a victory that could be a turning point with two weeks left on the schedule.

The next night, Jones hit two homers and knocked in five runs, Stone won his eighth straight and McGraw saved another as the Mets whipped the Pirates 7–3. The Mets moved into a third-place tie with St. Louis, one and a half games behind Pittsburgh and a half-game behind Montreal in the torrid four-team chase.

The *Times* called McGraw "the whirling dervish of the bullpen." Indeed, he was, with four victories and nine saves in his last 13 appearances.

"People don't know what I went through during those two months when I wasn't getting anybody out," McGraw said. "They think I planned it this way."

There was a bizarre footnote to the Mets' comeback story: the sudden disappearance of Willie Mays, the future Hall-of-Famer. Mays failed to show for one game, without explanation. It became a big mystery around the Mets' clubhouse. The center field great was teased in the local newspapers. "Willie or Won't He?" one newspaper wrote in regard to Mays's questioned reappearance.

When he finally did show up, there was more teasing from his teammates in the locker room, and Mays's disappearing act was never explained. But shortly thereafter he announced he would be retiring, ending his fabulous 22-year career in the majors.

"I've always said that I'll quit when it's no longer fun for me," Mays had said at one point during the season. That time had arrived.

His teammates were having fun, though, as they headed into the homestretch of one of the most exciting pennant races in history involving not two or three—but *five* teams.

The Mets tightened things further with a 4–3, 13-inning victory over the Pirates to carry them into second place, within a mere half-game of Pittsburgh.

When Seaver beat the defending division champions 10–2 with a five-hit, eight-strikeout performance the following night, the Mets moved into first place with a 77–77 record. Yes, break-even was good enough for the top spot.

Shea Stadium was jumping with a season-high 51,381 fans, many of them dancing in the aisles and holding up signs that said, "We're No. 1."

How sweet it was for a team that had been No. 6 for most of the season.

"It brings back memories of 1969," said Koosman, who won two games against the Baltimore Orioles in the World Series that season. "But it's as though this is the first time all over again. The New York fans are hungry, and they get your adrenaline flowing."

While the players could feel optimistic, Berra was cautious. He had been involved in too many pennant races not to be.

"If we had 20 games to go, I'd take my chances," he said. "But even Chicago is only two and a half games out, and they're fifth. We've been hot since the 17th of August, but I have to say it's still wide open."

Berra had a point. After beating St. Louis 2–0 on Matlack's four-hitter, the Mets improved their lead to one game over the rain-idled Pirates. But with New York, Pittsburgh, Montreal, St. Louis, and Chicago separated by only two and a half games on September 22, that could change at any time.

It did the following day when the Pirates swept a doubleheader from Montreal while the Mets were beating the Cardinals. The Mets' lead over the Pirates dwindled to a half-game.

On an emotional Willie Mays Night at Shea Stadium, the Mets nipped Montreal 2–1 behind the pitching of Koosman and McGraw and the hitting and fielding of Jones.

Jones hit a home run and helped preserve the victory with a defensive gem. "When I saw Willie crying, I felt bad," Jones said of Mays's sentimental farewell to the fans before the game. "It was a sad day for us all. And all I wanted to do was to get out there and play the game."

With the Pirates losing to Philadelphia, the Mets' lead improved to one and a half games.

Not time to celebrate just yet. A loss by the Mets and a win by the Pirates the next day reduced New York's lead back to a half-game as the teams headed into the final weekend of the regular season.

The Mets flew into Chicago for a four-game series while the Pirates were playing Montreal three times at home.

Suddenly, the weather threw the Mets a curve. Rain washed out their Friday series opener with the Cubs, forcing the Mets to play consecutive doubleheaders on Saturday and Sunday. The Mets weren't crazy about that.

"It's always tougher to win a doubleheader than a single game," McGraw said. "The reason is that the guys are more tired going into a second game and they don't have the normal rest they do between single games."

One thing in the Mets' favor: Pittsburgh lost to Montreal, giving them a tiny bit of breathing room.

But the race was still so painfully tight that a five-way tie was possible in the NL East. NL president Chub Feeney announced 10 different plans to settle any number of deadlocks.

On Saturday the Mets again weren't able to play because of bad weather, but it wasn't a total washout. The Pirates lost once more and virtually eliminated themselves from the race.

The Mets held a one-and-a-half-game lead over St. Louis and could clinch the East Division title with a doubleheader sweep of the Cubs on Sunday.

Close, but not just yet for the Mets. They lost a 1–0 heartbreaker in the opener before a 9–2 victory in the second game.

The division title was still up for grabs as the regular season went into an extra day, with the Mets facing Chicago in a rescheduled doubleheader.

© *Sports Illustrated.*

New York Mets' Rusty Staub on the run during the 1973 World Series.
Photo by Jerry Cooke.

They didn't have to play both games.

Jones homered and Grote singled in two runs to help the Mets take a 5–0 lead. McGraw came on when Seaver started to struggle and pitched three scoreless innings to nail down a 6–4 victory and the NL East pennant for the Mets. The second game was pointless.

The comeback was complete.

"It's a great feeling to have had to struggle," McGraw said. "It's like climbing a glass mountain and finally to be able to find some pine tar and lay it on that mountain and get to the top."

Following one of the most complicated pennant races in baseball history, the Mets defeated favored Cincinnati in a contentious National League playoff clouded by a fight between Harrelson and the Reds' Pete Rose.

In the Mets' riotous dressing room, Seaver shouted, "You gotta believe! We made it and I believe!"

The Mets ran out of luck in the World Series, losing to the Oakland A's. No wonder—they had already used up all their magic in the amazing National League race.

Better believe it.